FORBIDDEN INTIMACIES

GLOBALIZATION IN EVERYDAY LIFE

Forbidden Intimacies

Polygamies at the Limits of Western Tolerance

MELANIE HEATH

STANFORD UNIVERSITY PRESS
Stanford, California

Stanford University Press
Stanford, California

Printed in the United States of America on acid-free, archival-quality paper

Library of Congress Cataloging-in-Publication Data
Names: Heath, Melanie, author.
Title: Forbidden intimacies : polygamies at the limits of Western tolerance / Melanie Heath.
Other titles: Globalization in everyday life.
Description: Stanford, California : Stanford University Press, 2023. | Series: Globalization in everyday life | Includes bibliographical references and index.
Identifiers: LCCN 2022019305 (print) | LCCN 2022019306 (ebook) | ISBN 9781503627604 (cloth) | ISBN 9781503634251 (paperback) | ISBN 9781503634268 (ebook)
Subjects: LCSH: Polygamy--Government policy--Western countries. | Polygamy--Western countries. | Racism--Western countries.
Classification: LCC HQ981 .H43 2023 (print) | LCC HQ981 (ebook) | DDC 306.84/23--dc23/eng/20220516
LC record available at https://lccn.loc.gov/2022019305
LC ebook record available at https://lccn.loc.gov/2022019306

Cover design: Susan Zucker
Cover photo: shutterstock | Pixel-Shot
Typeset by Elliott Beard in Minion Pro 10/14.4

Contents

Acknowledgments

When I began this research, I had no idea how many years it would take to complete the project and write this book. Nor did I foresee the obstacles I would need to overcome in the process. That said, it was an amazing journey that opened doors to new experiences and offered a creative process that transformed me as a scholar and a person. None of this would have been possible without so many people who provided support throughout. The people I acknowledge here are among many who contributed to this project and inspired me along the way.

My deepest and greatest appreciation goes to all the individuals who generously shared with me their stories and insights. In Mayotte, I especially thank Askandari Allaoui, who so generously offered me his time, introduced me to dozens of officials and other participants, and hosted my partner and me for a weekend with his family. I appreciate the generosity of government officials and association directors—there are too many to name—as well as the people living in polygynous families who were willing to share their expertise and experiences. In metropolitan France the generosity and sincerity of association leaders, scholars, government officials, and especially those who were living in plural families were incredible. Jacques Barou, Claudette Bodin, Michel Farge, Pauline Gaullier, Saïda Rahal Sidhoum, Christian Poiret, and Catherine Quiminal were particularly helpful in providing insights based on their research on polygamy and decohabitation. In the United States and Canada I appreciate the willingness of government officials, lawyers, scholars, and activists to discuss this issue on record. I am eternally grateful to those in plural families and those who left polygamy who allowed me to spend time with them, opened their communities to me, and offered insights into their experiences.

I received generous support for the research and writing of this book from the Social Sciences and Humanities Research Council of Canada and from McMaster University. Material in this book appeared previously as "Espousing Patriarchy: Conciliatory Masculinity and Homosocial Femininity in Religiously Conservative Plural Families," *Gender and Society* 33 (6) (2019): 888–910; and "Judging Women's Sexual Agency: Contemporary Sex Wars in the Legal Terrain of Prostitution and Polygamy" (with Jessica Braimoh, and Julie Gouweloos), *Signs* 42 (1) (2016): 199–225.

As a large, comparative project, this research would not have been possible without the support of numerous research assistants. Julie Gouweloos and Jessica Braimoh were research assistants from the beginning of the project, and we worked together on a paper that we presented together and eventually published in *Signs*. Allyson Stokes and I worked on a paper that we presented at the Sexualities Studies Association Annual Meeting in 2013. Rebecca Ferrari was an amazing research assistant who conducted important interviews and transcribed them. I also thank Constanza Puppo for her support in transcribing. Many thanks to Magali Izzard for her fast and efficient work transcribing most of the French interviews in France and Mayotte. Jessica Braimoh oversaw a group of research assistants to code the English-language transcripts, working with me to ensure intercoder reliability. She and Nikki Brown were coders extraordinaire! A very special thanks to Megan Wightman, who did an amazing job coding the Mahorais transcripts. I also thank Claudia Aparicio, Deena Abul Fottouh, Ashley Belluomini, Martin Marquis, Alan Santinele-Martino, Jessica Rizk, and S. W. Underwood.

The evolution of this book benefited from numerous talks that I have given, and I am grateful for the probing questions and feedback I received from faculty and graduate students. My thanks go out to audiences at the École des Hautes Études en Sciences Sociales, Paris; Central European University, Budapest, Hungary; University Szeged, Szeged, Hungary; Oxford Roundtable of Religion, Oxford, UK; Webster University, Hill AFB, Utah; Western University, London, Ontario; Waterloo University, Waterloo, Ontario; and McMaster University, Hamilton, Ontario.

My editor at Stanford University Press, Marcela Cristina Maxfield, has been a rock, providing untold support and encouragement, especially considering that much of this book was written during the pandemic. I thank her for her belief in this project and for her thoughtful commentary. My appreciation also goes to editorial, design, and production director David Zielonka, assistant editor Sunna Juhn, senior production editor Emily Smith, and copyeditor Mimi Braverman, all of whom facilitated this book's publication with thoughtfulness and great attention to detail. I also thank series editors Rhacel Salazar Parreñas and Hung Cam Thai for including this book in the Globalization in Everyday Life Series. It is a perfect home for this research. I owe a debt of gratitude to my academic "mom," Judith Stacey, who has been an amazing feminist mentor and a sounding board for the ideas in this book. Colleagues at McMaster University have been very supportive of this project, and I am especially appreciative of Tina Fetner, Steph Howells, Karen Robson, and Marisa Young for being there for me.

This book benefited from amazing comments from two anonymous reviewers and from members of my writing group: Caitlyn Collins, Sarah Diefendorf, and C. J. Pascoe. I can't express how much I appreciate the support that I received from them while writing this book, especially once the pandemic hit. Martha Ertman and Jyoti Puri offered extensive comments on the final draft of the book, and they provided essential feedback for which I am deeply grateful. I thank Tey Meadow for her advice. Régis Schlagdenhauffen introduced the idea of including Mayotte as a case and offered important insights into polygamy in France. I am grateful to him for inviting me as a visiting scholar for a short stay at the École des Hautes Études en Sciences Sociales. Michael Stambolis-Ruhstorfer also provided important insights into the French context. Thank you to Erzsebet Barat and Dorit Geva for their support of my research. Jessica Braimoh and Julie Gouweloos provided feedback on various parts of the book. Nicole Iturriaga met with me early on and shared her experiences studying plural marriage in Utah. I am also grateful to Suzanne Senay, Terry Boyd, Marion Boyd, and Joseph Dudley for their comments and support.

A world of gratitude to my partner, Rémy Haardt, who embarked on this adventure with me without hesitation, shuttling all over Paris and its suburbs, voyaging to Mayotte, and helping me understand how the French think about things. To my family: Laurel, Isaac, Ben, and Nate, who supported me while writing portions of this book in California during the pandemic and being there for me. I will always treasure the time I spent with people who made this book possible, those mentioned here and those who are too numerous to list.

FORBIDDEN INTIMACIES

INTRODUCTION
FORBIDDEN INTIMACIES IN
GLOBAL PERSPECTIVE

[Plural marriage] is about intimacy. An intimate
connection is the greatest gift you can give
a human being. We need to honor that.
> —*Olivia, Mormon fundamentalist, Utah*

The question is not whether [polygamy] is the best
of all possible family formulations. The question
is, Does this form of intimate personal family
relationship inflict demonstrable harm such that it
is appropriate for the criminal law to intervene?
> —*Michael Vonn, Policy Director, British*
> *Columbia Civil Liberties Association*

Polygamy is something we must fight because it's a
social problem, it's economic. And it includes extreme
violence at the level of women and children.
> —*Awa Ba, founder and president of*
> *En Finir avec la Polygamie, France*

FOR SOME PEOPLE, POLYGYNY (OR plural marriage)—one man
married to more than one woman—is an important type of intimacy, a
family form that is central to the identities of those who practice it.[1] As
Olivia says, plural marriage "is about intimacy." She has lived in a plural
marriage for nearly thirty years and explains the "intimate connection"
between her husband, her sister wives—one of whom is her biological
sister—and herself as the "greatest gift you can give a human being." From
this perspective, forbidding it creates harm by forcing people to live un-

1

derground for fear that their families will be prosecuted. Michael Vonn, the policy director for the British Columbia Civil Liberties Association (BCCLA) in Canada, questions whether polygamy as an "intimate personal family relationship" does "inflict demonstratable harm" to justify prohibiting it. For the BCCLA the answer is no. Others, however, see polygyny as a harmful and violent patriarchal family structure that hurts all individuals involved, especially women and children. Awa Ba began an organization in France to fight against polygyny after her sister was subjected to it. She believes that forbidding polygyny is necessary to fight this "extreme violence at the level of women and children." These opposing perspectives have shaped how Western governments seek to regulate polygamy, an umbrella term for the practice of marrying more than one spouse at the same time.[2]

What can we learn from analyzing government regulation of polygamies? A growing number of scholars have studied how the state and sexuality shape one another.[3] Likewise, a broad group of researchers have looked at the interactions of intimacy, family, and state power.[4] In this book I argue that forbidden intimacies—intimacies that are prohibited based on the need to uphold the white, monogamous, heterosexual family ideal—contribute to how the state defines itself by determining its limits of tolerance. I spotlight how regulating conservative, patriarchal family forms enforces boundaries to demarcate intimacies that are favored and disfavored and how these boundaries are important in defining national identity. For many Western governments, polygyny has become the antithesis of what was once another forbidden intimacy: same-gender relations, now often characterized as progressive and forward-thinking.

In *Forbidden Intimacies* I contemplate how conceiving of polygyny as monolithic and exploitative masks the existence of polygamies that proliferate under the conditions of postmodern family life. The idea that polygamy is universally harmful to women, children, and society justifies prohibiting diverse plural families, some happy and successful and others difficult and violent. I will take you on a journey to consider the ways that forbidden relationships are lived and governed in transnational and national contexts. I bring together scholarly sources on sexuality, race, and the state; law and intimacy; and global and transnational sociology to uncover the unique challenges of regulating polygyny within specific transnational and national, religious, and cultural contexts.

Moving forward, I analyze how regulating forbidden intimacies constitutes similar and divergent racial projects based on national identities and transnational movement of laws and ideas across borders, determining what can be tolerated. To understand these racial projects, I examine the racialized and colonial histories that, even today, structure these intimacies and their regulation and how national logics shape regulatory strategies. I consider how *polygamies* in the plural are shaped and lived according to what I call labyrinthine love, how stigma and discrimination shapes different kinds of love, and how those in plural families have resisted these dynamics. Let's begin by considering forbidden intimacies and racial projects.

FORBIDDEN INTIMACIES AND RACIAL PROJECTS

How should we conceptualize forbidden intimacy? Often the focus has been on prohibitions against same-gender sexualities. Historically, nation-states banned same-gender sexualities and other forms of sexual "deviance," even designating the death penalty for those found guilty, such as in England and colonial America. By the nineteenth century the most important sex crime to be regulated in the United States was prostitution, and laws across the country banned it.[5] Although prosecutions of sodomy were far fewer under state laws, enforcement of these laws increasingly focused on men's consensual sex acts with one another. In the late 1880s prohibited conduct between men came to define what it meant to be homosexual, and sodomy laws represented a republican vision of America that excluded "inverts."[6] In prerevolutionary France the crime of sodomy was punished by burning at the stake. After the revolution France became the first country to revoke its anti-homosexual laws, dropping them from the Criminal Code.[7] However, France continued to treat same-gender sexuality as a crime, arresting thousands of men for "offenses against public decency with other males or for solicitation for the purposes of prostitution."[8] This history has shaped how Western nations police intimate relations.

Massive transformations in the organization and regulation of same-gender sexualities have challenged its forbidden status in many parts of the world. Numerous countries have decriminalized homosexuality and provided the equalization of laws relating to same-gender sex. In addition, many have institutionalized protections for LGBTQ+ populations from discrimination and violence and have recognized same-gender intimate relationships and parenting. By 2021, twenty-nine countries in the world had legalized same-gender marriage, and twenty-five of these are in Europe and the Americas.[9] At the same time, the regulation of same-gender sexualities has been important to state logics and their very definition. Historian Margot Canaday analyzed the U.S. federal government's influence on the construction of the category "homosexual."[10] Beginning in the early twentieth century, the state relied on policies tied to immigration, the military, and welfare to deal with the question of same-gender sexuality, leading to the postwar period in which the state came to define the citizen as decisively heterosexual. Over time, the federal government increasingly strengthened regulations to create a "straight state." Sociologist Jyoti Puri further built on this idea of regulating sexuality as necessary to state existence.[11] In analyzing why a colonial law introduced in the Indian penal code in the 1860s to criminalize "unnatural sexual acts" had rarely been prosecuted, Puri argued that, despite the lack of prosecution, the approach of the state was steeped in sexual meaning. In fact, the state expanded and justified its power by referring to "dangerous" sexualities as potentially disrupting the social order. Puri shines light on a colonial project that has criminalized racialized populations and individuals who are seen as sexually and gender-nonconforming in the Global South.[12]

Drawing on human rights discourses to support intervention and domination, actors from the Global North have increasingly pursued LGBTQ+ rights in the Global South, leading to what some have called gay imperialism.[13] Legal scholar Makau Mutua criticizes such approaches to human rights: "The human rights movement is marked by a damning metaphor. The grand narrative of human rights contains a subtext that depicts an epochal contest pitting savages, on the one hand, against victims and saviors, on the other."[14] By fueling a racialized contest over the meaning of human rights, postcolonial regimes regulate sexuality based on reified notions of culture and tradition, often leading to what sociologists call political homophobia to deflect attention away from undemocratic activities.[15] These backlash politics further stigmatize local LGBTQ+ populations that rely on organizations from the Global North for funding and support.

Although discourses of LGBTQ+ rights have fueled gay imperialism, the specter of polygamy has provided a different kind of racial and colonial project based on its perceived threat to heteronormative and monogamous ideals of family. Conservative politicians in Western nations have used the rhetoric of a slippery slope that slides from legal recognition of same-gender marriage to polygamy as a fearmongering tactic against the legalization of same-gender marriage.[16] In response, many LGBTQ+ and feminist actors have emphasized the differences between same-gender unions and polygamy, underlining the virtues of equality and monogamy for the former in contrast to the patriarchal and inegalitarian nature of the latter.[17] These actors argue that polygamy is antithetical to progressive, liberal, and democratic values and instead fosters authoritarian regimes. A prime example is E. J. Graff's nuanced analysis of what marriage is for, in which she seeks to dismantle arguments that assume marriage is the natural terrain of heterosexuals. Graff's counter to the slippery slope argument portrays polygamy as "precisely opposed to a democratic system."[18] For Graff, tribal and despotic societies foster polygamy by putting "kin first" and thus bear little resemblance to "democratic egalitarianism."[19] These kinds of sweeping generalizations are problematic because they link polygamy to racialized populations through orientalist and xenophobic logics, suggesting that these populations are backward and adverse to modern governance. Both gay imperialism and anti–slippery slope logics draw on homonormativity to incorporate homosexuality into mainstream and nationalist cultures, producing what Jasbir Puar calls "homonationalism"—the increasing inclusion of LGBTQ+ rights in predominantly Western conceptions of nationhood.[20] Polygamy, though, is a practice in which sexuality and nationhood are joined through racialized tropes of sexual perversity and excessive male domination.

In this book I examine governance of polygamy in comparative perspective in France (including the French overseas department of Mayotte), Canada, and the United States as a racial project, a framework that elucidates how Western states govern forbidden intimacies to define themselves against a repudiated, racialized other. Michael Omi and Howard Winant conceptualized racial projects as the processes by which "racial meanings are translated into social structures and become racially signified."[21] Racial projects often engage contemporary significations of whiteness that have "'overdetermined' political and cultural meaning."[22] Routinely, whiteness is unexamined in ways that allow it to remain invisible, an unmarked identity like heterosexuality.[23] In some circumstances whiteness becomes discernible and a source of anxiety, marking perceived threats to its privileged status. For example, white individuals participating in polygyny can inspire backlash against this racially repudiated practice.

Regulation of polygamy as a forbidden intimacy transforms ideals of hetero- and homonormativity, monogamy, and whiteness into racialized structures that organize law and policy to define national belonging. In Western contexts forbidden intimacies and practices marked as non-Western are labeled "cultural." Increasing transnational migration pushes states to regulate intimacies that are seen as offensive and other, and these practices often retain their moral disapprobation and collective nature in relation to the implicit whiteness of mainstream society. The prohibition of forbidden patriarchal practices provides an opportunity to juxtapose enlightened "Western" practices against practices from other parts of the world that are viewed as "barbaric." For example, in 2015 the conservative government of Canada relied on gendered and racialized narratives of culture and violence to adopt the Zero Tolerance for Barbaric Cultural Practices Act (Bill S-7). This bill focused on forced marriage, polygamy, and honor killing as cultural issues, stoking xenophobic and anti-immigrant fears about practices seen as coming from less civilized cultures.[24] Such attention to cultural practices that occur only in certain parts of the world or among certain communities perpetuates structural inequalities based on racialization and stigma. According to religious scholar Lori Beaman, "a desire to demonize the patriarchal practices of the illiberal other" can fuel anti-polygamy campaigns to deflect attention away from inegalitarian practices in mainstream society.[25]

In the following pages, you will learn about the racial projects of governments to regulate polygamy. Comparative research shines light on linkages between regulation of cultural practices, national belonging, and political inclusion or exclusion. Changing global dynamics—including the impact of globalization, conflicts in the Middle East, and terrorist attacks across the globe—have pushed many countries to contend with these insecurities by redefining national identity. For example, sociologists Anna Korteweg and Gökçe Yurkadul compared the ways that conflicts over the Muslim headscarf were central to understandings of national identity.[26] They argued that regulating cultural practices deemed as other, such as banning the headscarf or treating it as a problematic practice in the public sphere, provided the glue for defining national belonging. Scholars have also studied arranged marriage as a cultural practice in which dominant Western representations focus on negative cases, conflating arranged marriages with forced marriages.[27] This body of research points to the problematic and inconsistent ways that Western governments have dealt with patriarchal practices. Yet scholars have not fully examined regulation of cultural practices in the context of changing norms of intimacies that are forbidden.

My conceptualization of forbidden intimacies provides a critical lens on the racial projects that Western nations embrace to regulate families seen as patriarchal and oppressive. These projects structure ideals of intimacy—the quality of close association between people. The very conceptualization of intimate relationships—a closeness based on emotion, a feeling of mutual love, or a sexual connection—would seem to defy such patriarchal forms. How could patriarchal family structures that contain inherent gender inequalities provide such intimacy? Lynn Jamieson introduced the idea of practices of intimacy, pointing to the importance of how context matters in the ways that intimacy is negotiated.[28] This more nuanced understanding of intimacy is important to identify the range of practices that could involve close sexual or nonsexual connections. In the case of polygamies, these practices include conceptualizing love in the context of jealousy and harm.

POLYGAMIES ON A CONTINUUM: LOVE, JEALOUSY, AND HARM

Mimi Schippers, in her book *Beyond Monogamy*, argues that heterosexual culture has institutionalized the ideal of the *monogamous couple*. Monogamy demands that "a 'good life' of sexual and emotional intimacy" requires turning "away from other lovers."[29] Similar to the concept of heteronormativity—in which heterosexuality is institutionalized as the dominant sexual model of social, cultural, political, and economic organization—mononormativity institutionalizes the monogamous dyad as the only legitimate and natural relationship form. A growing movement called polyamory, which involves openly committed, emotional, and/or sexual intimacy of more than two people, has sought to challenge this mononormative ideal. Instead of being caught in the web of cheating or having covert sex with another person while in a committed relationship, polyamory is based on a philosophy that all partners are aware of each other and consent to the intimate relationship.

Legislators and practitioners often juxtapose polyamory and other forms of nonmonogamy as progressive and enlightened compared with traditional forms of polygyny. The idea that monogamy is more civilized, gender egalitarian, and associated with Western, Christian values is maintained through depictions of polygyny as uncivilized, gender inegalitarian, and associated with nations in the Global South.[30] Many view polyamory as free of polygyny's problems because participants choose to engage in the practice and because both men and women can have multiple partners.[31] Sociologists Meg Barker and Darren Langridge argue that polyamory and other modern nonmonogamies occur "within a context of new ways of relating that has developed with increasing gender equality, recognition of same-gender relationships, and related moves towards seeing relationship partners as equal with autonomous goals."[32] This conceptualization of polyamory suggests that it is equivalent to monogamy in offering a progressive form of love, in juxtaposition to the brutality of polygyny. Thus traditional forms of polygamy tend to be left out of theorizing on the changing landscape of love and marriage in relation to nonmonogamies.

I take a different approach to understanding polygamy and its regulation by examining how polygyny itself is occurring in the context of changing norms of sexuality and family life. I consider the consequences of regulating polygamies, or the multiple manifestations of nonmonogamy, by focusing on the forms that receive the most disapprobation. Rather than viewing polygyny just in terms of harm, I build on the idea of a continuum, which emerged out of feminist and sexuality scholarship, to conceptualize the multiple ways that polygamies are lived. Feminist theorist Adrienne Rich theorized how heterosexuality is "compulsory," in that it structures women's subordination. Heterosexuality perpetuates a patriarchal system that grants men, as "owners" of women's bodies, access to their labor and reproductive capacity—"the enforcement of heterosexuality for women as a means of assuring male right of physical, economical, and emotional access."[33] To oppose this system, Rich theorized the importance of a "lesbian continuum" to move the definition of what it means to be lesbian beyond the confines of how people identify themselves. A continuum illuminates the importance of nurturing social and sexual bonds among heterosexual and lesbian women as a means of empowerment.[34]

Conceptualizing how polygamies are lived and regulated on a continuum offers an alternative to the standard binary of monogamy versus polygamy, with monogamy considered the gold standard and polygamy considered harmful. Because monogamy, like heterosexuality, is compulsory in Western societies, conceptualizing polygamy along a continuum disrupts the idea that the heterosexual couple is always the basis for romantic and intimate relationships. Schippers explains that monogamy has been central to "social and cultural *regimes of normalcy* implicated in power relations and sexual stratification."[35] Considering how sexual stratification defines normal family life and sexual practice, polygyny falls far outside the "charmed circle," in the words of Gayle Rubin, that sets the standards of what is normal for moral—and therefore deserving—citizens.[36]

In conceptualizing this continuum of lived polygamies, I propose what I call labyrinthine love, a structure of emotions that blends varying types of love, jealousy, and commitment. Labyrinths are complex networks and are often used to describe a maze of intricate passageways and blind alleys. Labyrinthine love challenges the idea of a simple continuum from bad to good, pointing to how inequalities in society also structure the possibilities for love, jealousy, and commitment. Based on various types of nonmonogamies, labyrinthine love offers a more complex analysis of emotions that range from feeling structures in polyamorous relationships, with a focus on honesty and communication, to feeling structures in more coercive forms of polygyny, such as when a wife learns of her husband's marriage to another woman after the fact.

Love is a basic human emotion that has only recently spurred substantial sociological interest.[37] Sociologists understand love to be a social construction that has evolved historically. For example, during the nineteenth century economic considerations for entering marriage became less important, and ideals of romantic love—a concept that first took hold among the bourgeois—spread throughout much of the social order.[38] This ideal promulgated male dominance over women by reinforcing the idea of chivalry and defined women as weak vessels in need of men's protection.[39] In recent years, according to social theorist Anthony Giddens, a new form of love has developed: "confluent love," a type of love that is based on equal emotional exchange and the possibility of mutual sexual pleasure.[40] Confluent love is an idealized structure for polyamory, which does not require sexual exclusivity. Could confluent love also shape the changing structures of polygyny in line with other types of family transformation? I take on this question in this book.

Sociological analyses of love tend not to deal with another emotion that is often closely tied to it: jealousy. Like love, jealousy is a complex emotion combining other emotions, such as pride, betrayal, fear, anger, sadness, loss, and grief.[41] It can be defined as "a protective reaction to a perceived threat to a valued relationship or its quality."[42] Sociologist Gordon Clanton views jealousy as having an important defensive function against adultery, thereby protecting marriage and preserving the social order. His research examines the transformation of romantic jealousy. According to Clanton, before the sexual revolution, Western societies tended to understand jealousy as a "proof of love," based on the ideal of monogamy.[43] In contrast, the modern emphasis on personal freedom and choice has transformed jealousy into a negative emotion in a person who is "unduly possessive, insecure, and suffering from low self-esteem."[44] This perspective assumes that romantic jealousy is experienced in a monogamous relationship and that a third party is never welcome and always a threat.

Jealousy is conceptualized differently in nonmonogamous relationships, in particular, in polyamory. In polyamory, having other lovers is consensually negotiated and does not in and of itself constitute a reason for jealousy. Jillian Deri studied polyamory among queer women and found that they felt jealous "when their partner started to date someone new, when the partner fell in love, when the other lover was too similar to themselves, when there were overlapping roles, when they felt less secure in their relationship," and so forth.[45] This complex conceptualization of love and its connections to jealousy are central to my idea of labyrinthine love. Sociologist John Alan Lee outlined six broad styles of modern love: Eros (passionate, romantic love), Ludus (game-playing love), Storge (friendship-based love), Pragma (practical love), Mania (possessive, dependent love), and Agape (altruistic love).[46] Labyrinthine love involves various combinations of these styles. It also involves recognizing that jealousy is central to how love is experienced in monogamous and multiple relationships. Practitioners in the polyamory community have offered alternative language to reconceptualize sexual jealousy, such as "compersion," to capture the experience of feeling pleasure instead of fear or anger when one's partner has a sexually pleasing relationship with another person.[47] Thus, in the literature on nonmonogamy, jealousy is an emotion that can evolve into a positive feeling that adds to labyrinthine love. Moving beyond polyamory, we will think about how labyrinthine love, including jealousy, is important to conceptualizing polygyny in contemporary societies.

WHAT WE KNOW ABOUT POLYGYNY

Polygyny is accepted or enjoys legal status in many parts of the world. However, according to data gathered by Pew Research in 2020, "only about 2 percent of the global population lives in polygamous households."[48] Countries where polygyny was once legal now prohibit it, such as Tunisia and Benin, and other countries where it is legal have created more stringent rules for its practice.[49] If polygyny is a minority practice, why does it persist and even thrive in places where it is recognized and why is it lived underground where it is not? As a multidimensional phenomenon, no single reason can be identified. Being a deeply rooted sociocultural practice for some populations and even being permitted in some religions, such as Islam, certainly contribute to its persistence. In some cases polygyny is perpetuated by high-status men who desire more offspring. In other cases polygyny has economic advantages for women, or women support it when there is a lack of marriageable men, as Patricia Dixon-Spear found in her research on African American polygynous marriages.[50]

What does research on polygyny tell us about this family form? Legal scholars and philosophers have debated its harmfulness.[51] For example, legal scholar Martha Strassberg argues that polygyny is injurious to the liberal democratic state.[52] In contrast, Mark Goldfeder contends not only that polygyny reflects the legislative values and freedoms of the United States but that it can also be incorporated into our current legal system.[53] Empirical research provides evidence of polygyny's detrimental effects, though. In her book *The Evils of Polygyny*, Rose McDermott analyzed WomanStats Data and found that women are polygyny's primary victims; women experience increased violence and mental health problems, but men also suffer in societies where the concentration of benefits is relegated to a few men with the most economic, political, and social power.[54] She says, "The majority of poorer men have reduced reproductive access because so many women are monopolized by very few men."[55] Studies that have compared monogamous and polygynous marriages have found that polygynous unions tend to have a higher prevalence of spousal conflict, tension, jealousy, and stress.[56] Social scientist Alean Al-Krenawi has conducted numerous studies with colleagues on polygyny in the Middle East, finding in broad terms that women in polygynous marriages have more mental health problems and lower self-esteem and are unhappy compared with women in monogamous marriages.[57] In this context, jealousy is seen as a negative emotion that leads to poor mental health outcomes. Research in sub-Saharan African countries with high levels of polygyny has found a greater incidence of intimate partner violence among polygynous marriages than among monogamous ones.[58]

Although studies have attested to polygyny's harm, researchers have also complicated these findings. For example, even though some scholars identified polygynous unions as leading to higher levels of intimate partner violence, they also found that social context and environment are important.[59] For example, a recent study of polygyny in Nigeria found that unobserved selection effects concerning who enters polygynous unions were significant in determining different levels of violence between monogamous and polygynous marriages.[60] Comparative methodologies, as well as accounting for selection effects, have also been important to the debates over harm. A study of polygyny in Tanzania compared differences between polygynous and monogamous unions across and within villages to challenge the predominant view that polygyny is necessarily harmful.[61] The researchers found that, although polygyny was associated with poor child health and low food security when measured with all villages in the model, disaggregating the data showed that polygynous unions had better health outcomes and more food security, especially when children and fathers were co-resident. The prevalence of low food security and poor child health were "driven entirely by the tendency of polygyny to be more common in marginalized and ecologically vulnerable villages and ethnic groups."[62] Moreover, the researchers demonstrated that the costs of sharing a husband were counterbalanced by greater wealth (land and livestock) in polygynous households, suggesting that polygyny, even though gender inegalitarian in structure, might lend itself to gender equality in property rights for women who depend on men for resources. Another study on a fishing village in Sierra Leone also found that polygyny increased women's status and economic independence.[63]

Qualitative research offers further evidence that polygyny should not be treated as a singularly harmful structure. Focusing on France, Canada, and the United States—the three countries that I compare in this book—researchers have offered evidence that polygynous unions have their advantages and disadvantages. In France much of the research has considered the living conditions of polygamous families, who are often cramped into small, more affordable apartments in the suburbs of Paris.[64] Christian Poiret conducted interviews with families from West Africa, many of them polygynous.[65] The first wife in a Senegalese polygynous family talked of the security of having another wife at home when she was at work or if she fell ill. Her co-wife, however, said that she wanted to go back to Senegal, where she had lived well and not in a cramped apartment. Rivalry was a common theme that many co-wives experienced, but still co-wives would work together to care for the children and create a positive family environment. However, the issue of a lack of space was challenging for all.[66]

The most extensive research on polygyny in the United States and Canada has been on fundamentalist Mormons. Anthropologists Irwin Altman and Joseph Ginat conducted ethnographic research with twenty-six fundamentalist Mormon plural families in the United States, examining the ways that these families reconciled the communal ideals of the polygynous lifestyle with the need for intimacy.[67] They found that ideals of companionship among co-wives was one of the great attractions of plural marriage for women, along with sharing the responsibilities of housework and child care. Janet Bennion also conducted ethnographic research in a contemporary fundamentalist community in a town she calls Harker, Montana.[68] This group of roughly 900 people belonging to the Apostolic

United Brethren is highly patriarchal. However, Bennion details how these wives "find surprising sources of power and autonomy," though their lives are still "laced with certain serious compromises to their ultimate freedom and human rights."[69] Supporting the idea of multiple polygamies, Bennion found that women's experiences in these families varied significantly. Angela Campbell conducted in-depth interviews of plural wives in a polygynous community of about 1,000 people in Bountiful, British Columbia, Canada's only openly polygamous community.[70] She found that conjugal pluralism exists in the community and that fundamentalist Mormon women experienced varying degrees of choice and agency. Overall, these studies point to the tensions among these communities between religious obligations and a desire for intimacy and romantic love.[71]

In the United States, Hmong Americans, Muslims of varying ethnicities, and members of the Pan-African Ausar Auset Society practice polygyny.[72] Patricia Dixon-Spear conducted research on women in polygynous relationships in the Ausar Auset Society and among Muslim African Americans. The society was founded in 1973 to offer an alternative way of life for Africans in America and throughout the diaspora, with the objective of embracing an alternative lifestyle based on traditional African culture. Women in plural marriages in this society felt that, for polygyny to work, all wives must agree on bringing in a new wife and that polygyny must be practiced in a spiritual or social community that provides support, including counseling. Although Dixon-Spear found that many of the Muslim African American women she interviewed were not ready for polygyny, some embraced the practice and sought to nurture sisterly love among wives. Debra Majeed conducted ethnographic research on polygyny among practitioners of the African American Nation of Islam.[73] She identified three broad categories of experiences among polygynous women: Some made a conscious choice to enter polygyny and felt liberated by it; a smaller number chose polygyny as a strategy to share the burdens of marriage with another wife; and some experienced polygyny negatively, feeling coerced to accept another wife. Importantly, there were no cases of underage or forced marriage.

Some evidence also exists that transformations of intimacy are shaping global patterns of polygynous unions. A study of trends in marriage and spousal relationships in the Negev Bedouin society pointed to how broader social, political, and economic exigencies have shaped "neo-polygynous" unions with women outside their community, from Romania, Russia, Morocco, and Ethiopia.[74] These relationships were grounded in love, above all, pointing to the ways that traditional societies are transforming to embrace "choice, based upon emotion, attraction and Western notions of romantic love."[75] Another study examined how transnational migration shaped what is often thought to be static patriarchal traditions in Muslim polygynous unions.[76] Interviewing Pakistanis in Britain and Turks in Denmark, the researchers found evidence of great variety in the practice of multiple marriages, leading to "new permutations" of polygyny based on transnational migration and distance.[77] One example was a polygynous family that was established in Pakistan after the first wife developed arthritis and could no longer care for her children. She accompanied her husband to ask for the hand of the second wife. Later, the second wife and husband migrated to Britain with some of the children from the first marriage. As the father's health deteriorated, he needed to move back to the warmer climate in Pakistan. The second wife, who remained in Britain with the children, suggested that her husband marry again to have someone to look after him. The researchers interviewed the second wife's daughter, who was then in her 30s and had been born in Britain. She described the three wives "as having a good relationship, 'like sisters.'"[78]

This body of research suggests that polygyny is not monolithic and that complex systems of love may apply, as is the case for other nonmonogamies such as polyamory. Understanding this complexity is important to thinking about government regulation, particularly in Western nations that prohibit polygyny. Much of the research that has examined the complexities of polygynous unions and debates over harmful consequences either have not been empirical or have studied it in contexts where polygyny is permitted, such as in the Middle East and Africa. Here, I compare the lived experience of polygamies in the Western context where it is banned. As such, I examine the consequences of regulating polygyny as a monolithic practice.

STUDYING POLYGAMY IN THE WESTERN WORLD

What are forbidden intimacies, and how should they be studied? To date, there is a lack of research on how the state shapes and is shaped by intimacies that are seen as antithetical to "progressive" Western values. In this book I illuminate the debates over how to regulate patriarchal and outlawed family forms by providing a comparative analysis of government regulation. I take the cases of France (including Mayotte), Canada, and the United States, each with its own distinctive state regime, to uncover the dynamics of regulating the diverse lives of those living polygamies as forbidden. The goal is to illuminate the troubled relationship between laws that seek to curtail practices viewed to be harmful and how those laws are lived.

To accomplish this, comparative research is necessary to illustrate not only the differences but also the ways that ideas travel across time and place. Examining how polygamies are experienced and regulated in different places moves away from the simplistic dichotomy that focuses solely on whether or not polygyny is harmful. It allows us to conceptualize polygamies that are lived and structured differently based on social context, geography, and labyrinthine love. I move beyond assumptions of states as "bounded entities delimited by location," conducting instead a "relational ethnography" more concerned with fields and practices than places and bounded groups.[79] Consequently, I draw on transnational scholarship that theorizes on how law and culture move across borders and ponder how relations of forbidden intimacies are formed within and beyond country contexts.

In considering the movement of laws and culture, it is important to keep in mind transnational feminist critiques of global and international feminist tendencies to reify national borders.[80] Sociologist Vrushali Patil assesses the problematic way that patriarchy has been used in this literature, offering "homogenous, monolithic accounts of gender oppression."[81] She calls for more nuanced accounts of historical and contemporary patriarchies that are multidimensional and contextually situated, bringing to light the ways that colonization and decolonization shape gender dynamics and sexual hierarchy. In postcolonial relations the spatial nature of empire has been extremely important to maintaining gendered and sexual hierarchies that have privileged the heterosexual state.[82] By studying forbidden intimacies to understand cross-border movement of people, laws, and ideas and by focusing on historical and contemporary patriarchies, I illuminate the boundary work that Western nations do to structure their identities based on "progressive" ideals of intimacy.

The three countries and Mayotte that are the focus of this book offer important political and religious comparisons and opportunities to study the transnational movement of law and culture. The contemporary United States is exceptional for its strong "religious right" influence on political culture and legislation and for its strong focus on "family values."[83] The American version of the ideal "secular political order" incorporates a religious imperative to inhibit "the secularization of consciousness."[84] At the other end of the spectrum is France, with its principle of *laïcité*, or adherence to a French form of secularism that looks to the state to protect individuals from the claims of religion.[85] Its homogeneous republicanism places equal importance on marriage and family formation. The influence of religion on Canada's political system falls somewhere in between that of the United States and France. On the one hand, Canada has experienced a reduced role of religion in politics. The most extreme case is in Quebec, where the principle of *laïcité* is present, albeit with different manifestations than in France.[86] On the other hand, religion continues to play a strong symbolic role in Canadian lives.[87] The cultural and historical links between these countries allow me to theorize on the movement of law and culture across borders and how these relate to polygyny's prohibition.

Prohibition of polygamy in these countries is complex. In all three, marrying someone while still being lawfully married to another is bigamy, a criminal offense with varying penalties. However, laws concerning polygamy vary in their severity and enforcement, and regulating polygyny has historical and transnational links. Canada and the United States share an Anglo-Protestant heritage and face a growing concern over polygyny's practice among members of fundamentalist Mormonism, who predominantly live in Utah but also in communities in the other Western states, Western Canada, and northern Mexico. The estimated population is 40,000–60,000.[88] In Canada all forms of polygamy and some informal multiple sexual relationships are a criminal offense under Section 293 of the Criminal Code and are punishable by imprisonment for up to five years.[89] Polygamy is illegal in all fifty U.S. states. However, Utah is exceptional: Polygamy was once a felony, but in 2020 the state reduced the penalty to a misdemeanor, on the level of a traffic ticket, effectively decriminalizing it.[90] The three countries share concern over the growth of immigrant populations who hail from countries in which polygyny is legal and authorized by Islam or cultural tradition.[91] Transnational migration of polygynous families has often meant acceptance of its de facto practice among immigrants. France has the largest population of polygamous families in Europe as a result of French family reunification policies that authorized members of these families to immigrate to join their husbands and fathers from West Africa who were brought over as cheap labor.[92] With an estimated 200,000 people living in polygyny, the practice was tolerated for a time. In 1993, living in a polygamous household was banned under the Pasqua law. Naming polygamy an affront to women's rights, the French government sought to implement a policy where men must "decohabit"—live with only one wife—or lose their work permit.[93] France has also had to regulate polygyny in Mayotte, which became France's 101st department in 2011, making its inhabitants citizens of France. Ninety-five percent of its population is Muslim, and the traditional practice of polygyny was outlawed before Mayotte became a department. All these cases represent an incongruity between prohibition and practice.

I conducted ethnographic research over a period of four years from 2010 to 2016.[94] The study includes 145 interviews with 165 participants. I turned to the existing research conducted by sociologists and anthropologists in each country to identify central actors and used purposive sampling, seeking a wide range of participants. I contacted people who had written about polygamy or who had worked with polygamist populations to interview and help me identify key informants who could also introduce me to those living in polygyny, those having lived in polygyny, or those who had worked closely with these populations. I decided, when possible, to interview scholars who had studied polygamy in each country to gain more insight into the research that has helped guide my own scholarship. Often, we focus only on the populations we are studying, but I thought it important to include the voices of scholars who have helped shape the discourses concerning polygamy. I also interviewed government officials, social workers, lawyers, people living in polygyny, and people who had left their polygynous marriages.

The project began in Vancouver, Canada, in 2010, when the province of British Columbia initiated a reference case, submitting questions to the courts to ask for an advisory opinion on the constitutionality of banning polygamy in Canada. I spent three months attending the hearings and analyzed hundreds of pages of legal documents from the case, including affidavits, opening and closing arguments, and the final decision. In 2011 and in the summer of 2016, I conducted twenty-two interviews with lawyers, interveners, and leaders of feminist groups in Vancouver and Montreal. In 2013 I traveled to France to contact individuals working with polygynous families and to conduct initial interviews. I returned in 2015 to conduct forty-one interviews with forty-eight individuals, twenty-nine with government officials, organizations that advocate for polygynous families, and with groups that seek to end the practice of polygyny. I conducted nineteen interviews with individuals who were in or had left a polygynous family and/or had grown up in one. I visited the archives at the Ministry of the Interior in Paris to gather legal documents, reports, and media stories on polygyny. In the summer of 2015 I spent two months in Mayotte, conducting thirty-one interviews with government officials, including local and national representatives, organizations that dealt with the issue, and religious leaders. I interviewed eight people who openly discussed their polygynous lives (for a total of thirty-nine interviews).

My study of plural families in the United States spanned six months in 2014 and early 2015. I traveled throughout the state of Utah and northern Arizona to interview individuals living in plural families, those who had left, and government officials and organizations that worked with polygynous populations. I spent time in fundamentalist Mormon communities, including attending a dance, a church service, and a high school basketball game. I interviewed a plural family that was part of a sustainable community that had built houses into the rock of a canyon. Out of forty-three interviews with fifty-eight participants, thirty-seven were individuals and families that were currently in, had grown up in, or had left a plural family. I conducted twenty-one interviews with government officials, anti-polygamy activists, social workers, and lawyers who worked with polygynous populations. The diversity of people I interviewed in these three countries and Mayotte allows for an in-depth analysis of the relationship between regulatory structures and the effects of these on people's everyday lives.

In the pages that follow, I examine the regulation of forbidden intimacies at the limits of Western tolerance by mapping out the tensions between the diversity of polygamies that are lived and the state projects that seek to eradicate and/or regulate them. Comparatively, I investigate how understandings of national identity, whether based on ideologies of assimilation, multiculturalism, or republicanism, shape the legal approaches to regulating forbidden intimacies and consider how these ideas move across borders. I examine how homegrown and migratory polygamies are shaped and lived in the context of prohibition and map out the racialized and colonial histories that shape these intimacies and their regulation. I delve into the debates over patriarchy, theorizing in greater depth on the ways that patriarchies are lived and how agency is negotiated among women living in polygyny. Overall, my goal is to investigate how intimate citizenship is shaped by and shapes the state, examining national narratives of who belongs based on their choices of intimacy.

1 | RACIAL PROJECTS AND UNEXPECTED DIVERGENCES

> The [Constitutional] Council did not define "normal family life," but in its 1993 decision, concerning foreigners living in France, it stated that "the conditions for normal family life are those which prevail in France, the host country, which exclude polygamy."
> —*Françoise Monéger, former justice, France 2013*[1]

> White American Mormons were engaging in a practice thought to be characteristic of Asiatic and African peoples who were believed, at the time, to be civilizationally and racially inferior. . . . White American Christians, the Court implied, legislate monogamy.
> —*Judge Clark Waddoups, United States, 2013*[2]

> The harms said to be associated with polygamy directly threaten the benefits felt to be associated with the institution of monogamous marriage—felt to be so associated since the advent of socially imposed universal monogamy in Greco-Roman society.
> —*Chief Justice Robert Bauman, Canada, 2011*[3]

THE THREE EPIGRAPHS REFLECT GOVERNMENT logics that embrace the "superior" norm of monogamy to justify the right of government to ban polygamy and regulate intimacies. France, the United States, and Canada have each used this issue to elevate Western values over "uncivilized" nations. Looking more closely at these quotes, we can see that the first underscores the national logic of France that has banned polygamy for anyone entering its territory. Regulating polygyny as forbidden in France has depended on an imagined French family that is white, heterosexual, and ostensibly monogamous.[4] The preamble of France's constitution in 1946 defined what constitutes a legitimate family as the right to lead a "normal family life." Paragraph 10 states, "The Nation shall provide the individual and the family with the conditions necessary to their development."[5] This focus on the normal family offers a window into France's national logic of republicanism.

The second quote comes from Judge Waddoups's 2013 decision in *Brown v. Buhman* that found parts of Utah's anti-polygamy law unconstitutional. Waddoups refers to the 1879 Supreme Court case *Reynolds v. United States*, which upheld the first of four statutes of the law to force Mormons to abandon the practice of plural marriage and justified polygamy's prohibition in two passages that linked it to "Asiatic and African peoples" and "stationary despotism."[6] Referencing a global racial hierarchy, the *Reynolds* case laid the bedrock for all future determinations of polygamy in the United States.[7] This legal history shines light on the racialized national logic that views white, monogamous marriage as the central feature of social life.

In the final quote, Canadian justice Bauman, in his 2011 decision on the polygamy reference case, offers the rationale for why prohibiting polygamy is constitutional. The law criminalizing polygamy was passed in 1890, mainly to deal with Mormon families that had migrated to Alberta from the United States. Panic over Mormon polygyny was so intense that the Criminal Code prohibition on marrying more than one spouse cited Mormons in its text until the 1950s. Justice Bauman defended the law in stating that "harms said to be associated with polygamy" have the ability to threaten the institution of monogamous marriage, demonstrating the continued centrality of this institution to Canada's national identity.

In this chapter I consider how governments rely on Western ideals of "the family" to control and regulate the public order through racial projects that decide who belongs in the body politic. How these projects are instituted in each nation depends on national identity. Governments often rely on morality—tacitly or explicitly grounded in Christian values—to define legitimate and illegitimate intimacies.[8] Those practices deemed illegitimate have limited rights to privacy and are more susceptible to government intrusion. The idea that polygyny is a racialized practice makes its illegality appear commonsense and beyond doubt. Yet states apply such laws unevenly. I introduce the idea of *administrative ambivalence* to capture the contradictory nature of the racial projects that states use to rectify the tensions that arise from regulation. Administrative ambivalence is defined by a state's racial project that criminalizes forbidden intimacies as central to its national identity while at the same time inconsistently applying the law or ignoring it. It relates to the distinction made by legal scholars between "law on the books" and "law in action," or the gap between what is written and the "actual practices of legal officials and the public in cases of disputes."[9] Administrative ambivalence speaks further to policies that are likewise ambivalently applied.

In the pages that follow, I compare regulation of polygyny in France, the United States, and Canada to reveal the unexpected divergences in national logics. First, I consider France's focus on the "normal" family and the ambivalence arising from the goal of treating everyone the same. This approach leads to contradictory and often hypocritical consequences. Next, I turn to the United States and the attempts in Utah to address polygyny among white populations that are repudiated for participating in racialized and patriarchal family formations. Still, state officials are ambivalent about enforcing the law on a population that resembles the majority. Finally, I consider how Canada's national identity as a multicultural society has pushed it toward a more punitive approach. Even though Canada has declared tolerance of diversity, it has embraced an anti-polygamy stance that exceeds that of France or the United States. The comparison offers important perspectives on how racial projects define national identity.

REGULATING THE "NORMAL" FAMILY IN FRANCE

The racial project of regulating polygamy is centered on citizenship and belonging. In France the Civil Code makes explicit the need to deny French nationality when assimilation is insufficient: "The polygamous status of the foreign spouse . . . [is] proof of a lack of assimilation."[10] How did polygamy come to define a lack of assimilation in France? To answer this question, we must consider the national ideology and family policy that highlight tensions between pluralistic democracy and universalism. Since the French Revolution, the concept of *républicanisme* has been about a universal French community, which Jean-Jacques Rousseau characterized as the "general will," an absolute, indivisible source of political authority.[11] French universalism underscores the importance of sameness for achieving equality, understood as formal equality before the law.[12] Universalism complements *laïcité*, roughly equivalent to secularism, which demarcates separation of church and state, demanding that the state protect individuals from the claims of religion.[13] In recent years assimilation has come to literally represent the suppression of difference. Fearing that focusing on difference will disunite the nation, the French census, for example, does not record the race or ethnicity, religion, or national origin of the population living in France.

In contrast to universalism, the term *communautarisme* (communalism) emerged in the 1980s to deal with "difference," characterized by former colonial subjects from North and West Africa who migrated to France.[14] The French logic of integration rejects communalism for its emphasis on group over national identity. From this perspective, identifying more with one's group—for example, identifying with one's ethnic origins over national identity—impedes integration. Christophe Daadouche, a lawyer and member of GISTI (Groupe d'Information et de Soutien des Immigrés), a French nonprofit organization whose goal is to protect the legal and political rights of foreigners and immigrants, told me that communalism, often nurtured in ethnic enclaves or niches,[15] is not "an insult" in North America. In France, "If you say *communautarisme*, you have people pulling out their weapons!" Daadouche explained, "It's fear of the Anglo-Saxon model, but it's really crippling" to the point that "no community action is carried out." He outlined how certain racial categories are important to what counts as difference: "With the *kippah* [Jewish skullcap], no one is going to talk about *communautarisme*, but when it comes to other populations, suddenly we use that term" to demarcate immigrant or racialized people by their "non-Western" practices, such as polygamy.

Although Daadouche was critical of the way that *communautarisme* triggers surveillance of specific populations, Sonia Imloul, a social worker of Algerian origin and head of an organization called Respect 93, which works to prevent youth crime in the Parisian *banlieues*, described to me during our interview the need to ensure that young children of immigrants do not succumb to communalism. Her 2010 report on polygamy for the

Institut Montaigne, a liberal think tank, emphasized the threat of polygamy to France's social cohesion.[16] She told me:

> These situations are in any case catastrophic for children, and they are not going in the direction of social development or assimilation, like the French state desires. On the contrary, they risk generating great difficulties for integration, but also a regression which would lead young people to return to a form of *communautarisme*.

From Imloul's perspective the French state is right to forbid polygamy, because it will lead youth down a slippery slope to communalism.

Republicanism and the more recent rejection of communalism have shaped French family policies that propel a particular vision. For the French nation the state prioritizes the normative heterosexual, monogamous family, positioning it in the secular realm outside religious tradition or meaning. Historian Camille Robcis studied how the French emphasis on the normative family is central to its republican identity, a way to reaffirm its universalism in the face of changing societal norms brought on by postcolonialism and globalization.[17] According to Robcis, family activists in the first half of the twentieth century successfully prioritized the family as the most universal mode of representation for maintaining the public order. As a secular institution, the family facilitates social cohesion and is perceived as an institution beyond politics, capable of building political consensus. Still, as historian Judith Surkis demonstrates, republican conceptions of marriage are strongly tied to the Catholic Church and its problematic rapport with marital modernity.[18] For example, France's policy of annulment underscores how French law seeks to uphold *laïcité* while also allowing the specificity of annulment as an alternative to divorce.

A focus on democratic pluralism and integration has led the French government to regulate forbidden intimacies with administrative ambivalence, steering it to define the normative family in relation to what is prohibited while simultaneously tolerating this forbidden intimacy. Thus France reinforces its national identity (republicanism) by regulating "foreign family forms" in contradictory ways.[19] Beginning in the 1950s, pluralistic democracy became more important in shaping civil law to recognize the rights of individuals whose cultural norms differed from dominant French values.

For example, polygynous families migrating from countries where polygyny is allowed had some limited rights in France. The principle of attenuated public policy (*l'ordre public atténué*) was established in the 1953 *Rivière* case, in which the Conseil d'État (Council of State; France's highest court for cases involving public administration) recognized a divorce by mutual consent that was pronounced abroad but not recognized in France.[20] Legal scholar Michel Farge explained to me that this principle allowed France to "be less strict in the presence of a situation that had arisen abroad [such as polygyny]," allowing a "relaxation" in "defending our values, defending our policies."

The Conseil d'État then established a new general principle of law in 1978: the right to lead a normal family life.[21] The decision annulled a decree made in 1977 that suspended family reunification for family members who sought access to the labor market. The Conseil defined this right as ensuring that "the nation provides the individual and the family with the necessary conditions for their development."[22] In 1980 the *Montcho* decision confronted the question of whether this right applied to immigrant polygynous families. The case concerned a citizen of Benin who had married two women in Dahomey in accordance with local law. In 1967 the husband obtained a ten-year residence permit in France, bringing his first wife and children. A few months later, he brought his second wife and her four children. A French prefect in the district where the family lived ordered the second wife to leave the territory. Reviewing this decision, the Conseil annulled the prefect's demand for expulsion. Importantly, the Conseil ruled that polygyny was not in itself contrary to the French public order and was justified by the right to lead a normal family life. My interview with sociologist Isabelle Gillette-Faye, the director of an organization that deals with issues concerning excision and forced marriage, noted that France's initial approach to regulating polygyny was not *communautariste*, because "France remains very, very integrationist and assimilationist, but there was still a very, very great tolerance regarding the mores and customs of others." Her words point to the tension in France's republican approach that ultimately sought to recognize the rights of polygynous families and allow reunification.

France's tolerance of polygyny ended in 1993. The right-wing government headed by Édouard Balladur openly proclaimed a goal of "zero" immigration, passing the Pasqua and Debré laws. The goal was to roll back immigrant rights and limit the ability of migrants to settle in France. These laws applied restrictions for polygynous families to access and renew ten-year residence permits, which forced "secondary" spouses to choose one of three options: (1) divorce and *décohabitation*, requiring the wives to live separately; (2) continue to live together in polygyny, which could mean falling into irregular status; or (3) return to their country of origin. Anthropologist Catherine Quiminal explained to me during our interview, "The Pasqua law did not 'forbid' polygamy—one cannot forbid what is already illegal [obtaining multiple marriage licenses]. The law made it a condition to not practice it on French territory to obtain a residence permit." Polygyny was recognized as a form of *communautarisme*, a "foreign" family form that migrated to France as fundamentally *not* French. The 1995 decision of the Conseil Constitutionnel (the Constitutional Council; the highest constitutional authority in France) confirmed that polygyny could never be French. Its definition of normal family life read:

> The conditions for normal family life are those generally accepted in France, the host country, which excludes polygamous marriages; therefore, the restrictions imposed by the law on the right to family reunification of polygamous persons and the penalties provided for its enforcement are constitutional.[23]

Significantly, the decision did not specify what constitutes a normal family other than excluding polygynous marriages. Thus France's republican identity upholding normal family life is defined in the negative, as not polygynous.

A 1994 article in *Plein Droit*, a quarterly publication that analyzes the situation of immigrant communities in French society, criticized the Pasqua law for its implication that all immigrants are polygynous. The ideal family model that France upholds is "the father, the mother and the children (not too many!); a family that needs to be well integrated. Being integrated means living like other [families]."[24] In 2000 the Interior Ministry released a circular stating that the retroactive provisions of the laws did not apply to the first wife of a polygamous husband but only to his subsequent wives. Thus first wives could still receive ten-year residence permits. At the same time, the circular stated, "The prohibition of the principle of polygamy is based on the necessary respect for republican values, women's rights, and the integration of children"; thus it specifically linked the normal family to French republican values and national belonging.[25] Michel Farge elaborated that "polygamy crystallized all the difficulties of integration in France."

France's understanding of polygamy as attributable only to immigrant populations is a racial project. This project focuses on polygamy and other cultural practices to mark nonassimilability, such as wearing the headscarf and female genital cutting. In 1989 three French teenagers wearing headscarves at their high school in a Parisian *banlieue* sparked a fifteen-year debate that ended in banning headscarves from French elementary and high schools.[26] The debate focused on the practice's threat to French communalism. Likewise, debate over assimilation has focused on female genital cutting. In the European Union France has the most extensive jurisprudence on female genital cutting, systematically bringing cases to court. The government and media have attributed female genital cutting as a form of violence akin to rape or slavery.[27] These discourses work together to provide a picture of the unassimilable and racialized other, making immigrants and racialized practices appear as one and the same.

The creation of the racialized other allows France to ignore its own history, such as laws that include certain forms of polygamy. I interviewed Catherine Ternaux, who explained in her book *Polygamy, Why Not?* that "the French Revolution allowed successive polygamy: this is how divorce was qualified when it was authorized in 1792. . . . Certainly successive, but polygamy all the same, in the strict sense, married several times."[28] Michel Farge told me that pluralism in French policy tolerates nonmonogamy except in the case of polygyny for racialized populations: "One can say that either French law is hypocritical, or one can say that French law is tolerant of de facto polygamy." France tolerates multiple romantic or sexual relationships engaged in serially or simultaneously but not "polygamy." Catherine Quiminal discussed the racism of this approach: "Polygamy is not a fundamental problem in France. That's why I told you that racism was a reason, because there are ten thousand questions to deal with other than that." More pressing problems include immigrant women who cannot read and write. Associations provide some opportunity for women to learn, but they are left "pretty much at the level of a seven-year-old girl. It can't work, because even the cleaning ladies, they must be able to read and write. If they take bleach to wash the baby, there will be accidents!" Quiminal described how every time polygamy is put forward as *the* problem, "it produces racism."

Racializing polygamy as something that occurs only among other cultures allows the French government to maintain an administrative ambivalence that is harsh at times and tolerant at others. Social scientist Pauline Gaullier, who conducted extensive research on polygyny and the policy of decohabitation (requiring co-wives to live elsewhere with their children), discussed with me how the Pasqua law sent a signal to polygynous African families that they were no longer welcome on French territory and "must go back to their country." The legislation specified the "departure of all or part of the family," sending a signal to families migrating to France that they must live in accordance with France's customs, "in conformity with republican principles." The policy of decohabitation was another solution, because expelling families that had already settled in France would create a political quagmire. Some were not expellable, as they had children born in France. Gaullier explained that the state did not immediately set in motion the means to help families decohabit. "It was not put into place until the beginning of the 2000s. So, between 1993 and 2000, families were plunged overnight into illegality, with all the catastrophic consequences that this has in terms of salary resources, allowances, etc." Once the government did implement the policy, it did so in uneven and often punitive ways.

Decohabitation sought to help families exit from overcrowded housing conditions *and* required husbands to divorce all wives except the first to renew their residence permit. Quiminal explained, "With [former minister] Chevènement, they set up decohabitation. It required people to divorce, which is not very legal that the state forces a family to divorce. It's a fairly violent entry into the family." She described decohabitation as an "extremely strong control system," because it meant that social workers had to determine whether young women were children of the husband or one of several wives in the household. I asked sociologist Christian Poiret about the objectives of this government policy. He offered what he viewed to be the official government objectives versus the reality.

The official objective, it depends. It is to respect French legislation, which doesn't want the practice of polygyny on French territory. Then, you have a whole discourse on the principle of gender equality, etc. The reality is that if we had really wanted to implement a policy of decohabitation, we would not have only pushed women and men to divorce, but we would have given them [the means to live], which was not the case.

According to Poiret, many families have experienced great financial difficulty in maintaining more than one household. For some, it made decohabitation impossible.

More concerning to many of my participants was the disordered way that the state dealt with decohabitation. One social worker stated, "The difficulty is that depending on the prefectures, the understanding of the law is different. And I know that in Seine-Saint-Denis, for example, they applied the law in a strict sense, different from Essonne." In Essonne social workers had more latitude to work with families to find affordable housing without forcing divorce. She described the prefecture of Essonne as "quite tolerant on the issue." In other cases, even the terms of the legislation were not respected. Gaullier described how the legislation was supposed to protect first wives by ensuring renewal of their residence permits, but this often did not happen: "The first wives had their residence permit withdrawn to be replaced by much more precarious ones." She noted that this tactic "points to the question of discrimination against these families." The lack of a residence permit translated to precarity in jobs and social housing.

The conditions under which secondary wives were rehoused depended largely on the department and on the possibilities for finding housing. Christophe Daadouche, as well as many of the association leaders I interviewed, explained the challenges of undertaking the process of decohabitation, particularly in terms of being regularized: "There must be assurance that by moving away Madame can be regularized. If she cannot be regularized, the decohabitation cannot take place, because she cannot have a lease. So, she cannot get family benefits and cannot pay the rent. Thus, it is really necessary that all the conditions are met for the decohabitation to take place." Putting conditions in place meant an undue burden on secondary wives. The unevenness of the process translated into some districts allowing families to have two apartments on the same floor or in the same housing complex. In other cases departments required wives and children to be relocated far away from each other, even to other towns. Daadouche described the state's irrationality in forcing husbands to divorce secondary wives and then moving them to another apartment in the same housing complex.

> It makes me laugh! Republican morality is safe. Building A, apartment 1, there is a gentleman with a wife. Right across the street, in the apartment across the street, is the other wife with the children. That is to say that they are in the same stairwell, in the same building, one opposite the other. Republican morals and the law have imposed that, so they can say, "That's it, the family has decohabited."

Republican morality is key to understanding France's administrative ambivalence in supporting a policy of breaking up polygynous families to make them accord with French values in which secondary wives are, at least legally, treated as single mothers.

In the end, French officials did little to ensure that the divorce, when required, was real. According to Agna, an association leader who helped families to decohabit, the separation "remained only administrative for some, since the man continued to have his two wives, and have two dwellings, but one in which it was officially declared and the other in which it was not. While that did not necessarily solve the problem of polygamy, at least it did solve the housing problem." She explained that whether wives continued to share their husband had to do with "their intimacy—that doesn't concern us." The social workers I interviewed agreed that many men continued their relations with multiple wives, even if that meant commuting long distances.

France's administrative ambivalence toward regulating polygyny is also evident in how family benefits have been allocated to multiple wives. I interviewed the director of the family benefits department of the National Office for Family Allocations (Caisse Nationale des Allocations Familiales; CNAF), who explained to me that, although polygamy is an offense in France, still "it exists and therefore we must consider the factual situation. It does not matter whether one is married, cohabiting or otherwise. From the moment they are in a relationship, they are considered as a couple." Calling each wife and husband a couple underscores the republican imperative to treat all relationships as monogamous. The director emphasized this idea when I asked how CNAF would define polygamy. He replied, "We don't really have a definition, because like I said, there is no polygamy. We are really dealing with factual situations." Because by law polygamy no longer exists in France, there is no category for it in the family allowance system. He stated, "A man possibly has a spouse and a concubine; all other women are considered as other dependents." The state prioritizes supporting (French) children even in cases where polygynous families still live together. He explained, "Even if they are in the same accommodation, and they are really in a situation of polygamy, we pay benefits, because the whole system is in fact based on the best interests of the child." A circular issued in 1996 provided specifications for dealing with polygynous families. The family allocations must consider the resources of everyone: Secondary wives are entitled to support as a single person but must include their husband's personal resources. This contradictory approach views secondary wives as not married while making their support dependent on the resources of their "husband."

Another example has been France's approach to regulating polygamy in Mayotte. This island in the Comoros archipelago became the 101st French department in 2011, one of France's colonial legacies.[29] After departmentalization, the Mahorais gained status as French citizens and continued to have a special civil status under local law inspired by African customs and the rules of Sunni Islam, making this population among the last French citizens to enjoy a status distinct from that of common law.[30] In parliamentary debates legislators pointed to this personal status as one of the main reasons for rejecting departmentalization. Ending polygamy and repudiation became unconditional prerequisites.[31] Ordinances passed in 2003 and 2010 had a goal of "modernizing" the civil status of the local law. In 2005 the personal status was modified to allow only men born before 1987 to contract new polygamous unions, and in 2010 new polygamous unions were prohibited altogether. As sociologist Elise Lemercier told me, the law is just "symbolic." She stated, "Officially, there is no polygamy. But everyone knows that polygamy persists. What is practiced is a legal marriage recorded at the town hall, and the other marriages are conducted in front of a religious authority." She detailed how even women with high social positions and who are feminists are sometimes in polygynous marriages, which they have chosen, even after the ban. She traveled to Mayotte to conduct research on the issue after it became illegal. However, she found that "there was nothing to study." Her research considers public policy, and in Mayotte, "[polygamy] exists, but it's not a public issue." Whereas in metropolitan France the problem of the local civil status has been discussed, in Mayotte, "there is no public policy on polygamy." The judges who come to Mayotte from metropolitan France to oversee issues like polygamy stay only two years and "do not know what to do" about the issue.

Michel Farge described France's contradictory approach to me: "One of the difficulties, if you will, with the French system is that these different rights—civil law, the rights of foreigners, nationality law, and social law—do not necessarily have the same approach to polygamy." Different legal and administrative approaches to regulating polygyny have not held the same values or sought the same objectives. At the same time, France's republican identity and its desire to guard against communalism have shaped its overall approach. This fear of a lack of assimilation has propelled the state to use polygamy to control who belongs by revoking residence permits of those living in a state of polygyny. Its ambivalence, however, means that administratively polygamy is no longer recognized. Sonia Imloul explained that it is a "hot potato" issue that the French government "absolutely does not want to deal with." However, the government is perfectly willing to focus on polygamy as a problem when it benefits them politically. This tolerance-intolerance tightrope that the government walks has allowed polygynous families to persist in France, providing some with support and pushing others underground. France's republican identity requires families to be split up to form a configuration of a nuclear family and a single-parent family, mirroring "normal family life." In contrast, such a policy is anathema to the United States, which prioritizes marriage as a means of social cohesion.

MARRIAGE, ASSIMILATION, AND PLURALISM IN THE UNITED STATES

Popular television shows dealing with white polygynous families shine light on the racial project of regulating forbidden intimacies in the United States. In 2006 the highly acclaimed American drama *Big Love* aired on

HBO. Its five seasons told the story of a modern white polygamist family who blended into their suburban neighborhood of a Utah city. Barbara and Bill Hendrickson presented themselves as a married couple, and Bill's other two wives had houses next door, living as single mothers. The show revolved around the family's efforts to keep their secret. In 2010 the TV reality show *Sister Wives* began airing. The day after the show debuted, police in Lehi, Utah, announced that they had opened an investigation into Kody Brown and his four wives for possible charges of bigamy, which at that time was a third-degree felony and carried a possible penalty of twenty years in prison for Kody and up to five years for each wife. In a dramatic episode the Brown family fled Utah, moving to Nevada for fear of being charged.

The Browns' flight generated empathy, and the show has been a great success—it is airing its sixteenth season in 2022. The Browns are a white plural family whose appeal is to be "just like us," personal and relatable to other "mainstream" (white) families.[32] The population of Mormons in the United States are predominantly white, even though the U.S. population is becoming more diverse, and the demographic for fundamentalist Mormons is similar.[33] However, even with media efforts to make polygamists appear like "us," regulating polygamy in the United States has a long history of embracing racialized stereotypes of the other, calling into question the whiteness of anyone who practices it. Legal scholar Martha Ertman argues that the current ban on polygamy in the United States grew out of the view that Mormons had committed treason. First, Mormons were political traitors for establishing a separatist theocracy in Utah; then, they committed social treason against white citizens for adopting a supposedly barbaric form of marriage, one that was seen as natural for Africans and Asians but not for whites.[34] This history haunts the practice as it has been taken up by fundamentalist Mormons in the current era.[35]

Race and immigration scholars have shown how racial and ethnic boundaries are key in deciding inclusion. Richard Alba distinguishes between bright boundaries that make unambiguous distinctions between "us" and "them," and blurry boundaries that allow for more ambiguity around boundary making.[36] Whiteness contributes to this blurriness and points to how white fundamentalist Mormon families can be "one of us" but racialized because of their "barbaric" practice of polygyny. They are "one of us" as white Americans, but they are "race traitors" because of their practice of polygyny.[37] I interviewed a legal scholar and attorney who referred to the 1879 *Reynolds v. United States* case, which justified polygamy's prohibition by linking it to "Asiatic and African people."

> I think the orientalist perspective is really there. I mean, I've read *Reynolds*, and in fact, I've read all the Supreme Court opinions on polygamy because there were a couple more about taking wives across state lines, and the anti-polygamy cases have that strong ethnocentrism, right? We're Western, and we're evolved, and those of you that are Eastern are still living in the Dark Ages. I think it's not so clear that we are the end of evolution [*laughs*]; that our societies have a lot of downsides to them. Polygamy has been around since biblical times, and it was okay for Abraham, but it's not okay for somebody today.

Another legal scholar declared, "So, then it goes to the Supreme Court in 1878. When you read the *Reynolds* decision, you recognize how ridiculously biased it was when you read what they actually say. Ultimately, it was racist. They were also saying that they were comparing polygamy to all the dark races in the other continents. Really, it's offensive!" These quotes point to how blurry boundaries demarcate white plural families as not "bright" white or not white enough.[38]

Several people I interviewed articulated a view that pointed to how white plural families are racially suspect, especially the most recognizable group: the Fundamentalist Latter Day Saints (FLDS). This group is known for practicing spiritual marriages that involve underage girls and for their strict dress code. Women wear unicolor homemade long-sleeved "prairie dresses" and long stockings or trousers underneath. They keep their long hair braided in back with a Gibson wave in front. In the early 2000s FLDS church members, under the direction of their prophet, Warren Jeffs, built a temple near Eldorado, Texas, known as the Yearning for Zion (YFZ) Ranch, to be the new headquarters for the church. In 2008 a woman identifying herself as Sarah called a domestic abuse hotline, claiming to be a 16-year-old living on the YFZ Ranch who was to be married against her will. The call turned out to be a hoax, but it triggered a law enforcement raid and the removal of 437 children. Being highly mediatized, the court finally ordered the government to return the children. Later, investigators charged eleven FLDS men with prison sentences for crimes related to bigamy and sexual assault.

Sociologist Arland Thornton points to the racialized discourse used in the case of Texas's removal of children.[39] Dominant portrayals described a conflict between a backward, archaic group—akin to a tribe in Africa or Asia—clashing with the civilized and enlightened state of Texas. A social worker pointed out to me how this kind of racialized discourse was applied to refugees and fundamentalist Mormons. According to her, refugees in Utah were often "terrified" when they arrived because they did not know the culture. She stated, "We do this to the polygamists, to the FLDS." The goal is to make them "one of us."

> "Oh, here, let me save you. By the way, fix your hair. Cut your hair. Put on a different dress. Take that scarf off your face because, you know, that's not how we do things here. Let's change your whole identity, okay? And now guess what, oh gosh, polygamy is against the law here. And I know that your father was, let's see, he had a really big status where you're from. And he had six wives and so his status was way up here. Well, now you are here, and you are nothing but a bastard child, okay? Your mom is not here." You know, it's horrid what they go through.

Having worked with fundamentalist Mormons and refugees in the state, she recognized how polygamists are racialized in a similar manner, whether white or nonwhite refugees, building on the history of using polygamy as a forbidden intimacy to decide who belongs.

As a racial project, some officials made direct comparisons between racialized groups and polygamists. Mark Shurtleff, attorney general of Utah from 2000 to 2012, told me that he started calling the FLDS the "American Taliban," because "girls were taken out of school early, and that they were made to work. Kids were made to work, and women had no rights." Shurtleff builds on the racialized history of polygamy that portrays polygynists as race traitors, and in this case he compares polygynists to Muslim fundamentalist guerilla fighters.

Brian, who was raised in a plural family and had entered one of his own, discussed the injustices in America based on racial and ethnic boundaries.

He described learning in school about how African American populations "had to fight for equal rights and how they are still fighting for them." He asked himself, "Have we not learned these lessons yet? I mean, how many more populations do we have to move through before we realize that, you know, actually people should have rights? . . . To me, polygamy is still one of the bastions where it's okay to call names." Several people I interviewed mentioned the ban on interracial marriage that existed until the 1967 U.S. Supreme Court case *Loving v. Virginia* ruled that laws banning interracial marriage violate the equal protection and due process clauses of the Fourteenth Amendment. Grace, in her 40s and in a plural marriage, pointed to the decision, saying, "It wasn't that long ago!" Recognizing how so many things have changed, including being able to get a divorce, she declared, "I don't know, if you're going to embrace the abnormal [like divorce once was], why not embrace us, because we try to have a moral life. We try to live morality. It seems like you would want that in your society." Such conversations recognized the ways that plural families are not quite bright white, even as families were trying to live morally.

The racial project of regulating plural families created tensions as government officials sought to deal with a white population that embraced a racialized and repudiated family form. In the 2000s the issue became front and center. Former attorney general Mark Shurtleff explained that when he ran for office in 2000, polygamy "wasn't an issue." Then, the Juab County attorney had alerted him to "a group of polygamists living in his county, out in the west desert, openly. I think they went on an Oprah Winfrey–type show. And there they were basically announcing to the world that they were breaking the law in his county. So, he said, 'I'm going to prosecute them.'" Tom Green, who was spiritually married to five women, appeared on TV tabloid talk shows such as *The Jerry Springer Show* to discuss his plural marriages. The high-profile trial that followed led to his conviction in 2001 on four counts of bigamy, one count of failure to pay child support, and child rape, because one his wives had his child at the age of 14. In total he served six years in prison and was released in 2007. For Shurtleff, the *Green* case represented a definite boundary of wrongdoing. The attorney general's office then began investigating Rodney Holm in 2002, a police officer in Hildale. He was convicted in 2003 of bigamy and illegal sex with a girl he took as a third wife when she was 16. He was ordered to serve one year in the county jail with work release privileges and three years of supervised probation.

These two cases involved charges of bigamy (a felony in Utah) in addition to other criminal charges. Shurtleff recounted how he came to make the statement in 2002 that he was not "going to prosecute adult consensual bigamy." He told me, "We won't do it unless we might charge it in addition to another crime, like rape of a child." He just did not have the "manpower to prosecute tens of thousands of polygamists!" Instead, he decided to focus resources on "underage marriages, incest, and welfare fraud." Shurtleff stated:

> In the meantime, we started having other polygamist groups come to me and say, "We're not them. Leave us alone. We do not allow child bride marriages." And most of them, they brought proof of it. "This is something we absolutely prohibit," because I made that statement that I am not going to prosecute adult consensual bigamy.

The attorney general's office began to walk a tightrope on how to deal with the law, hearing complaints from those who wanted more prosecutions and those who sought decriminalization.

Elizabeth was a plural wife before her husband died, and she became a prominent spokesperson for decriminalization. She explained that the statement about not prosecuting bigamy unless other crimes were committed made it easier to feel safe.

> We would let [people in plural marriages] know, you don't need to be afraid of the government if you are not breaking any other laws, because Mark Shurtleff kind of set the precedent. And he said as long as you're not breaking any other laws, I'm not going to prosecute consenting adults. Two conditions—consenting adults and breaking no other laws. That was a great perspective I thought.

Still, many I interviewed described being afraid that they could be charged with a felony count of bigamy if something happened that would garner the attention of the police or authorities. One family told me about a time when one of their children had a terrible accident and had to be heli-lifted to a hospital that could care for her. The husband recounted the moment when investigators realized, "'Oh, you are polygamists.' Then they are heightened, like now they are heightened in what they are going to look for." This family was educated in how to deal with this kind of investigation: "We knew the language; we knew what they were looking for. The average plural family coming on that situation, terrified in trauma already, and having those kinds of questions, are going to then shut down." Others stated that you never knew if trumped-up charges could be used against a plural family. The investigation of the Brown family stoked such fears.

For the Browns the investigation was an opportunity to test the constitutionality of forbidding polygamy. They hired constitutional law scholar Jonathan Turley to file a complaint in the United States District Court for the District of Utah in 2011—*Brown v. Buhman*—challenging Utah's criminal polygamy law. In 2013 Judge Waddoups found that prohibiting the cohabitation of a married person with another was vague and overbroad and that it violated substantive due process.[40] One of the lawyers for the Browns explained to me:

> We borrowed heavily from the principles in *Lawrence v. Texas*. That was the case that decriminalized sodomy for consenting adults. And the underlying principles are the same, that the state doesn't have an interest in regulating this type of behavior between consenting adults. Its interest is not sufficient to overcome their desire to engage in this conduct.

Judge Waddoups declared a Fourteenth Amendment due process violation regarding religious cohabitation, because only religious cohabitation and not adultery and adulterous cohabitation were prosecuted at the discretion of the state.[41]

A unanimous three-judge panel of the U.S. Court of Appeals for the Tenth Circuit dismissed the case in 2016. Because the state and local prosecutors had declared a policy of not pursuing most polygamy cases in the absence of additional associated crimes, such as underage marriage, the court ruled that the Browns had no credible fear of future prosecution and lacked standing. In 2017 the Utah State Legislature then recriminalized polygamy, passing a bill that kept polygamy a felony and increasing the penalties for polygamists convicted of committing fraud and abuse. In yet another turn in 2020, the Utah governor signed Senate Bill 102 into law, reducing the penalty for the practice of polygamy to an infraction, except if other crimes were committed.

This history of oscillating between decriminalization and recriminalization echoes France's ambivalence over its polygamy laws. France began by allowing multiple wives to enter the country when marriages took place in former colonies where polygyny was legal and customary. Then, panic concerning racialized immigration in France led to new draconian immigration measures in 1993, including a ban on polygynous families living in France's territory. In the United States regulation of polygyny has applied less to racialized immigrants than to white fundamentalist Mormons. Still, anti-polygamy laws, together with immigration law, have played a critical role in establishing who is deemed unworthy of citizenship. Currently, U.S. immigration law reflects a nineteenth-century discourse that framed polygamy as "barbaric." Legal scholar Martha Ertman observed that federal immigration law has excluded "[a]liens who are polygamists or who practice polygamy or *advocate the practice of polygamy*."[42] Although the Immigration and Nationality Act of 1990 reframed the law to bar only those practicing polygamy from entering the United States, a 2007 decision excluded a Yemeni wife even though the other wife had died.

I interviewed Mark Henkel, who identifies as the National Polygamy Advocate.[43] Promoting himself as "pro-marriage, pro-woman, pro-Bible Christian," he leads the non-Mormon Christian polygamy movement. He discussed the *Brown* case and the idea of prosecutorial discretion.

> It should terrify you that any law that is unconstitutional can be on the books. A prosecutor can threaten you with it, you then file suit to say that law is unconstitutional, the prosecutor can publicly say, "Well, we won't go after you." And the court will say, "You don't have standing anymore." And so, the bad law stays on the books. That's a threat to the very liberty of everybody in America.

Henkel's words point to administrative ambivalence in dealing with polygamy. On the one hand, Utah's attorney general recognized the improbability of charging tens of thousands of individuals who lived in plural families and declared that he would not prosecute polygamy unless other

crimes were involved. Yet this declaration allowed the government to successfully appeal the *Brown v. Buhman* decision and recriminalize polygamy.
Utah ultimately reduced the penalty of living in polygamy from a felony to
a misdemeanor, but the law against polygamist cohabitation remains on
the books. One reason may be what is called the "irrevocable ordinance,"
which required Utah to prohibit "polygamous or plural marriages" in its
constitution to be admitted into the Union.[44] Thus Utah as a state must
prohibit polygamy.

Henkel's words also point to the ways that such laws are tied to American identity. For him, prosecutorial discretion threatens the foundation of
American liberty. For others, polygamy threatens American values. One of
the anti-polygamist authors I interviewed explained that polygamy reflects
the problem in America of too much religious tolerance.

> [Polygamists] are just—they are everywhere, and they keep cropping
> up! . . . The whole religious freedom thing has gotten so loosey goosey.
> And then we wonder, "Well, you know, why are these kids abused and
> trafficked, and married off at young ages, and raped, and not educated,
> you know, systematically and institutionally?" Because we've let this reli-
> gious freedom idea go completely beyond what it was really intended. You
> cannot violate human rights![45]

For this participant, America's commitment to religious freedom allows
crimes against children to be committed. Another anti-polygamist activist
pointed to her belief that democracy and polygamy cannot exist together
in America: "My life experience teaches me that it's slavery of women and
exploitation of children. It's antithetical to democracy. You cannot have it—
polygamy and democracy—in the same bed." These views on how the prohibition of polygamy relates to American democracy—as a threat to legal
standards or as a threat to rights—demonstrate how forbidden intimacies
define the boundaries of what it means to be American.

The ideal of heterosexual marriage—and the legalization of same-
gender marriage—was a key topic in the discussions on how to deal with
plural marriage. The 1879 *Reynolds* decision explicitly addressed the importance of marriage as a foundation of society that creates social obligations and responsibilities. It suggested that polygamy can create despotic

and repressive governments, in contrast to monogamy, which produces democratic governments.[46] I interviewed historian Martha Bradley-Evans, author of *Kidnapped from That Land: The Government Raids on the Short Creek Polygamists*, who discussed Utah's legalization of same-gender marriage in late 2013 and decriminalization of polygamy in 2014.

> But you know in Utah, it's so ironic that same-sex marriage is now legal in Utah, because it is an incredibly conservative environment both legally, socially, and culturally. So, I think that the government will do anything it can to tighten up the laws that they can control around marriage. It's not going to be an "anything goes" environment.

She thought that the appeal of the *Brown v. Buhman* decision would be successful and that the government would again reinstitute polygamy as a felony crime. Her prediction was correct. Fears concerning changing norms of heterosexual marriage propelled a backlash against plural marriage.

Mark Shurtleff discussed the connection he saw between same-gender and plural marriage. He was the attorney general in Utah in 2004 when voters approved Utah Constitutional Amendment 3, which defined marriage as a union exclusively between one man and one woman. At the time, he declared, " 'This is unconstitutional,' because then my job is, if it passes, I have to defend it." He was the only Republican in the state to openly oppose the measure. He reflected, "Can a state regulate marriage? That's the same question whether it's polygamy or same-sex marriages. Can the state define marriage? And we'd always defined polygamy as illegal or prohibited—same sex-marriages and polygamist marriages—based on historical precedent." Shurtleff recounted how U.S. law had long designated the "best family is a nuclear family with a mom and a dad. That's the bedrock of society." He felt that in the early 2000s this was no longer the case. He described how he was "torn on" the issue of decriminalization because he had seen it work but had also witnessed quite a bit of "bad on the other side."

Shurtleff's ambivalence over plural marriage reflects the broader administrative ambivalence that has led to its nominal decriminalization as a misdemeanor rather than a felony. On the one hand, the history of racializing some fundamentalist Mormons for their practice of polygyny continues into the present, such as calling the FLDS the American Taliban. On the other hand, individuals in consensual plural marriages can continue to live their open secret with less fear of prosecution. While the United States has little legal recognition of family diversity—although its legalization of same-gender marriage is a step in that direction—the lived experience of family diversity is quite remarkable.[47] For example, a recent study found that one-fifth of the U.S. population has engaged in consensual nonmonogamy at some point in their lives.[48] Marriage, which now includes lesbians and gay men, is entered into and viewed more favorably in the United States than in France, where options for entering civil unions for heterosexuals and nonheterosexuals has been in place since the Pacte Civil de Solidarity became law in 1999. The number of heterosexual couples getting civil unions hovers near the annual number of marriages.[49] In contrast, marriage is central to American identity.[50] Still, the regulation of polygamy provides a good example of how the government ambivalently tolerates de facto diverse family practices such as polygyny, publicly recognizing the difficulty of prosecuting consensual plural marriages when no other crimes are being committed.

There are substantial differences in the social context of regulating polygyny between France and the United States, such as the problem of housing in France but not in the United States. In the United States the administrative ambivalence of the government that targets the polygamous population has led to the toleration of plural families except in cases of closed groups, such as the FLDS, or in the presence of other crimes, such as underage marriage. Canada also has a history of regulating polygyny ambivalently, but after a provincial supreme court case found the criminal code outlawing polygamy to be constitutional, it prosecuted two fundamentalist Mormon leaders. Canada offers an important third example of the ways that regulating forbidden intimacies constitutes a racial project to define national identity and belonging.

MULTICULTURALISM AND THE PERILS OF DIVERSITY

The modern community of Mormon fundamentalists practicing plural marriage in Canada can be traced to Harold Blackmore, who purchased land in Lister, British Columbia, in 1946 and eventually moved there with his two wives. Blackmore legally married Gwen and spiritually married her sister Florence just before moving to the land that would eventually be called Bountiful. Journalist Daphne Bramham provides a detailed history of the emergence of the community in her book, *The Secret Lives of Saints*.[51] Winston Blackmore, son of Ray Blackmore, served as bishop of the FLDS in the Bountiful community of about 1,000 people for two decades, beginning in the 1980s, before Warren Jeffs, who became president and prophet of the FLDS after his father's death in 2002, excommunicated him. Blackmore is known for having at least twenty-four spiritual wives and over a hundred children. The community divided into two groups after his excommunication: About half remained with the FLDS under the new bishop, James Oler. The other half are members of the Church of Jesus Christ (Original Doctrine) Inc., an FLDS offshoot based on the teachings of Winston Blackmore.[52]

Like the United States, orientalist language has been used in efforts to abolish polygamy. I interviewed a journalist who told me how her focus had been on international trafficking of girls. She took on the issue after receiving an email from a women's rights advocate that stated, "[The polygamists] are trafficking women and girls into Canada to become concubines in Bountiful." The use of the word *concubine* conjures an orientalist discourse of harems and licentiousness.[53] This was not the only time I heard this language, including one anti-polygamy activist, who stated:

> There are mainstream Mormon men who are just waiting for polygamy to be legalized so that they can start living the true order of God in this life. And that's why I said on my radio interview recently, "If polygamy is legalized, you're going to see harems pop up like mushrooms." And I didn't mean just Muslim harems. Because in Canada, we have Christian fundamentalist polygamy, we have Muslim polygamy, we have Mormon polygamy, we have African polygamy, and we have Asian polygamy.

Bountiful, with half its population tied to the FLDS, has promulgated underage and forced marriages, including taking young girls to the United States or bringing them to Canada to marry older men.[54] Although it is clearly a feminist goal to fight against such practices, the orientalist discourses attributed to polygamy are problematic in drawing on racialized stereotypes.

When I discussed Bountiful with journalist Daphne Bramham, she told me about how when she first began writing about the issue, she shared the attitude of many Canadians: "A civil libertarian kind of view, which I didn't see this as a religious thing. I thought, 'If everyone's happy in this community, well maybe it doesn't matter.'" She described asking herself, "How much are we are going to tolerate? So, polygamy is really about how willing is a society to tolerate difference?" Canada adopted a federal multiculturalism policy in 1971, making it the first country in the world to initiate such a policy.[55] The law states that "the Government of Canada recognizes the diversity of Canadians as regards race, national or ethnic origin, colour and religion as a fundamental characteristic of Canadian society and is committed to a policy of multiculturalism designed to preserve and enhance the multicultural heritage of Canadians."[56] Scholars have argued that the United States and France differ from Canada because they embrace a liberal nationalist ideal of "passive multiculturalism" that restricts culture and family organization to the private sphere.[57] In contrast, Canada has an "active multiculturalism" that recognizes minority cultures in its policies and institutionalizes support for these in the public sphere.[58] Canada's Charter of Rights and Freedoms (1982) and Multiculturalism Act (1985) protect minority rights.

Fear of a slippery slope leading to legalizing polygamy fueled debate in 2005, when Canada became the third country in the world to legalize same-gender marriage. Stephen Harper, the opposition party leader who became prime minister the next year, declared, "I don't want to get into the polygamy debate, but I fear if we do this, the next thing on the Liberal agenda will be polygamy and who knows what else."[59] Later that year, Status of Women Canada, a federal government agency promoting equality between women and men in all aspects of Canadian life, published a series of reports on the legal and social ramifications of polygamy.[60] The reports were intended to assist the government in determining government policy regarding polygamy. Upon completion, they provided contradictory recommendations: Some of the study's analysts stated that Canada should consider decriminalizing the practice, as the ban might be unconstitutional, and others asserted that there was no justification to change the law. The reports reflected concerns over rights and belonging that are central to the framework of multiculturalism.

Following these reports, in 2006 the Royal Canadian Mounted Police investigated Bountiful, but unlike in earlier investigations, it now recommended criminal charges of the two leaders. Following this recommendation, two separate prosecutors advised that a decision from the Court of Appeal was needed to clear up the question of constitutionality. The attorney general found another special prosecutor who approved charging Blackmore and Oler in 2009. However, the charges were dismissed because the attorney general used an unorthodox strategy to search for special prosecutors, and the British Columbia government filed a reference case with the Supreme Court of British Columbia, an option in the Canadian legal system to get an advisory opinion on constitutional questions. The case was introduced at the trial level to provide evidence and witnesses, making it unprecedented in the history of Canadian law.

During the four months of trial beginning in late 2010, the governments of Canada and British Columbia defended the law's constitutionality and a court-appointed amicus challenged it. Lawyers representing eleven groups intervened. Chief Justice Robert Bauman issued his judgment in November 2011, ruling that the criminalization of polygamy was justified because of the inherent harm it posed for individuals who practiced it and for society in general.[61] In 2017 the government finally prosecuted individuals from Bountiful. Brandon Blackmore was sentenced to twelve months' incarceration plus eighteen months' probation, and Emily Ruth Gail Blackmore was given seven months plus eighteen months' probation for taking their 13-year-old daughter to the United States to marry Warren Jeffs in 2004. They were convicted under the sections of the Criminal Code of Canada that prohibits trafficking of a minor into another country for the purpose of an act that is a crime in Canada and for sexual assault on a minor.[62] Based on Section 293, which criminalizes polygamy, a British Colombia Supreme Court judge found Winston Blackmore guilty of having twenty-four wives and James Oler of having five in 2017.

There was no disagreement during the trial that crimes such as forced underage marriages needed to be prosecuted. George Macintosh, the amicus, explained to me that "the darker parts of the FLDS world" were not something anyone could defend. His argument rested on the fact that there were laws in place to deal with such crimes against women and children. However, in his view, this wrongdoing did not justify the law banning polygamy.

So, at the end of the process, I can stand up and say, "Look at this section [of the Criminal Code], it captures a whole bunch of people who are perfectly innocent, perfectly good, doing perfectly harmless things, and thus, it will infringe our constitutional rights of association and religion, and so on." And there are many good laws in place to handle the bad conduct which is complained of. And constitutional principle guides that you should look to those laws instead, so that the good conduct, or the acceptable conduct among other polygamists, can be allowed if it accords with our freedoms.

The other side disagreed. One of the lawyers for the group Stop Polygamy in Canada explained that it did not matter that some practicing polygamists were doing no harm.

And what we said in our final argument was that if you look at the evidence of Angela Campbell [a witness for the amicus] and the polyamorists and the anonymous witnesses from Bountiful, I could summarize what they say in one sentence, which is, "There are some people for whom polygamy doesn't cause any harm to them." And I would concede that to them, but so what? It's a test.

He explained that the court often must draw a line that is "somewhat arbitrary." For him, the point was to try to reduce harm in the best way possible.

These opposing arguments point to the ways that forbidden intimacies challenge a multicultural approach. Is the practice of polygyny something that should be allowed when it does not cause any harm to those who practice it? Is it about freedom of association and religion, or is it about harm to women, children, and society? The lead lawyer for the British Columbia attorney general, Craig Jones, described how he changed his perspective from one of civil liberties to focus on harm.

I came to see polygamy as an evolving animal, as a social force that we cage in the same way that we cage other destructive behaviors. But it's just waiting. And when it's given a bit of exercise, it gets stronger. And it armors itself, and it arms itself, and becomes protective, and develops these institutions, whether they are religious or political or economical in order to sustain, because it's an extremely successful reproductive strategy.

The idea of polygamy as an evolving animal reflects Jones's focus on evolutionary psychology and the biological drives that make polygyny a successful reproductive strategy. Jones told me, "When I read my way into it, the two that struck me were Steven Pinker and Robert Wright's sort of analysis of evolutionary psychology, and the societies that are more polygynist, and what happens with this cohort of unmarriageable males that become violent. So why a polygynist society is not a good place to live." To make his case during the trial, Jones relied on Joseph Henrich, an expert on evolutionary psychology. Like arguments of anti-polygamists in the nineteenth century, Henrich stated, "The possibility that normative (often imposed) monogamous marriage was causal in the successful global expansion of European (and European-descent) societies is something that becomes increasingly plausible when we examine the societal-level effects of monogamy."[63] Historian Walter Scheidel supported this view of monogamy's importance to democracy with his expert testimony on the development and consequences of "socially imposed universal monogamy."[64] Scheidel argued that in the Greek world, polygamy was regarded as a "barbarian" custom and a mark of tyranny. Likewise, legal scholar John Witte argued that monogamous marriage was instituted in the ancient world along with liberty, democracy, and the rule of law. This imperialist gaze that views Western democracy as imperative to society echoes colonial sentiments that have sought to impose monogamy as a form of domination over racialized and religious populations.

In his 265-page opinion Chief Justice Bauman carefully assessed the mountains of evidence provided in the trial. He acknowledged that the prohibition of polygamy was a violation of the guarantee of freedom of religion in the Charter of Rights and Freedoms but argued that it was constitutionally justified as a reasonable limitation to prevent harm to women, children, and society. The opinion largely focused on the perspective that polygyny is an innate biological drive that can be controlled only by the institution of monogamy. Bauman agreed with the attorneys general that, if polygyny were not prohibited, there could be a "non-trivial" increase in its practice in Canada.[65] Detailed legal and sociological analyses of the reference case have been made in recent years, both critical and favorable.[66] Those who are critical have remarked on the most surprising argument of Bauman's opinion:

the importance of the ban against polygamy to protect the institution of monogamous marriage, which he argued was the keystone of Western democracy. Bauman asked why Canada prohibits bigamy and not adulterous relationships, polygamy but not serial monogamy? His answer:

> When all is said, I suggest that the prohibition of [the ban against polygamy] is directed in part at protecting the institution of monogamous marriage. And let me here recognize that we have come, in this century and in this country, to accept same-sex marriage as part of that institution. That is so, in part, because committed same-sex relationships celebrate all of the values we seek to preserve and advance in monogamous marriage.[67]

Bauman's opinion draws a bright line between committed monogamous relationships and nonmonogamous gay couples—the so-called good versus bad gay people.[68] He stated, "The offence is not directed at multi-party, unmarried relationships or common law cohabitation, but is directed at both polygyny and polyandry. It is also directed at multi-party same sex marriages."[69] In this way, Canada's treatment of polygamy offers the clearest example of mononormativity in the twenty-first century that explicitly defines its national identity based on Canada's representation of progressive democracy in contrast to countries that permit polygyny.

Craig Jones discussed the boldness of this bright line. He assessed that the court decided what counts as polygamy "by basically saying, 'The flip side of polygamy is monogamy, and polyandry undermines monogamy just in the same way that polygyny does, so it's valid to ban them both.'" He described this stance as "pretty gutsy stuff," stating that, though more nuanced than the characterization he was about to give, Bauman's position was "rhetorically reminiscent of the sort of arguments against gay marriage that people made, that it undermined the institution and the value of this wonderful thing called monogamy." Although Jones supported Bauman's opinion, he did recognize the implications of the mononormative argument that has been used as a rhetorical strategy to fight against same-gender marriage.

Those who disagreed with Bauman's decision, and even some who agreed, were critical of its focus on evolutionary psychology and the importance Bauman placed on monogamy to creating and sustaining progressive civilization. Michael Vonn, policy director of the British Columbia Civil Liberties Association (BCCLA) and an intervener in the reference case, told me, "I was particularly concerned about the weight given to evolutionary science evidence. I was really taken aback by it. Our joking version is that monkeys are monogamous. Let's get the bonobo evidence to offset this. It was surprising how this highly suspect theory was allowed to shape this judgment." She expressed that we are basically "saying [a plural family] is an illegitimate family. We can't forget that there are families here. . . . These people are trying to live their lives." Others also thought it troubling to prioritize marriage and monogamy as the reason to ban polygamy. Rachel Chagnon, professor in the Département des Sciences Juridique at the University of Québec, Montréal, wrote critically of the decision.[70] During our interview, she stated, "It's a step backward for all the people who were hoping to have their situation acknowledged by the law and to open the door to a new approach toward what is a family, because the Bountiful affair brings us back to the nuclear family pattern! *La famille nucléaire*, with one mom, one dad and that's it." In her view the decision itself was a step backward.

Many discussed with me the fear of immigration as a motivation behind the judgment that justified the ban. BCCLA litigation director Grace Pastine told me that, though the trial focused on Bountiful, there was a nagging concern about racialized immigrants in the background.

> I think the subtext to this debate—I mean, this is focused on Bountiful in many ways, but what's in the back of everyone's mind is the seething hordes of nonwhite communities who engage in polygamy that are perhaps already in Canada or may want to come to Canada. And our view is that there is a real undercurrent of xenophobia within this debate.

Craig Jones discussed this fear in his memoir, arguing that polygamy represents a clash between Western values and those of the Muslim world. For him, the September 11 terrorist attacks in the United States justified thinking in terms of "less advanced societies" and "more advanced civilizations," and he argued for the need to guard against "Mormons and Muslims, who would see the rights revolution reversed in favor of patriarchal despotism."[71] During the trial, Jones proposed that evolutionary psychology could explain why polygamy might credibly spread throughout the Canadian population. One lawyer arguing for Stop Polygamy in Canada agreed: "One of the pieces of evidence in the case was that if Canada were to [decriminalize polygamy] that we would become a destination of choice for two groups really. One is Muslim immigrants who want to practice polygamy, and the other is mainstream Mormons."[72] These statements again reflect the orientalism that has shaped the debate.

This fear of the other resurfaced as the Canadian government passed the Zero Tolerance for Barbaric Cultural Practices Act under Conservative prime minister Stephen Harper in 2015. The bill introduced sweeping changes to criminal, civil, and immigration law and targeted three forms of violence against women: forced marriage, honor killing, and polygamy. Regarding polygamy, it banned the entrance of polygamists into Canada and permitted deportation of immigrants who engage in its practice.[73] However, polygamy was already banned for immigrants. Rachel Chagnon explained that the bill was not really against polygamy but immigration.

> It is a way to filter immigrants to find ways to leave Muslims at the door. . . . [The bill] goes in many directions, and when you follow all the tentacles, you realize where it does the most damage is in its immigration measures. The crux of that bill was in immigration, not in criminal law, which it was supposed to be about. It was publicized as something that would criminalize all these barbaric ways.

The implications of the bill as anti-immigrant were reflected in the parliamentary debates over its title that focused on the meaning of "cultural barbaric practices." Some argued that using the term *barbaric* is problematic in its historically racist context that is stigmatizing for immigrants of color.[74] For example, Senator Art Eggleton argued that the term "harkens back to a time of perceived Anglo superiority" in Canada.[75] He quoted Canada's first prime minister, John A. Macdonald, who in 1885 called Aboriginal peoples "barbarians that cannot be civilized."[76] The response of the conservative government was to focus on the universality of *practices* that are barbaric no matter who commits them, a problematic way of portraying some cultures as uncivilized. The Conservative immigration minister, Chris Alexander, argued that the bill targets any individual who forces others into marriage or is "engaged in polygamous relationships, which are disguised in our immigration programs and elsewhere as something else, as family relationships, as family reunification—'I'm bringing my sister or cousin.'"[77] This debate also reflected how ideas of citizenship and nationalism were linked to the family, enabling state power to penetrate "the most intimate domains of modern life" and decide who belongs in the nation-state.[78]

Although Canada has a far-reaching multicultural policy that would suggest the need to seek understanding of other cultures, it has approached issues such as polygyny in a particularly forceful manner that draws bright lines between "civilized" society and practices that are viewed to threaten civilization. It is especially interesting to consider the ways that Canada, France, and the United States have approached the issue. The United States and France maintain an administrative ambivalence that condemns the practice while largely allowing de facto polygynous unions to continue. The United States has witnessed several high-profile prosecutions of individuals practicing polygyny, such as Warren Jeffs, who was convicted of two counts of sexual assault against a child. Convictions of bigamy are in conjunction with other offenses. Canada, however, is exceptional in successfully prosecuting two leaders of Bountiful for polygamy as a stand-alone charge after a century of not prosecuting anyone.

Although Winston Blackmore and James Oler were found to be guilty of practicing polygamy, their sentences reflect the "expressive function of law," as Blackmore's six-month sentence and Oler's three-month sentence were served under house arrest—in other words, at home with their wives. The charges expressed public condemnation of polygamy, but at the same time the light sentences—practically nonsentences—ambivalently expressed Canadian law's support for the plurality of intimacy.[79] This outcome infuriated anti-polygamy actors who were hoping for a more stringent sentence to serve as a deterrent to other men who were spiritually married to multiple wives. Nancy Mereska, founder and president of the now defunct organization Stop Polygamy in Canada, wrote on her website, "Did we win the battle Nov. 23, 2011, and lose the war today? I think so!"[80] Likewise, Daphne Bramham called the sentence "a travesty." Trial evidence found that Blackmore had married and impregnated nine wives and Oler two wives who

were under 18 years of age. She stated, "Two men who are both polygamists and child sex abusers won't spend a day in jail." For Blackmore, the
punishment is "to carry on doing exactly what he's been doing for the last
30 years," spending "time in the company of at least some of his 24 wives
and 149 children."[81] The Canadian press reported the reasoning of Supreme
Court Justice Sheri Ann Donegan, who said of Blackmore, "He's made it
clear that no sentence will deter him from practising his faith."[82] The fact
that Donegan chose house arrest as punishment demonstrates the difficulty
of sending men to prison on the sole charge of polygamy.

How are we to understand Canada's more stringent approach to regulating polygynous relationships in a negligible population? The racial project of regulating forbidden intimacies is especially pronounced in Canada,
where its policy of multiculturalism means tolerating diverse populations
and practices. One of the lawyers in the reference case summed up what he
viewed to be the fundamental reasoning: "The way I put it is, you have the
freedom to choose as long as your choice is the one that I agree with. So,
you have the right to choose, as long as your choice is something that reflects Canadian values." Still, when it came to charging men with polygamy,
the Canadian government was successful, but administrative ambivalence
meant that the men did not go to prison. Still, Canada maintains a stern
stance, especially when focused on people of color by identifying their "barbaric" practices, which are seen as a threat to Canadian values. The result
of regulating polygyny racializes immigrants to ensure that only "good"
monogamous migrants are accepted. In sum, Canada's national identity
embraces its multicultural policy while drawing a bright line that rejects
those deemed uncivilized.

Canada's endeavors to regulate polygyny in its territory are perhaps the
most far-reaching of the three countries, but we have seen how France,
the United States, and Canada have cultivated racial projects by defining
forbidden intimacies to reinforce their national identity and identify acceptable and unacceptable populations. Each of these countries has incited
moral panic to justify this boundary making, and each has responded with
administrative ambivalence when faced with polygyny's regulation. One
reason for this ambivalence is the diversity of polygamies that governments

are faced with. In the next chapter we delve into thinking about the ways that polygamies are lived based on their social contexts, geographies, and citizenship status. These social contexts shape the possibilities for implementing racial projects in each country, particularly for France and the United States, which have the largest populations of polygynous families.

2 | LABYRINTHINE LOVE AND HOMEGROWN POLYGAMIES

> We went on our first date and got a hamburger, all
> of us [William, his two current wives, and Olivia].
> So, that was Thursday. Friday morning, he came to
> pick me up, because I told him it was a yes. He said,
> "Do you want a wedding?" And I said, "No." I had to
> help my sister and best friend do their weddings,
> and I did not want to go there. It was too much
> work.... And, so we got married that night.
> —*Olivia, Mormon fundamentalist, Utah*

> I decided to marry a polygamous man. He was already
> married, with children who are grown like mine—my
> children are all grown up—and I decided to get
> married. And it was sincere.... I met this man, the man
> I love, who I really love! I tell him all the time, "It is me
> who loves you the most, because I decided to leave
> everything: my principles, that I was anti-polygamist,
> I left my friends, I abandoned them just for you."
> —*Hamina Ibrahima, mayor of Chirongui, Mayotte*

OLIVIA, A WHITE WOMAN in her early 60s, was born and
raised in a Mormon fundamentalist family in Utah. She described to me
how at the age of 16 she had fasted and prayed over the decision of whether
plural marriage was right for her. She reflected on the way her entire family,
especially her mothers and father, worked together to make ends meet and
nurture family harmony. Olivia said, "Of course I grew up in it. It would
have been the natural thing for me to just do it, but being the personality
that I am, I had to know why." She spent the next two years searching for
"the right man." She described how she had been dating a boy her own age

for nine months. He was everything she could have asked for, but something just didn't feel right. She continued to pray. A few days later her father asked her whether she had considered William, a white man fifteen years her senior who had a successful business. She had not. She knew that he was already married to two women, one of them her older sister from another mother. She said that she would "give it a try." After spending time with the family and being impressed by how William cared for his children and respected his wives, even helping in the kitchen, she had a surprising feeling when this "huge yes came in." She became his third wife. Olivia's description of her decision to enter a plural marriage the very evening after her first "date" with the entire family, sits uncomfortably with dominant ideals of love and marriage in Western societies. Few would understand Olivia's *desire* to find a plural marriage.

Hamina, a black Mahoraise woman in her 40s, was born and raised in Mayotte. She grew up in a polygynous family and married at a young age, between 12 and 13 years old, a tradition that was once typical in Mahorais society but that has declined over the last twenty years. The wedding ceremony took place in Mayotte without the presence of her future husband, who was living in France. After the ceremony Hamina was sent to metropolitan France to join this man whom she had barely seen. Hamina continued her education in France and gave birth to three boys. When her boys were still young, she decided to divorce her husband and return to Mayotte. She recounted that she never asked for alimony from her ex-husband because *she* made the choice to end the relationship. Hamina raised her boys and remained single for ten years. She described how becoming mayor of Chirongui in 2008 was a sort of "second marriage," as it meant that she had less time for her boys. A few years into her first term as mayor, she fell in love with a married man. He had been in a polygynous marriage with two women—he and the first wife divorced ten years after he took a second wife—and he had three children with each. When he proposed to divorce the current wife to marry her, Hamina responded:

> I said, "No, you will not give up all your family, your roots. You've always been with them. . . . It's been 20 years." No, no, no! He has his two daughters [still living at home], by the way. I said, "These girls need you. And

even your wife, she needs you; she loves you. I love you. Listen, it does not bother me!"

She married him religiously to become his second wife, stating, "Really, I would be unhappy if one day you told me that you will leave the other."

These two cases describe different situations of polygyny and a different way to perceive love, as untethered from monogamy and exclusivity. The words of these women also dispute dominant views that focus on polygyny's harm to women and children. Western governments justify banning polygyny on the grounds that it subjugates women. However, each of these women *decided* to enter a plural marriage—in the first case as the third wife and in the other case as the second wife. My interviews with Olivia and Hamina also reflect different ways of conceptualizing intimacy other than the dominant "talk of love" that permeates Western societies.[1] Sociologist Ann Swidler argues that notions of romantic love reflect the ideal of being "unique and exclusive ('one true love'), embodying the uniqueness of the individual self."[2] For sociologist Chris Ingraham, it is the myth of romantic love that sustains patriarchal heterosexuality. This myth reinforces the belief in monogamous coupling that views women's submission to men's desires as a natural part of marriage and commitment.[3]

The reasons for how and why these women entered a polygynous marriage were individually based. At the same time, their decision-making processes were affected by how they were raised, how they entered their family situations, the spaces in which they lived, and the differing political and legal contexts. We know that the state relies on marriage and intimacy to manage the lives of its citizens.[4] Likewise, governments forbid polygyny to ensure that "harmful" family forms do not take root in their societies. For fundamentalist Mormons and the Mahorais, racial projects and postcolonial realities shape how polygynous families survive. Although most Western governments treat polygyny as a uniform, harmful cultural practice that must be eradicated, the reality is that homegrown polygamies—polygamies that emerged out of the cultures and societies in which they are rooted— encompass a range of experiences, as evidenced by Olivia and Hamina.

Place also shapes how polygamies are lived. Homegrown polygamies in the Global North have developed through racialization, which has motivated their ban and regulation. The history of racialization and colonialism is important to understanding polygamy's prohibition and to considering how desire, space, and religious belief shape the conditions of polygamist lives. In the Global South postcolonial relations affect the transformations of intimacy, diversifying the possibilities for homegrown polygamies to exist in such places as Mayotte.

By conceptualizing polygamies rather than a singular polygyny, I explore how they exist on a continuum from dysfunctional to thriving, a structural approach to understanding polygamies and how living them is shaped by labyrinthine love. I first consider the historical regulation of polygamy as a racial project in the United States and Canada and then delve into examining the multiple ways that polygamies are lived based on conditions of space, love, and desire. Next, I look at polygamies in Mayotte, where traditions are quickly transforming and affecting the ways that polygamies are experienced.

HISTORICAL REGULATION IN NORTH AMERICA

Polygamies arose in North America among Indigenous populations before colonization. The Inuit and other Native Americans practiced both polygyny and polyandry in ancient civilizations.[5] When the Europeans arrived, they condemned the practice of polygyny as part of a larger problem of promiscuity among Indian families.[6] Government officials in the United States viewed Native marriage practices as foreign and un-Christian. Officials were horrified that some Indians had several wives, in some cases living far apart from one another, and that the wives owned property in their own names, not in their husband's name. Historian Nancy Cott described the efforts of government officials to reform marital customs through the prohibition of polygamy, where they "consistently encouraged or forced Indians to adopt Christian-model monogamy as the *sine qua non* of civilization and morality."[7]

A similar imposition of Christian-model monogamy took place in Canada, where Native families were subject to massive surveillance. Missionaries and residential schools assisted a large bureaucracy that sought to transform Native women into submissive wives who obeyed their husbands. The practice of nonmonogamy among Native populations became a reason to exert control to a much greater extent than was possible with other communities.[8] Efforts by Canadian colonizers to prohibit polygyny in Western Canada among Native populations aligned with broader concerns of the colonizing world to discourage polygyny as barbaric and uncivilized. Before 2020 polygamy in Canada had been prosecuted only twice, once involving an Indigenous man and the other a non-Indigenous man in an adulterous relationship with a woman.[9] Historian Sarah Carter has outlined how the Canadian government convicted a Kainai man named Bear's Shin Bone for polygamy in 1899, based on the amendment in the Criminal Code that was designed to prohibit Mormon polygamy.[10] Mormon men were similarly racialized for practicing polygamy in the United States and Canada. Prime Minister John A. Macdonald stated in 1890, "Her Majesty has a good many British subjects who are Mohammedans, and if they came here we would be obliged to receive them; but whether they are Mohammedans or Mormons, when they come here they must obey the laws of Canada."[11] Fears of the spread of Native and Mohammedan "barbaric" practices through Mormons fueled the need for an anti-polygamy law.

Regulating Indigenous families upheld ideals of monogamous marriage that were important in building both nations. Common sense blended with political theory to sustain the view that monogamous marriage was each nation's moral foundation. Yet, as Nancy Cott has explained, monogamy at that time was a minority practice in the world. Thus moral philosophers and political theorists wrote about the importance of this institution to civilized life and exhorted it as the basis for political governance. Cott further observed that key to ideals of American republicanism, "the founders learned to think of marriage and the form of government as mirroring each other."[12] Although colonizers sought to assimilate Native Americans by seeking to eradicate polygyny and enforcing Christian-model marriage, it was the emergence of the Mormon faith that brought polygyny forward as a crisis.

Mormonism took root in the United States in the 1830s. This was a time of deep social change that reorganized family life as the agrarian social order disintegrated as a result of the Industrial Revolution. During the tumult, some religious groups introduced novel forms of communal and family living, such as the Oneida Community's commitment to group marriage. Joseph Smith, founder and prophet of Mormonism and the Latter Day Saint movement, followed this trend in seeking a radical restructuring of family life. His revelation in 1831 led to the practice of plural marriage among Mormons as an ideal family form, with procreation as its fundamental objective.[13] After the Mormons settled in Utah, Brigham Young publicly announced the practice in 1852. It wasn't long after that the government sought to ban Mormon polygyny; in 1856 the newly formed Republican Party condemned polygyny together with slavery as "twin relics of barbarism."[14] Legal scholar Martha Ertman has studied political cartoons to understand the racial aspects of anti-polygamy legislation. These cartoons depicted polygyny as a form of marriage that was "natural" for people from Asia and Africa but "unnatural" for descendants of white Northern Europeans. The politics behind the "twin relics" language portrayed abolitionists as fighting against racial hierarchy in favor of emancipation. In contrast, anti-polygamists had a goal of supporting white supremacy and racial hierarchy. She explained, "Many nineteenth century Americans condemned slavery for harming Blacks, and polygamy for harming Whites."[15]

In 1857 President James Buchanan dispatched troops to Utah to subdue what was seen as a religious rebellion. No law prohibited bigamy in the territory of Utah. Consequently, Congress enacted the Morrill Bill to proscribe it. Federal enforcement of "unlawful cohabitation" laws drove many Mormon officials underground.[16] *Reynolds v. United States* upheld criminalization and linked polygamy to "Asiatic and African people," as discussed in Chapter 1.[17] Mormon polygamists tried to evade the statute by marrying multiple wives simultaneously or in religious rather than legal ceremonies. The federal government amended the statute in 1887 to cover both simultaneous marriages and cohabitation with more than one woman. They continued to pressure Mormon officials to forsake plural marriage by enacting federal legislation that disenfranchised women and polygamist men, by putting church properties under federal receivership, and by threatening to confiscate Mormon temples.[18] In 1890 Mormon president Wilford Woodruff announced a manifesto to end the practice of plural marriage, making it possible for Utah to achieve statehood and self-governance. The Utah Constitution prohibited "polygamous or plural marriages" and enforced the continuance of the territorial statute that made cohabitation unlawful.[19]

Many Mormons continued to practice plural marriage after the manifesto. Church officials disagreed over church doctrine, ultimately producing a separate fundamentalist Mormon movement in the 1930s that adhered to the fundamental doctrines established by Joseph Smith.[20] This movement grew in isolated areas across the American West, Canada, and Mexico, with most adherents living in Utah and northern Arizona. A central tenet was the practice of plural marriage.[21] In response, state officials sought to suppress the practice through raids, which culminated in the siege of Short Creek, Arizona, in 1953. Polygamist men were jailed, and children were separated from their mothers with the goal of making them wards of the state. The American public was appalled by news coverage of weeping mothers and children who were separated from each other, and the bad press ultimately led to Governor Howard Pyle losing his reelection bid. Criminal charges resulted in short-term probations for twenty-six men, who pleaded guilty to committing unlawful cohabitation.[22] After the raids, feelings of alienation and a deep distrust of government and mainstream society swelled among Mormon fundamentalists. Internal tensions also arose about how to live in the world, and what was once a unified leadership split into groups hostile to one another.[23]

CONTEMPORARY NORTH AMERICAN POLYGAMIES

The most visible group that currently practices polygyny in the United States is fundamentalist Mormons. Plural marriage family activist Anne Wilde conducted a survey in the early 2000s and estimated that of the 38,000 individuals who participated, about 15,000 identified as independents who have no central leader.[24] The structure of fundamentalist Mormon communities is hierarchal, and the divine authority of religious leaders—all men—places them at the top. However, beliefs and practices are quite diverse. Some groups sequester themselves, whereas others move freely in mainstream society. Independents and Apostolic United Brethren denounce underage marriage, practice modern dress and mannerisms, and encourage women's education.[25] They constitute the largest number of those living in plural marriage in Utah. At the other extreme are the Fundamentalist Latter Day Saints (FLDS), who we learned about in Chapter 1. The FLDS has long practiced placement marriage—marriages arranged by the prophet. However, there is some evidence that underage marriage was not as common before Warren Jeffs, who seized control of the FLDS in 2002.[26] He was convicted of two felony counts of child sexual assault and is serving a sentence of life plus twenty years in Texas. Other groups exist somewhere in between these extremes.[27]

Other forms of polygyny exist in the United States. Although U.S. immigration law has banned polygamists since 1891, many individuals practice foreign polygamous marriages. In 2008 scholars reported that between 50,000 and 100,000 immigrant families are polygynous.[28] In the United States foreign polygamous marriages are rarely addressed in the broader public conversation. Instead, the focus of debates is on the more visible version of fundamentalist Mormons and other Christian variations.

I interviewed Mark Henkel, who has been influential in the Christian polygamy movement. He described to me the diversity of polygamies.

> You go outside of that Mormon land bubble, and you'll have Christian polygamists, Jewish polygamists, secular polygamists, and nonreligious polygamists. Polygamy is a neutral noun, just like the word "day" is a neutral noun. And the noun is modified only by the adjectives to which it is assigned. So, for example, Mormon polygamy is a different word and meaning than Christian polygamy than secular polygamy than Jewish polygamy, and so forth, just like rainy day is different from saying a sunny day. So, you can't assign an equality of value to the same word when the adjectives are changing or have different reasons.

For Henkel, conditions in the United States allow for the growth of what he calls UCAP, unrelated consenting adult polygamy, which allows individuals to enter polygynous relationships by choice rather than coercion. Henkel's particular brand of polygamy is based on biblical Christian principles. He explained how he came to embrace Christian polygamy by reading the scriptures carefully.

> I began publishing a newspaper on July 4th, 1994, called *The Standard Bearer*, and this was a newspaper that went out through southern Maine. I began laying down the doctrines of what would eventually be called Christian polygamy. And it was establishing that the doctrine of one-man, one-woman was invented centuries after Christ and appears no-

where in the Bible. And so, it was about not even about trying to have other wives; it was about simply truth for truth's sake—*Sola Scriptura*.[29] And that if Christians are going to say they believe in the Bible for what the Bible says, then the Bible absolutely never called polygamy a sin and never established an enforcement of government using marriage control to limit it only to one man, one woman.

Henkel created an organization for Christian polygamy called TruthBearer. org, and he told me that by the late 1990s, it had about 10,000 members. The group's challenge to the concept of one-man, one-woman marriage provides further evidence of the flourishing of multiple polygamies in the United States.

Another growing form of polygyny is among African American Muslims. The late Debra Majeed studied this phenomenon and attributed it to the racial context of the United States, which has disadvantaged Black people socially, economically, and politically.[30] She conducted ethnographic research in fifteen African American Muslim communities from 2003 to 2013, estimating that about 1,000 people practiced polygyny, but the number was growing. Majeed examined polygyny's impact on the lives of Muslim women and among Black communities as a solution to the "lack of marriageable (single, heterosexual, and available) men, and/or the high number of female-led households, and the continued economic disparity experienced by mothers and their children make the practice of polygyny both mandated and permissible."[31] She argued that there was a range of experiences of polygyny in these communities and that those living in polygynous relationships required support from their faith communities, which varied according to local context. The late Imam W. Deen Mohammed's association, Muslim American Society/Mosque Cares, has the largest number of African American Muslims. Imam Mohammed argued that polygyny can be practiced for the well-being of the community in cases where provisions for justice are taken, such as making the marriage public to the Muslim community and informing all involved.

Like the diverse polygamies that these actors describe, my research has uncovered varied perspectives on plural marriage among those who are currently or formerly in polygynous unions. Some were extremely negative and some quite positive. In the United States activists who fight against polygyny often have left the religion and their plural marriages. For example, Amelia was born and raised in the Apostolic United Brethren and described how she was molested as a child by two siblings and a cousin. At the age of 17 she fell in love with and married a man who was seven years older. Finding a second wife was a requirement, and her husband married her second cousin. The two women were friends and that made it easier. However, over time, Amelia became increasingly disillusioned with the religion and plural marriage. She described her inner struggle with her true feelings.

> Don't let anybody know you're jealous for heaven's sake because . . . I had to show my face in church. And I want people to think I'm this holy, righteous, good person that I want to be. And so, you put on a smile, and you dress up, and you go to church, and you go, "Oh, I love polygamy! I love my sister wives! I love this, it's so wonderful." And I called my mom's and my life "miserable happiness," because it fits so completely. We were so happy in our misery because we were going to get to heaven.

Ultimately, Amelia left the Apostolic United Brethren and got a divorce. She described her ex-husband as a "good man." She stated, "I think he was a victim, just like we were, of living it. I think he wanted the hell out of there. I can't tell you how many times he wanted a place of his own, a room of his own, a quiet space where he could go crash."

For some, living plural marriage is extremely difficult, even in groups like the Apostolic United Brethren that provide more choice in selecting who they marry and when. Several participants described to me that they were living a nightmare. Former fundamentalist Mormons have written numerous escape stories, especially those leaving the FLDS.[32] Groups that are more closed instill a strong sense of duty and loyalty that can compel members to grin and bear their family situations. In other cases sister wives are able to work through their feelings of jealousy to nurture a more positive family environment.

JEALOUSY AND LOVE IN PLURAL MARRIAGES

Amelia discussed the need to hide feelings of jealousy. Jealousy, as discussed in the Introduction, is an integral element of intimate relationships, including monogamous ones, but it can be especially challenging for people practicing nonmonogamy. The responses to this emotion are diverse. For some, it tears them up. Kerry, now in her 50s, was not raised in Mormon fundamentalism and decided to leave her plural marriage after raising her children. She and her husband had decided to practice the "fullness of the gospel" (plural marriage) together. She had faith that God would reward her for making this huge sacrifice. After agreeing to marry the second wife, she recounted how, standing at the altar, she wanted someone to just "stick a knife in me right now." She echoed the words of Amelia that it was frowned on to openly express feelings of jealousy.

Other participants discussed their own personal growth, giving them tools to deal with jealousy. Tammy, in her early 40s and married to Arch and Joan, told me that she views jealousy as a form of immaturity: "And I discovered that it truly is possible to love your sister wife enough, and to maybe grow up enough that there aren't the jealousy issues that tends to always be the first question, you know. 'How can you stand X, Y, Z?' And to truly just love that your husband loves your sister wife, because you love her too." Jealousy can be a form of insecurity that is fueled by a desire for closeness.[33] Forms of nonmonogamy, such as plural marriage, can stoke the flames of jealousy, compelling individuals to deal with this emotion as central to love and family life. At the same time, women explained the importance of what I call homosocial bonds among wives—strong bonds between women that attenuate the power of the patriarch. These are important to negotiating their family and work roles, allowing women to work outside the home and ensure that their children are well cared for by their sister wives.[34]

The space in which families lived was often an important factor in how they managed love and jealousy. I interviewed Tammy, Arch, and Joan in their home, which all three shared with their numerous children. It was spacious, with a large kitchen that the two wives shared. Because each wife had a section of the house, they learned quickly how to share. Large houses in Utah are not too expensive, and many plural families are able to live together in one house harmoniously. Often, one or more wives work outside the home, and one stays home to watch the children. One family with three wives that I interviewed was eventually able to afford three houses; two wives worked outside the home and the third worked from home while also watching the children. In other situations the wives would work together, taking turns on who would go to work. In all the families I interviewed, at least one of the wives worked outside the home.

Some families started out living in small spaces and eventually had to expand as more children arrived. I traveled to a remote area in Utah where families had built their homes into the beautiful red-rock cliffs that are a stunning feature of southern Utah. Each wife had her own house, but it did not start that way. Ellie told me that after she and Oliver decided to bring Julie, who was 18 years old at the time, into their family, they shared a small house. She explained, "We were sharing a very close space. That was a fun experience, to learn how to work together, and to bring somebody else in and open your home completely and just be able to go, 'Okay, my space is now your space.'" Eventually, as the families grew, they built a second house. Ellie said that they used cash, because they did not want to go into debt. The wives have a mail route that they share and take turns staying home with the children.

Participants described the ways that love can grow in plural families and that community is central to giving and receiving love. Julie described dealing with feelings of jealousy and love: "You come up with your insecure feelings, or your jealous feelings, or your . . . But, in the long run, when it is all said and done, I absolutely love living with Oliver and Ellie. I love sharing our lives together. Love sharing our children." Sandra, in her 30s, married at 18 years of age and is the second of two wives; she recounted:

> Anyway, sometimes people wonder if there's less love because the guy has to give a little love to this person, give a little love to that person. But that's the opposite of what happens. The love grows. The more people in the family, the more love there is to go around. It's like having children. I mean, can you divide your love between your children? Of course not. The more children you have, the more love you have.

She explained that the growth in love comes not just from the love between the husband and each wife but from the love that sister wives have for each other and for the other wife's or wives' children.

As I interviewed families, it became clear that their love was labyrinthine in combining various combinations of styles of modern love, such as passionate and practical love.[35] For example, Olivia, who was quoted earlier, eventually left her religion but remained in the marriage as the second wife because her husband is "one in a billion. He's that kind of guy. And even though today I don't believe in any religion, I stayed in the marriage because I have an amazing man that I love, deeply love. And I love my family; they are a loving family. And he's able to accept my changes." Her description draws on her passionate feelings for her husband even as she is now in her 60s. She also described a practical choice to stay in the family that she loves, even as she let go of the religious beliefs that made plural marriage a requirement to enter heaven. In contrast, families in which competition and jealousy are rife often involve game playing and possessive, dependent love. Avery and Jack had been in a plural marriage that went sour. The first wife was often overcome by jealousy after Jack took a second wife, and it made for misery. Avery explained, "There were times when I felt like it was a pendulum swinging back and forth. When she was pleasant and happy, I loved being around her. You know, she was engaging and fun. And then when she'd start to wig out, and get jealous, whatever it was that she'd give into those feelings, it would just be impossible to be around her." Jealousy could lead to children becoming pawns. Jack attributed this experience to people going crazy in their relationships: "You know, if really crazy people do it, then they are going to harm each other one way or another, just like crazy monogamist people harm each other in bad marriages."

Many of the participants described the love that they felt in terms of love based on friendship and altruism. By working on love as a form of companionship, plural families can make sure that there is plenty of love to go around. Harper touched on the importance of abundant love for building family and community. In discussing the benefits of her plural family, she provided an expansive definition of family: "The [benefits] are huge. . . . Every family is unique. When you talk about family and what defines a family, and you talk about the government's idea that a marriage is between one man and one woman in a family, and this is what the natural family looks like. . . . To me, family is the hub. It is the center of the core." Harper challenged the idea that the best model for family is monogamy. For her, family is about relationships, and plural marriage provides the opportunity for children to nurture relationships with many people who care for them.

> And I don't care what choices children grow up and make and choose for themselves, if that family core structure is solid, then the children are so much better off for it. And when I say solid, I don't say that it has to look like the defined nuclear family. A family is a group of people coming together for a common purpose, and raising children with common goals, common values. And, in a polygamous culture, that is magnified. . . . And here's a child that has an opportunity to have a relationship with mom, a relationship with dad, a relationship with siblings, a relationship with another mom, a relationship with other siblings, a relationship with yet another mom, a relationship with other siblings, a relationship with countless grandparents (laughs), and cousins. And the idea of family is just enormous!

Harper's definition of family fits the postmodern ideal of family based on variation and freedom of choice.[36] For fundamentalist Mormons this expansive understanding of family is key to the styles of love possible: Romantic love is shared between the husband and each wife, but love also grows between the husband and all the wives, allowing them to work together and become more considerate. Samantha, a woman in her 40s who had participated in a plural marriage for over twenty years, discussed her growth as a person and her personal evolution that required maturity and a recognition of her selfish actions: "I hadn't been married very long, and something happened, and . . . I did a thing. . . . I went into my room, and I looked in the mirror—I realize how cliché this is—but I looked in the mirror, and I just remember looking at myself and saying, 'You're selfish. That was so selfish.'" Learning to prioritize the needs of others and to deal with jealousies that arise with sister wives is central for women in plural marriages. Her ability to reflect on her selfishness made it possible to nurture relationships with wives that were positive and fulfilling.

Muslim polygynous families are also diverse in their structure and the ways they are lived, drawing on the complexities of labyrinthine love. Debra Majeed's research on African American Muslim families found that the happiest ones were those in which the first wife (and subsequent wives) was involved in the decision to take another wife. Building a relationship with a new co-wife was key. She offered the experience of Rabi'a. A successful academic, Rabi'a was married to a man for nine years and had three children with him when the two began to seriously discuss bringing in a second wife. This was something that she and her husband discussed before they were married, and her requirements were at least seven years of marriage and an annual income of over $100,000. He had met both. According to Majeed, Rabi'a felt that "her husband was 'the type of person who could do' polygyny, that he was emotionally, physically, and financially mature enough to take on the additional responsibility."[37] They identified a woman at their mosque. Cases such as Rabi'a's exemplify successful polygynous families, where all members have chosen to participate. However, Majeed also found that polygyny can have negative mental health consequences for all involved when the families are not working well, especially when men take on multiple wives but are not able to live up to their responsibilities. The women in these marriages might have limited economic options and might accept polygyny grudgingly. This can pose problems for women who marry as the second wife in a religious ceremony that is not recognized by the state. Having no legal recourse in cases of abuse or divorce, these women must rely on their religious communities for support. Living polygamies in African American Muslim communities are thus complicated by the social context in ways that are similar to those of Mormon fundamentalists.

For plural families living in North America, the social and legal conditions under which polygamies are lived make a difference in the ways they are experienced. Closed groups such as the FLDS tend to practice placement marriages, which are often forced, as well as underage marriages. Although it is important to fight against such practices, not all polygamies are harmful. Even among the FLDS, I learned of families in which members were happy in their plural marriages. Participants described that jealousy and competition can be central to plural marriage, but different styles of love and ways of dealing with jealousy—labyrinthine love—mix to determine how plural families work through these challenges. Conceptualizing how love is like a labyrinth shines light on the difficulty of regulating forbidden intimacy. As a continuum, different manifestations of polygamies make assessing harm more complex than most approaches account for. In the

next section we will consider another example of homegrown polygamies—
Mayotte, in which the legal and social conditions have changed over time
and polygamies are growing.

TRADITIONAL MARRIAGE AND MUSLIM POLYGAMIES IN MAYOTTE

The practice of polygyny in Mayotte goes back centuries. The island was
first populated by several civilizations, predominantly of Bantu origin,
an ethnic group from southeastern Nigeria that migrated to Mayotte between the fifth and eighth centuries.[38] At the end of the eighteenth century,
a Malagasy tribe from Madagascar invaded, bringing a Malagasy dialect.
European colonial influence began when the Portuguese and French landed
in Mayotte in the fifteenth century and Mayotte became a supply point of
the Indian Ocean trade routes. The French gained colonial control over the
island in 1843, and it became a province of the colony of Madagascar, along
with the other islands of the Comoros archipelago, in the early twentieth
century.[39]

Muslim and customary laws mix in Mayotte to regulate gender relations, sexuality, family life, and social mores. Muslim ideology places
men at the top of the social and moral hierarchy. The gender division of
labor obliges the husband to have an income to maintain his family and
makes him the head of the household. However, although Mahorais society is patriarchal, its kinship structure limits men's authority. Many of my
participants discussed Mayotte as a matriarchal society in which women
"wear the pants." Researchers have found this claim to be somewhat ex-
aggerated,[40] but family life in Mayotte does include a tradition of matrilineal residence; it is organized around women who are the central pillars
of the family. Among family relationships the mother-daughter bond is
supreme, and women are central to sustaining other family relationships.
Traditionally, the father and brothers build a house, called a *dagoni*, on the
family grounds, and the sisters of the same family will live there with their
husbands after they are married. Customary law obliges men to ensure
that their female kin are supported financially.[41] Moreover, young men are
forbidden from living in the maternal home after they become teenagers.
Instead, they live in *banga*s, mud-built huts that are often painted in attractive and colorful patterns. Because daughters are given a house that is

guarded throughout their lives and remarriages, sons are obliged to find a wife to share a house, unless they have the means to build their own. Matrilocality provides stability for women, because divorce is common. An older woman generally has two to four husbands, and a man may have many more wives.[42] In this sense, matrilocality provides women some power to resist the authority of men who enter the home of the bride. Society expects women to marry, and being single is accepted only as a transitional state between two unions.

Social reproduction is a key organizing principle in Mahorais society, exemplified by the customary celebration of weddings, called the *grand mariage* (great marriage), once based on marrying a young (what we think of as underage) virgin bride.[43] Over the past ten years, wedding celebrations have transformed and become more extravagant and costly with several hundred invitees. Named the *manzaraka*, brides no longer marry very young.[44] The ceremony begins with the groom, dressed in beautiful traditional costume, marching with a large group of men surrounding him and women following behind, also in traditional costume. The procession moves across the village while Islamic poems are sung and accompanied by tambourines. A sumptuous feast is served separately for men and women, which is followed by dancing and chanting. The typical cost is exorbitant—20,000 euros or more—and often the young couple pays more than the parents.[45] Overall, participation in and the timing of the great marriage has become more optional. Many individuals elect to have a simple religious ceremony (*mafounguidzo*) and do the *manzaraka* later when they have the financial means. I was invited to participate in the prewedding celebration of one great marriage, helping to make jasmine garlands for the ceremony with other female family and friends. I met the bride, who sat on the bridal bed with exquisite makeup and attire during the preparations, waiting for the banquet to begin. Although she participated in these traditions, the bride told me that she worked a full-time job and supported gender equality in her marriage and in Mahorais society. She, among other young women I spoke to, represented a new generation of educated women who sought a balance between tradition and autonomy. More consumer-oriented weddings represent a mixture of Western and Muslim rituals. Moreover, celebrating a great marriage has not meant more permanence in these relationships, as the society's matrilocal structure supports having children from different fathers.

Paradoxically, polygyny has been one aspect of this matrilocal structure. Combo Abdallah Combo, a sociologist and training manager at the Institut Régional du Travail Social in Mayotte, described a correlation between the ritual of great marriages and polygyny that existed in the past. In particular, the necessity of participating in a marriage with a virgin girl sometimes meant becoming polygynous. He described the example of a young man having a sexual relationship with a young woman and marrying her as prescribed by religion and custom. This, however, could not be a great marriage because the bride was no longer a virgin. Later, the mother would pressure the son to do a great marriage.

> My mother is going to tell me, "My son, you're my boy, and you haven't had a great marriage yet. So, I expect you to have one." I already have a wife with children—three, four, five children—that I just formalized religiously because it is compulsory. . . . What does this mean? It means that I must marry another woman. So automatically, my mom encourages me to be polygamous.

In the current era in which marrying a virgin no longer defines great marriages, men may feel less obliged to marry more than one woman to meet society's (and their mother's) requirements. However, these evolving norms have not necessarily meant a large decline in the number of polygynous unions. According to estimates from a 2015 survey by the National Institute of Statistics and Economic Studies, between 9% and 11% of households surveyed in Mayotte were polygynous.[46] This figure is slightly lower than the 13% of the population that practiced polygyny in 1991. Yet it still represents roughly 27,000 individuals and perhaps more, given the difficulty of measuring the exact number of Mahorais men who have more than one wife but would not appear in these data, as the other wives live on Madagascar or other islands.

Traditionally, polygynous families in Mayotte do not live in the same household. My participants described a system in which wives often lived in different villages and even on a different island—Petite-Terre or Grande-Terre. Ali, a government official and the son of a polygynous family, recounted how couples lived separately in Mayotte, unlike other parts of Africa where the wives lived in the same enclosure. He described how in most cases, even if the wives did not get along as co-wives, they sought to get along as co-mothers who have children from the same father. When this was not the case, the wives could turn the children against each other. This created a difficult family situation. Ali recounted that in his own upbringing all the children and mothers got along.

> My father was polygamous, but he taught us all to live together. That is to say, I could go to the other mother's house, live at the other mother's house, just like I was at my own mother's house. And the other children also came to my mother's house to live with us in the same way. . . . My dad had four wives, two of whom were senior. So, all the children of the four women, we all lived together.

Still, men and women alike told me that Mahoraise women did not live polygyny well on the islands of Mayotte, even when they managed to get along.

Nael described how he had taken a second wife, whom he had met at work. He grew up with his first wife in his natal village and had three children with her, but he had no children with the second wife. He recounted the challenges in making both women happy because of conflicts and jealousies, especially because the first wife had not been able to adapt to being in a polygynous marriage. Even though the women did not necessarily express their jealousies openly, Nael, in his early 30s, described his struggle to make sure that each wife felt she was being treated fairly: "I built a house for the [first wife], so I absolutely had to do the same [for the second]. So, situations like that can lead to the two being in conflict. One thinks that I spend all my money on the other, and I don't do enough for her." These kinds of jealousies were echoed often in my interviews, and the ways that husbands and wives dealt with them determined the harmony in their households.

In contemporary Mahorais society, women's dependence on men has shifted, because many women work full-time jobs and are self-sufficient. Yet polygyny persists. Soifaouya identified herself as a "Mahoraise woman" to highlight how she resembled many women in Mahorais society but asked me not to use her real name. She has a career that pays well and later decided to enter a polygynous family. She explained, "I have everything I need, but I am living in polygamy. Basically, I do not accept it, but I live it anyway. And why? One moment, one says psychologically, it's not easy to be single in society." Because it is frowned on for women to remain single, many women feel pressure to marry, even when they are in their 40s or 50s. Some fall in love with men who are already married and are willing to enter a polygynous marriage. Soifaouya's case was like that of Hamina, described earlier: Both fell in love with a man who was already married. Unlike Hamina, Soifaouya had hoped that this man would leave his first wife, which he had promised to do. In the end, he broke his promise, and she became his second wife.

Soifaouya described a fundamental evolution in society in which more women support the husband, especially in polygynous marriages.

> Well, it is still the man [who mostly supports the family]—we should not exaggerate. But there is also this side that thank god women also work; they have responsibilities. Here, it is the reverse of what was at the origin of polygamy. In fact, the system has remained, but the reasons are no longer the same.

She elaborated: "And more and more women who work, I would say who 'maintain' the man more than the man maintains the woman. In the end, women sometimes compete to please the man. . . . She'll buy him a shirt, go to him. So, he has nothing to do in the end. He is the king." Over time, the freedom to have sexual liaisons with multiple people opened up. Yet families see it as "immoral to go with several women." Thus even young men who might be less likely to become polygynous are still marrying multiple women to satisfy their families. Parents might also pressure a man to marry their daughter after the onset of a sexual relationship. These dynamics continue from the past, but today we see women who have the means to live without a husband marry into polygyny. Elise Lemercier, a sociologist who studies the family in Mayotte, confirmed that many elite women are in polygynous marriages: "Even women with very high social positions, very feminist, etc., are very much in polygamous marriages, which they have chosen after its prohibition in Mayotte."

Thus the reasons to enter polygyny are complex. Some women discover that the man they have become involved with and who they planned to marry is already married. I interviewed Chayma, a Mahoraise official in her 30s, who recounted the case of a girlfriend who became the second wife because she discovered too late that the man she loved was already married.

> We are not all from the same village, so we do not necessarily know who is married or not. Me, I have a girlfriend who lived in Petite Terre at her father's house—her polygamous dad, and so, when she came back to live with her mother when she was in high school, she met a man. She did not know that this man was married, and by the time she learned it, she was already attached to him. So, she still married him.

Chayma's story points to how accepted it is for men to begin a relationship with another woman without telling her that he is married.

Noera Mohamed, the regional delegate for women's rights for the prefecture of Mayotte, explained that many young people of her generation, in their late 20s and early 30s, were in polygynous marriages. According to her, polygyny was practiced for multiple reasons, including women who submitted to it because they needed the support of a husband to survive. Some women felt that it was better to be married in a polygynous union than to remain single. Finally, some women of her generation saw polygyny as providing more freedom than monogamy.

> I met women of my generation who told me, "For me, it's a way of life that suits me because I'm free. He comes only two, three times a week, and the rest of the time, I do what I want." So, these are all the opinions that I heard, and I did not judge them at all, because everyone does what she or he wants. But we realize that despite everything, it does not change. There are still people today who enter in polygamous unions.

Noera described how surprised she was that polygyny persists in Mayotte, because she thought that women today would no longer accept it. But that was not the case; for some, polygyny provided more freedom in a society that still required them to marry. This reasoning points to the pragmatism of entering a polygynous union and is related to the complexities of labyrinthine love.

In discussing her own situation, Noera vacillated a bit on whether she would be willing to enter a polygynous union. She is Mahoraise but was not born in Mayotte, having migrated from metropolitan France with her parents when she was 13. This gave her a somewhat different perspective. For example, she told me that she is still single at 33 years old, something frowned on by her family and Mahorais society. She stated, "I'm telling you that unless I'm really on the verge of despair, I can't see myself sharing. . . . Well, I have a vision of the family with a husband, children, the father who is there, who is present, and not one that I share with someone else. But the future, I don't know. One never knows what will happen tomorrow." As a professional working for women's rights in Mayotte, Noera provided a nuanced perspective on women living in polygyny and remained somewhat open to considering it herself. These multifaceted reasons for entering polygyny illuminate the complexities of labyrinthine love that are integral to polygynous relationships. These include negotiating jealousies, deciding whether to stay in a polygynous relationship, or choosing it as a way of maintaining one's freedom.

This continuum on which polygamies exist captures a vast array of experiences, most of which go unrecognized by the state. By treating polygyny as a racial project, states tend to regulate polygyny as a singular structure that is solely defined as gender inegalitarian and backward. Identifying the diverse experiences of homegrown polygamies will help to find ways to support both plural families that work well, such as Sandra's family, which she conceives of as producing more love not less, and those that include elements of abuse, such as in Jack and Avery's family, where jealousy solidified into hate. Although racial projects to regulate forbidden intimacies often focus on a state's own citizens, polygyny also occurs in populations that are migratory. When it is transported into a new national context, the polygynous experience becomes something else altogether. In the next chapter I address this question of migratory polygamies.

3 | MIGRATORY POLYGAMIES

Racialization and Colonial Reckonings

> I was happy. After that, it's true that there is always
> rivalry between the two wives, if that's not obvious. But
> in any case, when we lived together, I was happy. In fact,
> it went well. Of the two wives, neither was working at
> the time. My father was working, and it was going well.
> —*Mariam, daughter of first wife, Paris*

> In Senegal, we call the other wife my mother's rival,
> because for her, she was a rival. So, she took care of
> me because she had no choice. I was in the house, but
> she didn't take care of me [like a mother would].
> —*Abdou, son of second wife, Paris suburbs*

MARIAM WAS BORN IN PARIS in the late 1970s; Abdou was
born in the Paris suburbs in the early 1980s. Both were roughly the same
age, but their upbringings differed substantially. Mariam's father migrated
to France in 1960 from Mali, during the years of increased migration in
France. He brought over his first wife in the late 1970s and the second in
the early 1980s under France's family reunification policy. Mariam was the
first child born to the first wife. During her upbringing, the family lived
in a two-bedroom apartment in northern Paris. In the years to come the
two wives had a total of sixteen children, all raised together in their small
apartment until Mariam was 18. She described how as the family grew, the
space also grew increasingly cramped. Although her memories of a happy
childhood predominate, she recounted that the most difficult aspect of her
upbringing was the overcrowded apartment: "In terms of our accommoda-
tions, it was very difficult, because being so numerous in a small apartment

is complicated. Even to do one's studies, it was complicated. There was a lot of noise, there were a lot of people, and it was difficult to concentrate. I remember that I had to go out in the hallway of the building to have quiet and do my homework." Still, Mariam remembers that her family was like many others in Paris near where she grew up, and it did not seem unusual to have a small accommodation for a large family. Many nonpolygynous families also had large families living in small apartments.

After the 1993 law prohibited living as a polygynous family, Mariam's family began a process of decohabitation in the late 1990s. She was studying at university at the time and was married in her early 20s. She described how the second wife had to divorce her father civilly. Religiously, however, both wives remained married. Both were required to stay at a hotel with the children until social services could find each separate low-income housing. It took four years, and the cost was exorbitant—the two hotel rooms cost 4,000 euros a month. Mariam's father had to pay 1,000 euros, a large sum at the time. He stayed with a friend and would visit the family periodically. Despite these difficulties, the family stayed close. The two apartments were not too far from each other, and her father divided his time between the two, one day with Mariam's mother and the other with her "aunt." Mariam described how periodically they organized family dinners at one of the wives' households. Mariam felt closer to her biological brothers and sisters, but she also felt close to her half-siblings. When I asked whether there was a strong connection between all the siblings, she replied, "A connection? Yes, of course! They remain my brothers and my sisters."

Mariam's happy memories and current connections to her biological parents, her other mother, and her siblings contrast with the upbringing of Abdou, whose family was split apart. Abdou's father arrived in France in the early 1970s from Senegal. Abdou's mother became the second wife and joined her husband in the early 1980s when she was pregnant with her first child, Abdou. Each wife had seven children, totaling fourteen. All of Abdou's full brothers and sisters were born in France except one, who has born when his mother was in Senegal. Abdou explained to me that his father never allowed both wives to be in France at the same time, even though in the early 1980s it would have been legal to do so. The two wives took turns going back and forth to Senegal until Abdou was 8 years old. At this point, his father sent his mother back to Senegal for good with all the children except the two oldest boys. Abdou visited Senegal three times, and he was there for two and a half years on the third visit. For ten years Abdou was raised by the first wife in France, and his mother died when he was 18 years old.

Unlike Mariam's family, who packed into a small apartment, Abdou's household was not as crowded. The first wife had her first two children in Senegal, and they were older by the time she came to France. Five of the first wife's children were born in France, but two returned to Senegal, later returning to France to marry. Thus the household after his mother left for good consisted of Abdou's father, the first wife, his biological brother, three half-sisters, and himself—seven members in total. He told me, "It's a complicated way of life." On the surface, theirs was a "normal" monogamous family. Underneath, there was a darker truth. Abdou described being maltreated by the first wife: "It was very difficult because I was not only with my father. I was with my father and another wife. This is what is complicated, in fact, because she mistreated us." He explained that the rivalry between the two wives spread to mistreating the children: "Well, in fact, it was my mother who was the rival, but since my mother was no longer there, it was necessary to have another rival. So, it became the kids. They are the ones who suffer." This toxic jealousy at the limits of labyrinthine love created an infernal environment for Abdou's upbringing. Abdou never thought of the first wife as his mother but as "another woman." Being forced to care for her rival's children, she abused them. Abdou's experience reflects harm stories of failed or failing polygynous families: relationships between wives characterized by unsolved conflicts, tension, and animosity that can lead to violence among co-wives and the other wives' children.[1]

These two different experiences of growing up in polygynous families reflect the diversity of polygamies that are lived in various migratory contexts. It might be hard to imagine that Mariam's family could be successful in the cramped circumstances they endured for many years. Abdou, on the other hand, lived in a more ideal situation, with more space and better economic circumstances, except that he was deprived of his mother and abused by the first wife. Abdou was not sure about the decision to leave the older two boys with the father and first wife. He told me that his father was not one to discuss these kinds of issues, and his mother died before they were able to discuss it. Still, he knew that she would have preferred to live with all her children in France. Her relationship with her sons eventually became one of mothering from a distance, until her early death.

How do we understand these polygynous families whose experiences have been shaped by migration and polygamy's ban? We have learned that polygamies take on a certain shape and form when they are homegrown and practiced as part of a culture or religion, but polygamies that move from one country context to another are often lived quite differently. A polygynist family migrating from and to countries where polygamy is legal might not experience much dislocation. Polygamies that migrate from a country where it is legal to where it is banned present different challenges.

Migratory polygamies mirror certain dynamics of transnational marriage and motherhood, which bring challenges to families, especially in cases of mothering from a distance.[2] Mothers and the children left behind experience emotional distress and physical deprivation when mothers are compelled to migrate and live for extensive periods of time far away.[3] The different ways that individuals experience transnational family life vary by gender. Dominant gendered norms in most societies designate mothers as the primary caregivers, with the expectation that they are physically present to perform their duties.[4] For migrant mothers who are unable to meet these standards, guilt and stress are prevalent. Children whose mothers live elsewhere often report feeling excessive sadness at the loss of having their mother physically present. Many migrant women take jobs that are precarious in which they endure abusive employer relations.[5] Such patterns of distress can be exacerbated in polygynous families that are divided between the country of origin and the host society, particularly for the wife or wives and children left behind.

We also know that migration shapes and is shaped by sexuality and family life. For example, sociologist Hector Carrillo has theorized on the importance of sexuality to the migration processes of immigrant gay men, and research on sexual migration has uncovered how sexuality shapes migratory patterns and state structures.[6] Carrillo has argued that cultural and structural explanations for migration are important to move past the problematic idea that gay men migrate from sexual cultures that are "backward" to more "progressive" ones. In fact, migrants can use their cultural backgrounds to challenge the discrimination they often experience based on such factors as race, ethnic background, and sexuality in the host country. Even for sexual migrants who migrate to places where same-gender relationships are legal, sexuality can still place them in precarious circumstances.

For polygynous families it is also necessary to challenge the idea that they move from backward to more progressive countries. In countries such as France, colonialism has structured the possibility of living polygamies in the Global North. Just as in North America, colonial logics not only helped to define polygyny but also regulated "backward" practices; the legacy of colonialism has also shaped migratory processes and the regulation of migrant intimate lives. This historical trajectory shapes perspectives on polygamy in general and has influenced legal structures that regulate forbidden intimacies.

Considering the prohibition of such family structures as polygyny, we know little about how forbidden migratory intimacies are lived. Just as with homegrown polygamies, migratory polygamies are shaped by colonial, legal, and national structures of the host society, and issues of space and class can make migratory polygamies untenable. These factors affect the ways that labyrinthine love is lived and how jealousy is managed. In examining migratory polygamies in France, I first consider the colonial circumstances that have shaped the ways that polygamies are viewed and received by the broader society. I then examine how labyrinthine love is experienced for transnational polygynous families. Finally, I consider the experiences of migratory polygamies that remained in France after the Pasqua law took effect in 1993. Overall, stories of migratory polygamies reflect the challenges that families face in living forbidden intimacies as noncitizens as well as the increased possibility for deception to occur.

COLONIAL ROOTS AND CIVILIZING PRACTICES

Polygyny in France is tied to colonialism and migratory patterns in which workers from former colonies brought over multiple wives. France's colonial past focused on regulating family not only in metropolitan France but also in its colonies, a history that has continued to shape its conceptualization of the social contract.[7] According to historian Alice Conklin, France's rhetoric of Enlightenment was used to justify its empire, specifically referred to as its *mission civilisatrice*, a mission to civilize "primitive" peoples.[8] The notion of a civilizing mission has had special meaning in France, as the word *civilization* itself is a French invention of the eighteenth century.

The civilizing mission's apex occurred during the Third Republic, from 1870 to 1940. The end of the nineteenth century and the beginning of the twentieth witnessed a period of growing nationalism in Europe. The French desire for national glory and nationalist sentiment, especially after the defeat of the Franco-Prussian War, pushed France to look overseas to Africa, Southeast Asia, and Oceania to expand its empire. The stated goal was to improve the living conditions of colonial subjects, such as building railroads. Importantly, rather than an expectation of full assimilation, France sought to develop republican values within the specific cultures of the colonized. However, practices that specifically offended republican principles were targeted for eradication. "Barbaric" customs were largely attributed to sub-Saharan Africa and Oceania. Conklin argued that the ideal of civilizing populations rested on contradictory principles that colonial subjects were "too primitive to rule themselves but capable of being uplifted."[9] Elevating colonial subjects meant regulating offensive practices such as polygyny.

The issue of polygyny became a focus of colonial governance early on in Algeria. Colonial administrators used polygyny, in addition to other practices such as child marriage and repudiation, to mark a distinction between the French and Muslim juridical systems, drawing a boundary to delimit French national belonging by the absence of these practices.[10] According to historian Judith Surkis, in the early days of colonial administration polygyny was seen as a vice that derived mainly from economic considerations; once a man had enough money and power, he would marry multiple wives.[11] Colonialists conjectured that the material gains proffered by the imperial project in the colonies would one day vanquish polygyny as men perceived that it was expensive to support multiple households. This perspective was later contested, as the definition of polygyny came to be understood as a religious "right" that was intolerable to civilized peoples and represented the difficulty of applying French law to Jewish and Muslim subjects. France's personal status laws that were assigned by religion allowed Algerian Jews and Muslims legal access to polygyny and divorce. At the same time, this personal status blocked the ability of these populations to become citizens. Whereas the personal status of North African Jews was removed in 1870, giving them the possibility for citizenship, Muslims remained inferior "subjects" of France and objects of French law.[12] Despite periodic attempts at partial reform, the treatment of Muslim Algerians persisted until after the Fourth Republic in 1946.

Over time, polygyny came to represent the heart of "Muslimness."[13] This perception was not supported by reality. In fact, the number of polygynist men had decreased in Algeria, from 16% in 1886 to 3% in 1948, likely because of the increased financial difficulty of having more than one wife.[14] Reforms that would allow Algerians to vote led to the passage of the Jonnart law, which regulated Algerian access to full citizenship, requiring them to renounce aspects of Muslim law, including polygyny. Those who would not renounce Muslim law or who the French government deemed unworthy of citizenship would remain French subjects but would still have the right to vote in local elections.[15] The debate over polygyny and French law is captured in the words of Senator Claude Alphonse Delangle from a report published in 1896: "[Polygyny is] incompatible with public modesty, with morality, with the good order of the families . . . . It is not possible to have contradictory rights on the soil of the homeland."[16] The definition of "homeland" was quite slippery: A 1916 law bestowed citizenship to the inhabitants of the four communes of Senegal, justified by their conscription during the war. In this case the colonial administration recognized the Muslim community's submission to Koranic law and their polygynous marriages in 1912 while granting full citizenship.[17]

Colonial perspectives of Arab and African sexuality focused on its "hypersexuality," symbolized by polygyny and the harem. With the disintegration of France's empire and migratory flows of Arab and African male workers from former colonies, polygyny would become an issue to regulate not just "over there" but also on France's doorstep. Thus the contradictions of regulating an "anti-republican" family structure in faraway colonies found its way into the French public consciousness. During and after World War I, France's immigrant population began to diversify as France recruited immigrants from colonies in Indochina, sub-Saharan and

North Africa, and elsewhere to serve in wartime industries.[18] France's depopulation crisis put migrants in the spotlight of administrative attention as a possible solution.

The history of immigration in France is extensive. Its immigrant population nearly doubled between 1870 and 1890, and by 1931 France had the highest foreign population in the world, exceeding that of the United States.[19] The ordinance of November 2, 1945, became the first significant regulatory policy on immigration, creating the National Office of Immigration, which established residence permits with durations of one, five, and ten years. Migrant male workers were allowed entry between 1945 and 1975; they worked in poorly paid jobs in industry, construction, and agriculture, initially as temporary guest workers who were expected to return to their countries of origin.[20] These men were housed in *bidonvilles* (shantytowns) with no electricity or running water or in squalid and overcrowded hostels, hotels, or apartments. The fact that they were fully employed and living on the outskirts of cities made them largely invisible to the French public. Sweeping change occurred in 1974, when the French government terminated foreign labor recruitment and annulled bilateral agreements that had permitted former colonial subjects to move freely in and out of France. Men began to bring their wives and children to France, authorized by family reunification policies, and large numbers of immigrants moved into public housing apartments (*cités*) that were once largely inhabited by white French working-class families. Thus their presence became more visible and motivated intense debate over whether and how sub-Saharan and North African immigrants could assimilate into French society.[21]

North and sub-Saharan African immigration to France is historically linked to administering its overseas territories. By 1962 African immigrants constituted nearly 15% of the total immigrant population in France, with the vast majority from the Maghreb (11.6% from Algeria, 1.1% from Morocco, 1.5% from Tunisia, and a mere 0.7% from all other African countries).[22] The proportion of immigrants from sub-Saharan Africa increased to 6.6% by 1990. Polygynous families are predominantly from two regions in West Africa: (1) the Senegal River basin, bordering Mali, Mauritania, and Senegal and inhabited by the Soninke and Toucouleur ethnic groups; and (2) Casamance, bordering Senegal and Guinea and populated by the Jola

(Diola in French).[23] Polygyny in West Africa is not just a religious practice but is an accepted aspect of the traditional culture and kinship systems observed by Christians, Muslims, and adherents of native religions alike.[24] Urban sociologist Pauline Gaullier has pointed out that there are no statistics on the exact number of polygynous families in France, and researchers and government officials have provided a wide range of estimates, from 3,000 to 20,000 families.[25] A 2006 estimate from the National Consultative Commission for Human Rights concluded that between 16,000 and 20,000 polygynous families existed in France in 2006, with upward of 120,000 individuals.[26]

Polygyny became a central focus of debate over assimilation as multiple wives entered France under family reunification laws for families from West and North Africa. Fear of the nonassimilability of African families led to the 1993 Pasqua law, which put an end to polygynous family reunification and made it illegal to live in a polygynous family on French territory. Many polygynous families fell into a legal gray zone, being neither regularizable nor deportable. Some men never brought all or any of their wives to France. Others sent wives back for various reasons. Polygynous families from former colonies often were transnational, creating unique challenges involving jealousies and distance.

TRANSNATIONAL POLYGYNY

Individuals I interviewed emphasized the idea that polygyny works better in cultures that support it as traditional. Jean Marie Ballo, a French citizen originally from Mali, founded the organization Nouveaux Pas (New Steps) to help polygynous families improve their living situations in France. The son of a polygynous family himself—his father had three wives in Mali—he explained the reasons that polygyny was part of traditional culture in rural Africa.

> In Africa, and elsewhere, polygamy exists because it is accepted in the population, tolerated in the culture. Not by religious principles but by tradition. Polygamy is used by different rural societies as a means of production because labor is needed in the fields, because the means of production are not mechanized. We needed manpower in the fields.

The mortality rate of children is high in many parts of Africa, and the need for large families made polygyny a good solution. Ballo explained that children are "a kind of social security because the means of production do not exist. Thus I can understand the politics of polygamy but without tolerating it, without accepting it, because I have also known that this practice makes women completely objectified." He emphasized that polygyny is more complicated when it migrates to countries where it is prohibited and not tolerated.

Dealing with polygamy's prohibition often means that migratory polygamies are lived under difficult circumstances. Many families are transnational, as was the case for Abdou, whose mother was sent to live permanently in Senegal. In general, migration plays a substantial role in how polygyny is lived. When the husband leaves his wives in the country of origin for long periods of time, the "rivals," as polygynous wives call each other in Senegal, tend not to get along. Although labyrinthine love could be possible when the women decided to work together to unite their families, living polygyny transnationally seemed to place more strain on relationships that could already be difficult to manage. Moussa offers a good example. He migrated to France in 1971 to work at a factory. He married his first wife in 1978, a cousin whom his mother selected. She stayed in Senegal, and Moussa would migrate to France for up to two years to make money, and then return to Senegal for a period. He and his first wife had their first child in 1983. For fifteen years, no new child arrived. Moussa wanted more children, and in 1997 he married his second wife. He explained that, traditionally, if the first wife is unable to have more children, marrying a second wife might help. Moussa spoke some French, but Sakou, a Malian leader of an African community group, was present to translate. He explained the reasoning: "Often there are old women who work in the occult sciences. [According to them,] once married to the second wife, the first can get pregnant." And this is exactly what happened. In the end, Moussa had three children with the first wife and five with the second.

In general, cultural factors and familial pressures are the main motivators that lead to taking more than one wife. Moussa married his first wife to fulfill his family duty. Sakou explained how Moussa viewed the family as central to life in Senegal.

The West African family is the big family. It's the tribe. Everyone who has the same grandfather lives in the same yard. These are big houses. For example, his cousins he calls brothers. His paternal cousins, they are the same family. There is no difference between his blood brother and his other brothers [cousins].

The second marriage was the "marriage of love." The two wives lived in a big house, which was part of the housing complex of the fraternity. Each wife had three rooms. Working in Paris allowed Moussa to send home enough money to sustain a comfortable lifestyle. In Paris Moussa lived in a migrant worker hostel with other Senegalese men who were in France to work. Four men shared a small room. Moussa had recently retired. Sakou explained that, in France, Moussa had his music and television. For Moussa, "my children and wives are everything," and he preferred to be with them. However, returning to live permanently in Senegal would decrease his pension. He thus continued to make the journey back and forth from Senegal to Paris.

His transnational family presented its challenges. When in Senegal, he would spend one evening with each wife. Jealousy played a big factor. According to Moussa, "The downside [of polygyny] is when the wives don't agree with each other. This is serious. But when they agree, it's perfect." Unfortunately, Moussa told us that the wives did not agree 90% of the time. He declared, "It is complicated!" When Moussa was away, the two wives got along better. The problems arose when he was there. Normally, he would leave one wife early in the morning to join the other. When there was a problem between the two women, often his mother would intervene. The following exchange demonstrates Moussa's reliance on his mother while also claiming his own authority:

> Sakou [translating]: When there is a problem between his wives, he has total respect for his mother. It's the mom's decision that matters. In the case of something contentious, it can be said that it is the mother who decides. But with your wives, when there is something to decide in the family, who decides between you and them?
> Moussa: If I say I don't agree, that's all.

On the one hand, Moussa's mother is a key figure in keeping the family together. On the other hand, Moussa hints at his patriarchal family structure in which he is the final decision maker.

Like Moussa, both of Oumar's wives lived in Senegal. Again, how polygyny is lived depends on context. Oumar married his first wife in 1976 and migrated to France in 1980 to make a better life. Working in France allowed him to achieve certain financial objectives, such as building a house and buying livestock in Senegal. He drilled a well in his village. In 1996 he married his second wife when she was just 18 years old. Oumar explained that having two wives made it possible to expand his family, and each wife had separate cattle to breed. The first wife had five children and the second six. The transnational nature of their family presented challenges. Oumar would spend two to four months in Senegal and then return to Paris for sixteen to eighteen months to work. For him, much of his life was one of celibacy. Sakou summarized: "There is no life with his family, with his wives and children. So, it is a life without affection. You live at a distance from the family."

Oumar said that he knew of many polygynous families that worked well; there were no differences between the wives or children. But his family did not work well. The age difference between the women could account for why the two women did not get along. The wives lived in the same house but never shared meals. Everything was separate between them. Sakou explained:

> He says that polygamy is delicious, but it is difficult to manage two wives and support them financially. It's horrible. He says that every day, between the girls, there are problems. He says there is jealousy, and then if he must give gifts, they must be the same. If he is to fill a suitcase with gifts, each woman must have her suitcase and the gifts must be equal.

The idea that polygyny is delicious but horrible demonstrates the complex feelings of some men who bring a second wife into their family. It was attractive to marry a much younger woman, but Oumar's decision caused friction in the household. He would have preferred that each wife have her own house, but he could not afford two separate households. Oumar told us that when he was living with his two wives in Senegal, the problems subsided. However, he had to manage the conflicts that emerged when he returned to France. Thus the structure of living transnationally put further strain on the family.

In contrast to Moussa and Oumar, Mamadou brought his two wives to live with him in France in 1975 and 1978. They lived in the same apartment for six years, but Mamadou explained that living together in crowded conditions was problematic. Sakou translated: "There were jealousies, there were a lot of problems, and finally he decided to send them back to Senegal." The first wife had seven children and the second five. Four children were born in France and are French citizens. Mamadou told us that French society and its structure stoked conflicts between the two women. Sakou translated:

> He said that when they were here, it was because of social organizations such as social workers and the like that the two women had a lot of problems with each other. In Senegal, there are practically no quarrels between them. So, according to him, it is because of those who perhaps asked them to revolt. In the end it had become too difficult.

It is not possible to verify whether the social workers or others encouraged the women "to revolt," but this perspective demonstrates the challenges of living migratory polygamies. Living in France might give wives the means to question their polygynous situation, whereas in Senegal it was traditional and less likely to be challenged.

Bijou, a mother of four children in her late 30s, told me that polygyny permits men to lie. She recounted how easy it was for men to use migration to enter in polygyny. Originally from Senegal, Bijou became a French citizen in her early 20s. At the age of 28 she returned to Senegal to marry a man she had known since childhood. According to Bijou, her future spouse was in the process of getting a divorce when they decided to marry. Because many marriages in Senegal are performed religiously and not civilly, the divorce was also done religiously. After one year of marriage, Bijou was able to bring her husband to France under the family reunification policy. To be eligible to migrate to France, her husband signed a form at the city hall declaring that he was monogamous.

Bijou later learned that he never divorced the first wife, which meant that Bijou was unknowingly living in a situation of polygyny. She was angry but had been raised in a polygynous family, so she decided to endure. She explained, "I am a person who believes very much in marriage. So, once

I was in my marriage, once I knew that he was polygamous, that he had another woman, I already had a child, and I did not marry to raise my children alone." She tried to tolerate the transnational polygynous quagmire that she found herself in. Her husband returned to Senegal whenever he pleased to be with the first wife. Finally, when he told her that he had decided to marry a third wife in Senegal, she had had enough. Bijou hired a lawyer and turned her husband in for fraud. He had declared the children of his first wife in Senegal with French social services to get extra benefits. The French government quickly rescinded his residence permit and issued an order for him to quit the French territory. However, because he was the father of French children, he was able to get a temporary permit to stay in France if he provided support for them. He did eventually return to Senegal. None of this was ideal for Bijou, who was left to raise her children on her own. She lamented, "France is very hard; I did not see myself raising my children alone!" But that is where she found herself.

Distance made dishonesty possible so that a wife who thought she was in a monogamous relationship ended up in an undesired polygynous marriage. Such complications introduce challenges for governments seeking to protect the rights of women. Often these rights are provided as justification for criminalizing polygyny, yet as will become clear throughout this book, women's rights are unevenly addressed. One of the most interesting aspects of Bijou's case is the fact that fraud compelled the government to act quickly to rescind her husband's residence permit. She noted that an acquaintance was in a remarkably similar situation in which her husband had lied about his polygynous wives in Senegal. However, neither were French citizens, and the government was decidedly silent concerning her complaint. Thus cases of transnational polygyny make wives more vulnerable to feelings of isolation, neglect, and rivalry as well as to outright deception.

BREAKING UP IS HARD TO DO

Although some polygynous families remained transnational, numerous West African men brought over second and third wives in the 1970s and 1980s, when it was legal to do so, and these women were often granted ten-year residence permits. As the two vignettes at the beginning of this chapter suggest, the ways that polygyny is lived in France when all the wives are present is varied. Space became the central issue for being in a polygynous household. Large numbers of West African immigrants worked at the Renault and Citroen factories on the outskirts of Paris and required housing as their families grew. For many who had limited incomes, affordable housing often meant renting a small apartment in the *cités*, the colossal concrete housing projects that were built in the postwar decades as utopias for white working-class French families. Once immigrant families moved into these projects, white flight occurred, and the *cités* became concentrations of poverty and social isolation.

Polygynous families were some of the largest families to need housing. Some families lived in large houses, but those were exceptional cases. Sociologist Christian Poiret, who studied the issue of polygyny among African families, described one such family to me: "I remember a *marabout* in Mantes-la-Jolie who had the means to have a large house with separate apartments for each wife. This is the exception." In contrast to these exceptions, I heard many stories about circumstances of large numbers of people living in tiny apartments, such as Mariam's family, described at the beginning of this chapter. I interviewed Catherine Quiminal, an anthropologist who has extensive publications on migratory West African families. She discussed the difficult housing situation for polygynous families: "So, there is always a big problem of living in polygamy for migrants, especially since there are even some who continued to live in migrant worker hostels with their wives." The French state created these hostels in the late 1950s and 1960s as a short-term housing solution for what was meant to be a temporary migrant labor force.[27] These hostels still exist today, housing an aging cohort of men who are "geographically single."[28] For the most part, migrant men who live in these hostels have left their wives and children in their countries of origin, and even in retirement they travel between the hostels and their families. However, according to Quiminal, some men have brought their wives and children to France: "It was a disaster because—I don't know if you've ever visited a hostel—but it is at best nine square meters [about 97 square feet]." She explained:

These hostels are normally for single men. They [the men] made them [the wives] come clandestinely, because family reunification obliges you to say that you have an accommodation, in principle, sufficient to accommodate your wife and children. And so, well, they gave the address, but after they didn't have [a sufficient accommodation] because the question of housing is quite difficult in France today. So, they were in the hostels, and there are still some polygamous families in the hostels.

The inability to find housing meant that wives and children suffered in cramped conditions that required children to spend most of their time outdoors.

I interviewed Agna, a Malian immigrant who founded an association in the early 2000s to help African families, especially women, learn to speak French and to acquire skills to survive in France. Some of these families were polygynous. She recounted situations of overpopulation that were unthinkable for most families: "When I arrived, as I told you, I saw women living in polygamy in a small [accommodation]. Sometimes I saw families in a studio. There is just the curtain." She described how this could be especially difficult for the children, who had to do homework and attend school.

One of the families that left a deep impression on me was a family of eighteen, and they were in an F3, a two-bedroom apartment. The two women had their room and then the smallest children went to sleep with their mothers. However, the older children had to wait for everyone to go to bed to sleep in the living room. So, suddenly in the morning, they had trouble waking up. They were late to school, or they would sleep in school. That's when we said to ourselves, "We must look for a solution. How can these families live like that?" Because, I mean, polygamy, for me, it is not adapted to France, because an apartment is a room in Africa. We live in the open air. So, for me, how can eighteen people live in a room?

This sentiment was shared by Jean Marie Ballo, described earlier, who told me that, although polygyny might work in Africa, it is not easily lived in France.

This practice is not at all adapted to Western living. Because in Africa, in these countries, people each live in their own space. Everyone here lives under the same roof. And I remember when I met women from polygamous households, they were unhappy. They said to me, "Mr. Ballo, if you don't help us, our heads are going to go through the roof." Translated literally, that means that our heads will explode!

And living in cramped quarters did cause some wives' heads to explode. Agna told a story from a colleague about two wives who "beat each other practically to death, tearing one's ear, tearing the other's lip." She explained that, even when the women are raised to live in a polygynous household, being separated by just a wall becomes untenable in many cases.

Some families were able to manage in cramped quarters, and the wives got along. These families resented the need to decohabit. I interviewed Lamine, who migrated to France in 1971 and worked for Renault. He married his first wife in 1974 in Senegal, a cousin, and brought her to France in 1977. He married his second wife, also a distant cousin but someone he had not known until the marriage was arranged, in 1988 in Senegal and brought her to France. At the time, both wives were given a ten-year residence permit. The first wife had six children; all were born in France except for one that was born while they were staying with family in Senegal. The second wife had four children, all born in France. The family lived together in a five-bedroom apartment, bigger than some families were able to afford. In 2007 the neighbor's apartment caught fire and the building was too damaged to be habitable. At that point the French government required Lamine and his family to decohabit, and each wife moved into her own separate two-bedroom apartment. Lamine insisted that the family of thirteen (Lamine, his two wives, and ten children) got along very well living together. "They get along very well, my two wives. There is no problem. My children, the children of the first and the children of the second, are all united." The first wife was gravely ill, and she was in a hospital bed on the other side of the room where our interview took place. He told us that the second wife came every day to help care for her. I was not able to ask either wife to confirm this account; the first was too ill to participate, and the second was not there at the time. However, the social worker who had facilitated the interview was present, and she confirmed his account, having worked with them for many years.

Lamine and his family had decohabited unwillingly, and he was paying for two apartments: "It's too expensive, two apartments on one salary. It's really hard. I called my second wife and told her that they just called me at the office. Well, the government decided that we must decohabit. I'm going to go with my first wife, because the lease is in both of our names." He had refused to divorce one of his wives, so even after the family had decohabited, Lamine and his second wife were not able to renew their ten-year residence permits. The following exchange illuminates the situation.

> Lamine: Well, yes! [The first wife] got her ten-year permit.
> Melanie: Always?
> Lamine: Always, always. She got it in 2000, 2010, and now, until 2020. It's 2015, her card is valid for another five years. But me, every year, I renew and then I pay dearly. We pay 106 euros! Every year, 106 euros! [The first wife] who is not [seen as] polygamous, she pays 260 euros for ten years.

Lamine expressed his anger at the French government that they would allow his family to migrate and to raise children in France and then suddenly make their status irregular: "We should have French nationality, but we can't. They even deprived us of the ten-year permit. To get it, you must divorce. We are not going to divorce our wives! There must be a reason to divorce, but you're not going to divorce your wife for a residence permit problem, no!" Over and over, I heard a similar story concerning residence permits.

In my research I found that the government did renew ten-year residence permits for a few men and women but not for most. I interviewed Fatoumata, a second wife, and three of her daughters in their four-bedroom apartment on the first floor of a large public housing complex. The living room was bright and cozy, with masks and Malian art on the walls. Fatoumata had migrated to France from Mali as the second wife shortly after marrying her husband in 1975. In France she had nine children, and the first wife had five; they lived together in a four-bedroom apartment until 2005. The large family got along well. Fatoumata described that each wife cooked two days in a row, and the entire family ate together. The three daughters who were present, now in their late teens and early and late 20s, described a happy childhood in which the children got along. Because there were two generations, the oldest children moved into their own apartments while the youngest ones were growing up. At the time of the interview in 2015, the oldest child of the first wife was 44 years old. Hawa, the youngest, who was 19, told me that her oldest sisters helped her with school. Although the conditions had often been crowded—at the extreme fourteen children living in two rooms—they made it work. In 2005 the old towers in the public housing complex in which they were living were demolished, and the family was required to decohabit. The husband was not happy about this, but Fatoumata explained that she and her co-wife were grateful to have their own space. Fatoumata moved into another four-bedroom apartment, and the first wife moved into a three-bedroom apartment, as she had only three children still living at home in 2005. The two families lived close to each other and continued to eat meals together. The wives continued to take turns cooking and doing dishes.

Overall, the decohabitation had been successful for this polygynous family. Fatoumata moved into her new apartment right away, and the first wife moved six months later. The children still saw each other regularly. The main problem that Fatoumata encountered was the revocation of her residence permit and the ability to pay for her apartment. The first wife had become a French citizen before the decohabitation, and the husband had always been able to renew his ten-year residence permit. The state, however, would issue Fatoumata only a one-year permit. Aicha, in her early 20s and who had a daughter of her own, explained: "It was really the prefecture; they said that she had to divorce for naturalization." Fatoumata told me that her husband would not accept the divorce, and this meant that she could neither become a citizen nor keep her ten-year residence permit. Every year, her daughters had to help her renew her permit, like Lamine and his second wife had to do, a costly and time-consuming process. Aicha declared, "It is such a hassle! She decohabited, and she came here legally!" Fatoumata and her daughters declared their frustration that "this had lasted for now *fifteen* years!" They had called an association that helps African families to see whether something could be done, but so far, they have not had any success. The other challenge for Fatoumata was the increasing costs of paying for the apartment and utilities. When she first moved into her own apartment, Fatoumata received government assistance, as she had minor children at home. Over time, the cost of the apartment and utilities increased. Once all her children were grown, she was forced to pay most of these expenses on her own. She is disabled and receives a bit of government aid. The daughters expressed that many others in the complex were complaining about the increased utility expenses. Still, Fatoumata was glad to have her own apartment.

Hamsetou's situation was similar to that of Fatoumata. As the second wife, she had legally migrated to France in 1985 under the family reunification policy and had six children. She also lived in the same housing complex that was demolished. She and her daughter, Micheline, who was 29 years old at the time of the interview, described a happy family life in which the two mothers successfully shared a four-bedroom apartment. In 2000 the government would not renew Hamsetou's ten-year residence permit, whereas the first wife was always able to renew hers. Instead, she was given a one-year renewable permit. In 2005 she and the first wife were keen to participate in the process of decohabitation to have their own apartments. Micheline told me that the children were sad to be split up, but the two wives appreciated living in their own space. Before the decohabitation, Hamsetou said that a woman from a government agency promised that, if she decohabited, she would be able to receive her ten-year residence permit. However, this never happened. After ten years Hamsetou still had to go the prefecture every year to renew her permit. She was not sure why she could not receive her ten-year residence permit and did not discuss divorce.

Representatives from associations that work with polygynous families described many cases of successful decohabitation. The association leader Agna, who had helped at least a dozen families decohabit, was confident that in most cases the wives were happier and lived in better circumstances. She stated, "We did not have people who said to us, 'Because of you, now I am no longer married.'" However, many families had to wait for long periods—six to ten years—to get an affordable apartment, and some were never able to decohabit because of a lack of available housing. The husbands of Fatoumata and Hamsetou decided to return to Mali after the decohabitation, as they were retired and felt that managing two households was too difficult. This also made the financial situation of the two women living on their own in France more difficult and put strain on the children to support their mothers. I also learned that husbands of families that had decohabited continued to live with both wives, often spending a couple of evenings at one home and a couple at the other.

Djénabou, who started her own association, felt that women must make their own choice about whether to continue a polygynous relationship. She was raised in a polygynous family in Guinea and was sent to the Netherlands to marry a 45-year-old man when she was 14, becoming his fifth wife. Three wives were in Guinea, and Djénabou was surprised to find that her husband was also married to a Dutch woman when she arrived after the marriage. She experienced three miscarriages before she was 18, the third one after she and her husband had migrated to France. With the help of a social worker, she finally left the marriage. She attended university and became an activist to end female genital cutting. She also worked with many women in France who were in polygynous families. As part of her studies, she interviewed several women in polygynous marriages.

> I met young girls who were born here, who grew up here in polygamy. Those who say they are completely against polygamy, and those who say, "No, it depends. Sometimes it goes well. The stepmother—the second wife—can be nice," etc. My conclusion is that I am always against polygamy, but we cannot generalize. This is a very broad, very broad question, because it depends on the country.

Djénabou's words iterate the idea that social context shapes the way that polygyny is lived.

Migratory polygamies are often precarious because of elements that speak to their transnational nature, and polygamy's continuum must be conceptualized with this in mind. On the one hand, it may be easier for men to deceive wives into believing that they are in a monogamous marriage when they have other wives elsewhere. For wives left in the country of origin, the fact that they have so little time to spend with their husband when he does visit can put further strain on their relationships. A different kind of strain is put on polygynous families when all or most of the wives have migrated to France. Financial considerations become key, and families have been crowded into small apartments, creating conditions that are difficult not only for the families themselves but also for their neighbors. The large number of children living in the confined quarters means that even the youngest spend substantial amounts of time outside without parental supervision. This problem has been addressed through the policy of decohabitation, which often benefited the wives in giving them an apartment and more independence. At the same time, the government sought to enforce breaking up the family through divorce and taking away the residence permits of husbands and secondary wives if the family refused. Different government strategies for regulating polygamies are based on racial projects organized around national logics of "Western" ideals of intimacy. These projects constrain and enable what I call suspect agency of women in polygynous unions who can choose their husband within constraints. We turn now to consider women's agency in the context of polygyny.

4 | GENDER, POWER, AND AGENCY IN FORBIDDEN INTIMACIES

> We women are not victims. We are not brainwashed
> and incapable of making an intelligent choice.
> This stereotype frankly offends us.
> —*Samantha, plural wife, Centennial Park*

> If you've been brainwashed, and your parents
> said that for seven generations you will be
> a polygamist, that's all you know.
> —*Amelia, former plural wife, Apostolic United Brethren*

SAMANTHA AND AMELIA FUNDAMENTALLY DISAGREE about women's agency in polygynous relationships. For Samantha, the stereotype of being brainwashed is offensive. Samantha, a working mother in her 50s who earned five post–high school degrees, readily defended her decision to choose plural marriage. She was raised in a plural family and described her admiration of her mothers, who always worked together, demonstrating a successful plural marriage. She married as a plural wife at age 18 and never regretted it. She described how an interviewer asked her whether plural marriage had lived up to her expectations. Her response was, "No!" He was shocked, and she explained that plural marriage had surpassed her expectations: "I had no way to comprehend all that it could be when I was making that choice." Entering a large family with many children was a "blessing," and she loved being a mother to all, even as she had her own children. Her plural family supported her while she was completing her higher education, and she was a highly respected professional in her community.

In contrast, Amelia felt that she was brainwashed by her upbringing. Her story is one of anguish and anger. She described her upbringing in a plural family as dominated by "a mean mom who was supposed to be taking care of us while my mother was at work." As a teenager, she began to question whether she wanted to be in a plural marriage: "No, I don't want to, but I have to. And if I want my family, and if I want my children, and I want to be with my parents, then I have to do this." She explained that she chose her husband, and "he chose me, because in the [Apostolic United Brethren] group, the majority of the women had choices." The greater freedom of the Apostolic United Brethren did not make up for the hardships of living in a plural marriage. Amelia fell into a suicidal depression at one point, and a friend helped her get into therapy. She said, "I knew I wasn't supposed to be seeing an outside therapist, but I believed what she was telling me . . . that it was okay for me to stick up for myself, and it was okay for me to defend my kids, and it was okay for me to have a voice." Amelia eventually left her husband after her children were grown. Some of the children blamed her for breaking up the family and did not speak to her for years.

How can we reconcile these two positions between choice and coercion? The anti-polygamist perspective casts doubt on Samantha's assertion of choice. If polygyny is all one knows, how does one make an intelligent choice? Is consent possible? Yet many women I interviewed asserted that plural marriage *was* their choice. At its core, polygyny is about patriarchy, which sets it on a collision course with feminists who fundamentally disagree about what constitutes women's agency. Anti-polygamy feminists argue that polygamy is based on a patriarchal kinship structure that is grounded in fundamental gender inequalities. In this view, women are coerced or have false consciousness—they are unable to make choices because of their socialization—and polygamy creates conditions in which women and girls are exploited sexually. On the other side are feminists who put forward a nuanced analysis of agency that resists the dichotomy between choice or coercion. This view seeks to understand how women—and all human beings for that matter—make choices in the context of relationships that are constrained within varying social contexts.[1]

Debates over women's agency connect to sociological and philosophical understandings of structure and agency. The structure-agency dualism offers two extremes of agentic choice that oscillate between agency's complete negation and its radical liberation based on essentialist beliefs.[2] This dualism is fundamentally gendered and racialized, being based on assumptions of masculine sexual prowess and feminine receptivity. It translates into global racial relations in which imperial powers—as rational, sturdy, masculine—have colonized countries marked as feminine and mysterious. It is tied to Enlightenment thinking that automatically labels other cultures as in need of civilizing. The dominant Western paradigm of "saving" women has justified imperialist and military actions, such as justification for the war on terror and the need to save burqa-wearing Afghan women from the perils of patriarchy.[3] Anthropologist Lila Abu-Lughod argues that the arrogance of Western projects to save women needs to be challenged because it perpetuates Western superiority rooted in Christian missionary ideals.[4] Controversies over women's subordination, such as the veiled Muslim woman in need of saving, draw on the problematic assumption that white men must save "brown women from brown men."[5]

Polygyny, as a forbidden intimacy, offers an important window into the ways that state regulation and transnational processes shape discourses of agency that enable and constrain women's sexual and familial choices. In previous chapters we examined how each country has a specific racial project regarding polygyny based on its history and national logic. Here, the discourses concerning patriarchy and polygyny are applied across the country context. In each case the nation focused on racialized perceptions of the other, such as attributing polygamy to slavery or trafficking, to endorse the nation's "enlightened," Western values. In addition, governments used discourses of "saving" women to divert attention away the negative consequences of polygamy's prohibition and regulation on women and children. In what follows, I map out what I call suspect agency, an approach to regulating women's agency that fundamentally relies on gendered and racialized understandings of the structure-agency dualism. Suspect agency is based on racialized ideas of patriarchal cultures, assuming individual responses to power relations and making women's agency dubious. I consider how women in polygynous relationships understand their agency when it is suspect.

IT'S ALL ABOUT PATRIARCHY: RACIAL PROJECTS AND SEXUAL SUBORDINATION

The practice of polygyny brings into view legitimate concerns over patriarchal power and its perpetuation in societies. Discourses concerning polygyny also connect to government racial projects that rely on racialized discourses of patriarchy, ignoring gender inequalities that persist in each nation. Governments rely on essentialist and liberal understandings of women's agency that focus on the structure of polygyny, which negates the possibility for choice. In our interview, legal scholar Michel Farge succinctly presented this logic in France when he compared polygyny to the debates over the headscarf: "The question of the veil, it is much more complex. . . . It concerns the symbol of everything that one attaches to the veil, whereas the question of polygamy, it is almost arithmetic. A man can legally have two wives, and the reverse is not true." Craig Jones, former attorney general of British Columbia, referred to "polygamy's cruel arithmetic."[6] The fact that a woman must sexually share her husband with other wives creates a compulsory subjugation of women.

The concern over patriarchy and gender inegalitarianism in polygyny renders women's sexual agency suspect. Several of my interviews provided a convincing argument for this perspective. Jean-Marie Ballo, who was raised in a polygynous family in Mali and who fought against polygamy in France, explained the difference he saw between having an "adventure" and polygyny as one of choice.

> A lover and a mistress, they are two adults who choose to live a sentimental adventure, without any commitment to children, without any constraint on the family. And I find that it is not at all the same thing, that polygamy is imposed on women. . . . The consequences are not at all the same and most people who want to have a love affair, lover, or mistress, well, they compartmentalize, I think. That is, they choose. And [with polygyny] the woman does not choose; it is imposed.

In his view, polygyny was compulsory; women would never make such a choice willingly.

Yolande Geadah, an independent researcher who has written on issues of gender equality for many years, wrote a report on the harms of polygyny as an intervention for the polygamy reference case in Canada by the Conseil du Statut de la Femme du Québec (Quebec Council on the Status of Women), a government advisory and review body to promote the rights of Quebec women. Based on her research, she shared with me her perspective that the "negative impacts are inherent to polygamy, to the polygamist system, because it's a patriarchal system." She views polygyny as "a subjugation tool," which "serves to subjugate women in marriage." Although some women might benefit from polygyny, "the majority of women are losers in a situation where polygamy is admitted." In speaking directly to the idea that the sexual rights of women are negated by Canada's ban on polygamy, she stated:

> On the contrary, I think polygamy is a negation of women's sexual rights, because a woman with a polygamist husband will have one quarter of a husband or one tenth of a husband only. So, her own sexual needs won't even be satisfied, because, of course, she must remain faithful to the husband. This is a patriarchal institution; it's not just a sexual arrangement. So, I totally disagree with people taking it on the angle of sexual freedom.

As a feminist scholar and activist who fights for women's rights, Geadah offered thoughtful reasons for why this patriarchal institution hurts women.

According to Geadah, women's agency is suspect in the case of polygyny in the same way that it is suspect in the case of prostitution.

> And I also wrote a second report, which was about prostitution, that was during the *Bedford* case. And I see some parallels, because it's always presented as being the choice, the free choice of women. But we cannot talk of free choice when you have no alternatives and when you are vulnerable. So, of course, I support free choice, but you must look beyond this simple argument.

For Geadah, conceptualizing women's free choice in highly patriarchal institutions is complex and must attend to structural issues, an important intervention. As a feminist, she wants the state to consider the more complex outcomes of patriarchal structures. This feminist stance participates in the contemporary sex wars that can be traced back to the 1982 Barnard Conference, where conflict exploded over issues relating to sexuality—pornography, erotica, prostitution, lesbian sexual practices, and sadomasochism—and whether such practices are dangerous or pleasurable for women.[7] The sex wars demonstrated the importance of identifying structural constraints and recognizing the possibilities for women's sexual pleasure within these constraints.

A discourse that emerged in my interviews is the idea that polygyny serves as a form of slavery. In Utah one Mormon feminist, who had been a women's studies professor and fought for support of the ERA in the Mormon faith, provided the radical feminist perspective on polygyny that I heard often: "You can't see as many people over as many decades as I have and say there's anything good about polygamy. At least, I can't. My life experience teaches me that it's slavery of women and exploitation of children." In France Sihem Habchi, president of Ni Putes Ni Soumises (Neither Whores nor Submissives), a French feminist association founded in 2002 to fight the violence that women of color have experienced in Parisian neighborhoods, offered a similar perspective. She told me that a new type of polygyny was taking hold in France that she called "voluntary slavery." According to her, fundamentalist French Muslim women, as well as immigrants, are voluntarily entering into polygynous relationships: "It is a choice—not a choice—an abandonment, that's for sure. But it is all the same slavery. I mean, it is women who do nothing other than be at the service of a man." For Habchi, women can make a choice to abandon themselves as "slaves" in a polygynous relationship.

The language of trafficking is also a predominant discourse that makes women's agency suspect. Amelia, quoted at the beginning of this chapter, stated, "It's about women who are being trafficked by their fathers and their mothers and told that they will marry whoever they are told to marry. It's about trading. The women that say it's a choice, and I used to do the same thing, I don't buy it." There is truth to her words: The polygamy reference case registered thirty-one underage girls whom FLDS leaders sent between the United States and Canada for the purposes of polygamy. In the United States it is a federal offense under the Mann Act to transport women across state boundaries for "any sexual activity for which any person can be charged with a criminal offense."[8] As we learned earlier, a Canadian fundamentalist Mormon couple was convicted under the sections of the Criminal Code that prohibit removing a minor from Canada for the purpose of an act that is a crime and for sexual assault on a minor.[9] Cases of trafficking involving minors are rightfully charged and speak to the idea of consent within constraint.[10] A girl of 13 may consent to being married to Warren Jeffs, but the parents' power over her, being underage, and her religious beliefs all constrain this choice in extreme ways. Underage and forced marriage of other underage FLDS girls married under the prophet are similar, whether or not they move across borders. As with all discussions of consent, there are gray areas. For example, can a 17-year-old girl who wants to marry her 19-year-old partner make this choice? The idea of constrained choice helps to place such decisions in context.

Although these kinds of crimes should be and have been successfully prosecuted, the language of slavery and trafficking also points to the problematic racial projects that paint polygamy as barbaric. Social scientist Kaye Quek writes about fundamentalist Mormon polygamy as a form of "marriage trafficking," not just in cases where underage girls are moved across borders but in and of itself. Applying the three elements for trafficking outlined in the 2000 Palermo Protocol of international human rights, she argues that the "custom should be recognised by states and the international rights community as a case of human trafficking."[11] For Quek, the socialization of FLDS women makes "female subservience to male authority the norm,"[12] an idea that implies that women's agency is suspect. Her focus on custom and culture is key to the othering of plural marriage, in which Quek takes the extreme case of the FLDS under Warren Jeffs and applies it to all fundamentalist Mormons. At the same time, Quek recognizes that some women report choosing their plural marriages and that these accounts should not be discounted. However, she points to "the broader context in which these positive accounts appear" as "one of an openly patriarchal culture . . . in which women are valued for the ways in which they can be exploited (sexually, reproductively and domestically)." For her, polygamy can be identified "as trafficking, even if there are individuals within the group who do not identify it in these terms."[13] This characterization of an "openly patriarchal culture" of exploitation underscores the othering of plural marriage, suggesting that it exists outside the broader patriarchal culture that continues to produce gender inequality in Western societies. Let's explore how different governments make women's agency suspect.

REGULATING SUSPECT AGENCY TRANSNATIONALLY

Internecine feminist debates over sexuality and agency influence the state's delineation of danger and pleasure in women's lives.[14] Engaging in these debates, state actors frequently use the law to challenge, restate, and redefine the relationship between harm and expressions of human sexuality and intimacy.[15] Some critics suggest that feminists have sought legal recourse in a manner that has expanded the scope of an already intrusive state.[16] With polygyny, state intrusion has not only rendered women's agency suspect but also erased women's voices in plural unions. When examining state discourses and policies that prohibit polygyny based on the need to "protect" gender equality and women's human rights, the consequences of prohibition can cause harm to women living in polygynous unions. Canada and France have different national logics in prohibiting polygamy. However, as will become evident in what follows, laws and policies that prohibit polygamy have similar outcomes in making women more vulnerable and further limiting their agency.

In Canada women's intimate sexual agency was implicitly, sometimes explicitly, on trial during the polygamy reference case.[17] One of seven interveners in the case who argued for upholding the law prohibiting polygamy was West Coast LEAF, a feminist nonprofit organization located in British Columbia that is tied to the national Women's Legal Education and Action Fund (LEAF). LEAF's purpose is to advance women's substantive equality rights through litigation, law reform and public education.[18] In its submission to the court West Coast LEAF argued that "the practice of polygamy violates the fundamental rights to autonomy and equality of women and girls."[19] Its main objective in intervening in the case was to ensure that the government fulfilled its duty to safeguard women and girls of faith from exploitation.[20] Thus the question of women's sexual agency was central to West Coast LEAF's objectives.

In contrast to the arguments of the attorneys general of Canada and British Columbia that focused on the inherent harms of polygamy and its threat to Western democracy and civilization, West Coast LEAF asked the court to consider a narrow interpretation of the law as constitutional in criminalizing polygamy only "insofar as the practice of polygamy exploits women and girls."[21] Specifically, the organization argued that the harms of polygamy arise out of patriarchal relations of power and that freedom of religion is not infringed by the law as a result of the need to prevent these harms. In the organization's view the law must consider whose equality rights are at stake, that is, those "who may be subject to the coercive force of a religious leadership that subscribes to authoritarian rule and entrenched patriarchy."[22] West Coast LEAF argued that the sexual abuse experienced by women and girls "cannot be discussed as personal deviations. . . . The power and control exercised by men over women and girls in polygamist unions creates an environment conducive to sexual abuse."[23] These critiques of patriarchal power that can exist in a small, closed religious fundamentalist community provided the justification for West Coast LEAF's assessment of women and girls in polygynous families as victims of patriarchal power with little capability to choose or resist their sexual victimization.

West Coast LEAF sought a delicate balance in the case to support diverse sexual and family relationships while simultaneously fighting against women's exploitation. For example, the organization argued that the law does not capture relationships tied to a philosophy of polyamory. The Canadian Polyamory Advocacy Association, an intervener on the side of the amicus, argued that polyamory differs from polygyny by supporting equality and self-realization. According to West Coast LEAF, "The law does not prohibit multiple spouses per se; rather, it prohibits the exploitative practice of polygamy."[24] In our interview, Kasari Govender, the former legal and executive director of West Coast LEAF, articulated the importance of determining social context for what kinds of polygamous relationships should be criminalized.

> The Canadian Polyamory Association were saying just sort of what I've outlined around the state has no business in the bedroom of the nation. That this is about freedom of choice, and about the kind of equality that they practice in their relationships as a matter of the philosophy of polyamory. And that's a very, very, very different context than it is in the argument about polygamy in Iran, for example, which is very much about a traditional society. Now, here [in Canada] we have both of those things. We have a traditional society in Bountiful in fundamentalist Mormonism saying this is our tradition, and we should be allowed to follow our

tradition. And we also have people on the same side of the argument, but the other side of the coin [the polyamorists], really, which is, this isn't tradition. This is a very progressive lifestyle, and we've made these choices.

Govender conceptualizes tradition to demarcate who has freedom of choice and who does not. She explained the argument: "That the state shouldn't have a role in the bedrooms of the nation, except where there is exploitation, where that bedroom door has been closed in order to hide it from view, and that constitutional law can't be used to protect men's ability to exploit women." For West Coast LEAF, tradition has led to the closure of Bountiful's bedroom door, where men have free rein to exploit women.

As noted, the polygamy reference case did provide evidence of harmful and illegal activities associated with some Bountiful community members. However, the exploitation perspective also ignores evidence that not all women are exploited, even in Bountiful. In her memoir Mary Jayne Blackmore described how after Warren Jeffs split her community, there was more openness on the Blackmore side, allowing journalists to enter—including a 2010 exposé by *National Geographic*—and improving the education system of Mormon Hills School, where Mary Jayne Blackmore was a vice principal.[25] When I visited Bountiful, I gave a presentation on how to apply to university. This more open polygyny, however, was not represented in the reference case. Winston Blackmore's side did not participate because of financial constraints, and this half of the community's perspectives were not included except in the presentation of Angela Campbell's qualitative interviews with wives in the community.

In his decision Justice Bauman sided with the argument that polygamy is a form of exploitation of women and children, citing expert witness John Witte's evidence that the reason anti-polygamy laws in the United States were passed was the concern over "the exploitation and enslavement of women, the concern about creating rivalry and violence in the household."[26] Here again the language of slavery points to the racial projects concerning polygamy. In the conclusion of his decision explaining why the polygamy law is constitutional, Justice Bauman stated:

> The challengers also urge that s. 293's [the anti-polygamy law] overbreadth is starkly demonstrated by the fact that it criminalizes all participants in

the illegal union, including the "victims" (overwhelmingly, the multiple women).

I question whether the capable consenting spouse is a "victim." To the contrary, she can be seen to be facilitating an arrangement which Parliament views as harmful to society generally.[27]

Rather than seeking to save the "victims," Justice Bauman viewed women who were willing to remain in their plural marriages as criminals who were facilitating harmful practices. A journalist covering the case agreed with women's culpability in remaining in their plural marriages: "Initially, I really thought, you know, there should be all sorts of social programs to help the women because these poor women, and I came to the conclusion that most of the women can't be saved. Most of them will never leave." Thus, for her, they should be captured by the law.

Justice Bauman emphasized the need to protect (some) women—at least those willing to leave their plural marriages—but his decision minimized their voices and made their agency suspect. In the reference case he allowed witnesses from the FLDS side of the Bountiful community to provide testimony anonymously, and his decision briefly addressed "the positive aspects of life in Bountiful" that these witnesses recounted.[28] Several discussed the benefits of having sister wives and their religious beliefs that motivated their participation in plural marriage. However, Justice Bauman placed doubt on this testimony.

There is a certain disconnect between their positivism and some aspects of these witnesses' realities. Witness No. 2 confirmed that no one from the community has graduated to become employed in any of a multitude of professional careers. Witness No. 3 is now attending summer sessions at Southern Utah University. She values education highly but admitted that because Grades 11 and 12 at BESS are not certified, she did not receive her Dogwood diploma [graduation certificate].[29]

Although one witness did recount several women who had received postsecondary degrees in the FLDS community in Bountiful, the cross-examiner for the attorney general of British Columbia inquired about a long list of professions that were not represented in the small community (e.g., banker, computer technician, veterinarian, physiotherapist, psychologist, lawyer).

This line of reasoning suggested that polygamy held back community members from achieving professional careers. Justice Bauman discounted another witness's account of a happy life in Bountiful after she recounted being sent to Canada to marry a "stranger on a half-hour's notice." As discussed, underage marriages in the FLDS are a grave problem. Still, this problem does not exist only in this community. The Canadian Civil Marriage Act was updated in 2015 to prohibit marriage before age 16, but girls can legally marry at the age of 16 or 17 with parental consent. The 2016 Canadian census recorded 22,115 individuals between 15 and 19 years of age who were married or in common law partnerships.[30] Justice Bauman participates in the racial project of using polygamy to emphasize the problems of the other while ignoring the country's own inequalities. Failing to identify the broader context in which child marriages take place, as well as using it to discount positive accounts of plural marriage, is part of that racial project.

As is the case regarding many criminal laws whose goal is to protect women, the Canadian law prohibiting polygamy criminalizes all polygynous wives age 18 years or older. Justice Bauman provided an exemption of the law for anyone married under the age of 18: The law "is consistent with the Canadian Charter of Rights and Freedoms except to the extent that it includes within its terms, children between the ages of 12 and 17 who marry into polygamy or a conjugal union with more than one person at the same time."[31] Once these minors turn 18, they are captured by the law. Michael Vonn, who was the policy director at the British Columbia Civil Liberties Association (BCCLA), an intervener in the case, told me how shocked the BCCLA was by the criminalization of wives in plural marriages.

> Thoughtful people can disagree what can be best for the protection of women and children, but it was the reasoning of the decision that really caught us off guard. From the perspective of the equality advocates, the question for us was how to condone this reasoning: the upholding of the criminalization of all parties to plural marriage. . . . The decision offered a small carve out for those 12 to 17 years old but would nevertheless still mean that a multiple wife married at 16 becomes available to be criminally prosecuted the minute she turns 18. . . . This smacks of the kinds of misguided reasoning in the war on drugs and other morality defenses. In other words, the harms are greater than the purported benefit.

Vonn criticized how Justice Bauman disregarded women's voices in the decision. She described participating in a panel workshop at the University of Victoria where one of the panelists decried the fact that Canada was prepared to criminalize the victims. Vonn stated, "It is amazing how little weight was given to the voices of the women affected." One panelist surmised that the logic of the decision appeared to be from the nineteenth century. Suspect agency was one of the deciding factors in the case's outcome. One expert in the case offered her assessment of the reasoning, reflecting the language of the justice: "I think the voices of those who were oppressed are more important in this issue to understand the real impact on their lives than those who defend it simply because they are still living in it, and they cannot denounce it publicly." In this view, women can only be victims when they leave their plural marriages.

Although polygynous women's voices were suspect, so too were those of the two women scholars who sought to introduce the importance of accepting the wives' accounts in the court case. Angela Campbell, a legal scholar from McGill University, was an expert witness for the amicus. She had conducted twenty-two interviews with women from Bountiful about their experiences living in polygynous marriages.[32] In his decision Justice Bauman pointed to the more positive picture of polygyny that Campbell's research portrayed. However, he dismissed her research, like the testimony of Lori Beaman, a professor of classics and religious studies. Beaman did not conduct primary research in Bountiful or any other polygynous community but instead focused on research she had conducted on the issue of harm. Bauman dismissed the testimony of these two scholars as "sincere, but frankly somewhat naïve in the context of the great weight of the evidence."[33] He suggested that Campbell's research was problematic because the community either selectively chose who participated or because the women were coerced to participate. He further criticized Campbell for believing informants when they asserted that underage marriages no longer occurred in Bountiful, taking their claims "at face value."[34] He cited evidence from the YFZ Ranch in Texas. While acknowledging that the Blackmore side of Bountiful had broken off from the FLDS, he rejected these women's accounts. Legal scholar Rachel Chagnon summed up the paradox of Bauman's decision: "It was in order to protect [the women] that the judge decided in the end that it was right to criminalize polygamy, which makes no sense." However, the fact that women's agency was automatically suspect provides the rationale.

Canada's court case concentrated on polygamy's harms to women and children in addition to its harms to society and the institution of monogamous marriage.[35] In contrast, France justified its prohibition of polygamy not to protect women but to guard against polygamy's threat to the public order. Even though the 1993 Pasqua law did not address the need to protect women, a 2000 circular stated, "In fact, the prohibition of the state of polygamy is based on the necessary respect for republican values, women's rights, and the integration of children."[36] Thus later justifications for banning polygamy expanded to include women's rights.

Reflecting the case in Canada, the way that the French policies touted respect for women's rights *and* criminalized polygynous women is ironic. In our interview, lawyer Christophe Daadouche outlined the hypocrisy of France's prohibition: "Now, a law which officially was a defense of women, which sanctions polygamists and wives in the same way, you will admit that there is something wrong!" GISTI (Groupe d'Information et de Soutien des Immigrés), the nonprofit group he works with, had aided many women, especially first wives, whose husbands had chosen the younger wife and left them to fend for themselves. He stated that the men "kept the youngest and they kicked the first wife out." Many were left "on the streets due to the enforcement of a law that was supposed to protect them." Sonia Imloul, who conducted research on these families, also pointed to the irony of the state's approach to assisting women: "The state manifests itself by saying, 'Here, in France, your situation is prohibited and if you are a victim, we can help you live serenely and quietly.'" But, in fact, she stated, support was complicated and often nonexistent. Siham Habchi, former president of Ni Putes Ni Soumises, further discussed the state's ineffective implementation.

> The most forgotten are the women, because decohabitation has been painful and difficult. These women have suffered or have found themselves alone in raising their children, with an absent father who has returned home [to his country of origin]. And often the husband has another wife in that country.

The fact that many women lost their residence permits made them more vulnerable.

On the surface the French policy appears to empower women who choose to decohabit to become more autonomous. The reality is that France lacked the political will to implement the policy of decohabitation in a manner that would support wives who were living in cramped and untenable circumstances. Anthropologist Catherine Quiminal was critical of the government approach: "I think for women who were already in a process of empowerment, it helped them. But there are so few of them." She explained to me that the reality was the reverse of ideal. The women aided by the policy were those already in a process of empowerment and who already had basic language and work skills to live more independently. Sociologist Christian Poiret agreed.

> I think that the main effect was to make [the women] more precarious, since from the moment you are forced to divorce to keep a residence permit, you are encouraged to decohabit, and you are not given the means to do it. You find yourself in a situation where you are even more at the mercy of your husband.

France's implementation of the polygamy prohibition in Mayotte had the same effect of making women's lives more fragile. A second wife who I interviewed in Mayotte told me that the ban hurts the "woman who has no resources and is told 'from now on, no polygamy.' And yet, we do not offer her anything" to help her survive. This fragilization of polygynous women's place in society because of the ban on polygamy was repeated in interviews in all three countries and Mayotte.

In the French context women's agency was suspect when they could not become completely autonomous. Women's associations helped some women find housing and become independent, but as Quiminal assessed, a large number were left to fend for themselves. The assumption that decohabitation provided the opportunity for all polygynous women to become autonomous meant that those who were unable to do so became invisible and/or were blamed for their lack of integration into French society.

The case of France has been used as a transnational worst-case scenario of the consequences of letting polygynous families enter a country's territory. The Canadian polygamy reference case pointed to France to demonstrate the likelihood that there could be a substantial increase in the number of polygynous families in Canada if polygamy were decriminalized. Justice

Bauman argued that criminalization was justified to ensure that a similar situation of harm to women did not occur in Canada. He cited the expert testimony of Dr. Rebecca Cook.

> Concerns came to be raised with respect to the poor living conditions of polygynous wives. These concerns included co-wife competition, spousal neglect and coercion into marriage at a young age. Privacy harms were aggravated because living costs meant that separate living arrangements were not economically feasible for most polygynous families. In addition, second and third wives at times had difficulty accessing public health care and social security benefits despite having the necessary documentation.[37]

Rather than discussing the failure of the state to support polygynous women in France, Justice Bauman and expert testimony made their agency suspect to justify criminalizing the practice to keep polygamy out of its sovereign territory. The case of France furthered the tortured logic of protecting women as a reason to criminalize them. Many women, however, resisted efforts to make their agency suspect.

GENDER RELATIONS: FIGHTING SUSPECT AGENCY

Much has been written about how women negotiate patriarchal relations and principles. Some scholars argue that women accept a "patriarchal bargain" by embracing gendered beliefs detrimental to gender equality but enabling individual power and agency.[38] However, a broad swath of researchers have found that the interactions between gendered beliefs and patriarchal values are more complex.[39] Ethnographic research on the lived experiences of religious women points to the ways that they subvert, resist, and often embrace conservative gender ideologies to their own benefit.[40] Scholars have also begun to examine how social context and interlocking systems of race, class, gender, and sexuality constrain and enable choice.[41] Recent scholarship has found more diverse sexual agency within patriarchal relations than previously assumed.[42]

In thinking about women's agency, many of my participants were concerned more with patriarchy than plural marriage. In Utah I interviewed historian Martha Bradley-Evans, who has written extensively on the history of Mormonism and plural marriage. She provided the following nuanced analysis.

You know, from a feminist perspective, I think polygamy works against women, right? Because it creates this sort of superstructure of patriarchy that's present in every aspect of their life. And I've been fighting patriarchy my whole life. . . . One of the reasons I find Warren Jeffs so interesting is he's clearly kind of a mentally ill, egocentric narcissist, and he's also the president of their church. So, when you combine two, three things, of course you're going to have all kinds of terrible abuses of that power, but it really is just patriarchy gone wrong. If there's that much power in any single individual, even in the context of a family, it creates opportunities for things to happen that shouldn't. So, for me, it's not polygamy that's the problem; it's patriarchy that's the problem.

Polygyny, according to Bradley-Evans, is "patriarchy on steroids. . . . It's your worst nightmare, patriarchy." This understanding does not attribute inherent harm to polygamy but carves out patriarchy as the problem.

Interviews in Mayotte also presented the problem as being about patriarchy. In Mayotte some men marry additional wives without the first wife's consent. Actoibi Laza, an academic in Mayotte, explained, "When you're going to marry a second wife, you must ask for the permission of the first. In Mayotte, this is not the case. In Mayotte, you tell your wife." Daourina Romouli-Zouhair, who was Mayotte's economic and social environmental adviser, noted that nothing had changed in Mayotte in terms of polygyny, even after its ban. Young men traveling to France for their education would come back, marry, and later take a second wife: "The young men haven't changed at all. . . . He doesn't see that his father made his mother suffer and say, 'I'm not doing that.'" Another Mahorais government official, who preferred to remain anonymous, explained the reasoning. She stated, "What the second wife gives me, my first wife does not. And by sticking with both, I have it all." The idea that men do not ask permission and want to "have it all" underscores this patriarchal power some men hold.

At the great marriage I attended in Mayotte, I interviewed several young women in their 20s who offered their perspective on polygyny. One pointed out that polygyny's perpetuation depends on women who marry men who they know are already married. According to her, many women of her generation and older remain in their marriages even after their husbands take a second wife: "Sometimes they say to themselves, 'Why leave my husband? There is no one who will come and raise my children.' In fact, we suffer. In the end, the man wins because he has two wives, but we suffer." This suffering surfaced several times in my interviews. Hamina Ibrahima, mayor of Chirongui, described her own plural marriage as happy. In reflecting on its practice in Mayotte, she told me, "For women who suffer, it is very bad." Both her older sister and sister-in-law were in polygynous marriages, and Hamina told me that they are miserable.

> My sister who is at home, she doesn't want for anything financially, because the family is there—my brothers, myself, her children—but she is unhappy because her husband married another woman. And it's been 20 years. Her husband didn't marry the other woman yesterday; it's been 20 years!

This suffering even after so much time has passed shows the depth for some of the pain when their husband takes another wife. Yet women decide to stay in their plural marriages.

In Canada there were also nuanced analyses of agency. Mary Jayne Blackmore is the fifth child of Winston Blackmore's 150 children who reside in Bountiful, Canada. The community in which she was raised was a branch of the FLDS. In her memoir, which details her journey to becoming a feminist, she described the horror that her community experienced during the raid on the YFZ Ranch in Texas in 2008.[43] When the mothers went on *Larry King Live* to plead for the return of their children, Blackmore agreed that the raid was a form of religious persecution. Still, after having been raised in the FLDS, she acknowledged that the women's claims to have made their own choices rang hollow: "I know these women and how they think. At least I used to. But listening to them say they have choice—I now disagree with this pretty strongly. If you have two choices and one is family and heaven and the other is loneliness and hell for eternity, those are not choices."[44] When disobeying the prophet can mean going to hell, choices about marriage and family are made within limitations. Blackmore's words underscore the importance of thinking about agency as constrained within social contexts.

Scholars have problematized the apparent dichotomy that the structure-agency debate offers within patriarchal relations. Saba Mahmood's study of the Egyptian piety movement examines how women's participation is not founded on resisting male hegemony but instead on nurturing virtuous living based on issues ranging from veiling, circumcision, and interacting with men.[45] The need to decouple conceptualizations of agency from those of resistance provides important insight into how agency can be negotiated in conservative and religious contexts. Women's negotiation of suspect agency depends on many factors, including upbringing and cultural background. For those raised in an environment where polygyny is a norm, entering a polygynous marriage may not be viewed as oppressive. In France women's organizations have worked to help women living in polygyny, and several have offered a nuanced assessment of women's sexual agency and choice.

Djénabou, whom we met in the previous chapter and who had been in a polygynous marriage, offered a more complex perspective on women's choice to enter such unions: "I meet some [polygynous wives] and when I say, 'I am against polygamy,' there are some who look me in the eye and say to me, 'I am for polygamy.'" She explained that they had been raised in an environment where "we have been told that this is what is important." Women in polygynous unions told her, "It is you who became white, you became French, you changed your culture. That's why you're against polygamy!" From Djénabou's perspective, it is important to accept where women stand on the issue, "getting down to their level and trying to speak their language to help them." This does not require rejecting polygyny.

A social worker in Utah who worked with refugees described discussing polygamy with a polygynous wife from Syria.

And I said, "So tell me a little bit about plural marriage in your culture." And she just laughed at me. She says, "It's not called plural marriage! It's marriage! It's normal! You are going to have another wife, and there are rules around it. I mean, he must provide equally for each wife. And there must be equality. It has to be the same type of a life the first wife has."

Many feminists would disagree that there could ever be equality in a polygynous union; however, some polygynous wives claimed a different kind of equality.

Whereas some interviewees distinguished patriarchy from polygyny, others pointed to how women resist efforts to make their agency suspect.

One plural family outside Salt Lake City defined themselves as feminist and progressive. The Cloward family had left fundamentalist Mormonism but remained together. The following conversation exemplifies the tension in thinking about women's agency in polygyny. Randy described his decision to become fundamentalist and how it changed over time as a result of the patriarchal structure of the group.

> Randy: So, I chose to convert to fundamentalism, and then I chose to convert to progressivism. But again, I think that we're socially constrained and guided by the nose. And there are so many different things from the fundamental influences of just patriarchy. And it's because of this ancient tradition of patriarchy where the boys, well, they are strong enough, or maybe they hold the priesthood, right? Which is just an institution of patriarchy. But the girls don't have access to that except through their father. . . . Blatantly, the women are denied a choice, and the men supposedly have a choice. I still think it's either choose this or choose hell.
>
> Meagan: But it's kind of offensive to me that people look at it that way all the time, because women, we have brains!

Meagan's intervention to tell Randy that the perspective he describes is "kind of offensive to me" points to the frustration that many women in plural marriages feel when they are portrayed as unable to make choices or as lacking brains. For Randy, polygamy and patriarchy cannot be conflated, and it is patriarchy that constrains women's choices. Meagan, however, sees more nuance—women have brains and make choices in patriarchal relationships or societies.

Many women I interviewed self-reflexively explained their view on suspect agency, focusing on performing gender relations that resisted stereotypes and embracing labyrinthine love in its complexity. Some fundamentalist Mormons recounted their desire for a plural marriage and being involved in the choice of a second wife. Julie was not born into the fundamentalist Mormon religion but became the second wife to Oliver in her mid-20s. They are independents, and by 2017 they had seventeen children. She recounted how important it was to her that it was Ellie and not Oliver who approached her about joining the family.

I think the way that Oliver and Ellie went about it, Oliver was very re-spectful. I could tell he wasn't trying to "woo" me or win me in any way. Ellie was the one who came to me and said, "Oliver and I have been pray-ing about you." She was the one who asked me. That meant a lot to me in our family setting and situation, to where I was the one who told Oliver we were engaged.

She recounted how entering the family in this way allowed the two women to nurture a friendship.

Harper, a young first wife who helped decide the entrance of the second wife, described her decision as a form of soul searching.

I chose into this culture. Umm, I always wanted it. I mean, I remember a lot of soul searching as a teenager, determining, "Is this for me?" I was raised this way, yes. And what child doesn't—raised up in any certain culture—have to evaluate how much of this is something that I truly want, or something that I am doing because my parents have taught it to me. And I felt very early on that I wanted to live this way.

On the one hand, Harper's words indicate that her upbringing led her to make the decision to continue in fundamentalist Mormonism. She re-counted how people would tell her that she would have a plural marriage because that was all she knew. Her response: "That is not true! Uh, we have every opportunity in front of us that anyone else has. And not only that, but this isn't a lifestyle that you're going to choose . . . lightly [*laughs*]." This idea of making a choice that could not be made lightly was often repeated by women in polygynous unions.

Several conservative Mormon fundamentalists self-identified as femi-nist. Samantha discussed how she viewed the feminist dilemma that society presented concerning her choices: "I'm a feminist, so I might be the odd person here to be talking about patriarchal marriage and the patriarchal order, because it seems it's opposite of [society's definition]." However, she emphasized her right to choose to live in such a marriage: "At the heart of feminism is the word *choice*. And I think it means defining who you want to be, and if it means you want to be this way, that's fine." Samantha recog-nized that other women may want feminism to look a different way from the choices she has made. "You don't want me to have ten children, because

I wouldn't have ever done that on purpose. You're absolutely wrong." For her, the patriarchal order is about responsibility: "I see it as a set of responsibilities on a man to bring certain things into a family unit that women can use. I told a reporter once, I'm like, 'You don't want us out there.' I said, 'You will not meet a group of women who have higher expectations for men.'" Hannah agreed that the patriarchal order was not for irresponsible men.

> They must be big, big-hearted men. To take on that much responsibility, that is huge. To be responsible for huge families, and all those relationships, it takes quite a man. When they first had *Big Love* come out, I saw the first previews of it and I said, "Bill Paxton doesn't even begin to have enough to him to be a polygamist. He just doesn't."

Fundamentalist Mormon men and women discussed the importance of men's accountability and the challenges of being the head of the household when there are multiple wives.

The ideological organization of many fundamentalist Mormon plural families in the United States parallels that of evangelical Christians where the husband is the established head of the family. Samantha described how the husband is a "masculine mirror" for women to see parts of themselves that they would not see otherwise: "I think that what happens in these spaces is that we become a fuller version of our self." Thus the husband holds the mirror to more than one wife, but each wife has her own special relationship to the husband. And in families that are successful, the wives act as a group to ensure that men live up to their responsibilities of prioritizing and nurturing family relationships. In other words, being a breadwinner is not enough and requires what I call a conciliatory masculinity that paradoxically mixes normative masculine standards of leadership with nonnormative ideals of emotional labor and conciliation.[46] Men who act more as dictators or who do not treat all wives equally tend to head families full of strife and contention. The men and women I interviewed described the effort that men must make to create family harmony.

To soften rough edges as the husband seeks to meet the needs of all wives, conciliatory masculinity requires a high standard for acting as head that is shaped in relation to femininity. James, a Centennial Park member and husband of three wives, described the analogy that he tells those outside the community.

I give a metaphorical description of rocks that are put into a tumbler, and all their sharp edges and corners get worn off. And when you take those rocks out, there's this beautiful smooth rock. . . . I've had a lot of rough edges knocked off, and I've had to give up some of the things that I probably would have pursued career-wise, or at least interest-wise, for the lifestyle and for the raising of a large family.

James suggests that the wives and husband get tumbled together to produce a "smooth" masculinity where the husband prioritizes his large family over more individualist pursuits, such as advancing his career. Whereas in families that hold gender-traditional beliefs the wife most often compromises her career, men in plural families also make career sacrifices that allow them to spend time with their families.

Masculinity is shaped in interaction with femininity as men do "emotion work" to be good husbands.[47] Terry, an independent who has two wives and eight children, discussed the emotional elements that required him to grow and learn.

You know, I hear a lot of men say, "I would never live polygamy. That's ridiculous! How can you handle more than one wife?" You don't handle wives anyway . . . but if you can look at it as relationships, and experiences, and growing, and learning, and learning to work together, and really learning to sacrifice of yourself. I'm not trying to get a four-door truck, or a snowmobile, or, you know, retire by this certain age. . . . We're about a longer view.

Terry eschewed the idea that wives should be "handled" and rejected a worldly perspective that focuses on getting material possessions—a snowmobile, a four-door truck—that many men covet as central to their masculine identity. Instead, it is necessary to prioritize the family to spend time with their children. Terry explained his priorities, saying, "I'm involved with the family. Someone asked me once, 'Well what about your children, doesn't that really rob them?' And I said, 'Well I don't watch TV. I spend more time with my kids than most monogamists I know.'" Having large families means that men must spend time and energy to have relationships with their wives and children.

Successful plural marriages further require men to perform a masculinity that is considerate of the feelings of multiple wives. According to

Hannah, "If a man can keep his family together, and everybody will work together towards that, he grows in leaps and bounds just like the women do, and they are better and better husbands, and they're better and better fathers." Samantha stressed the importance in her experience for the husband to be thoughtful and a good listener, qualities not usually associated with male headship that orients men toward leadership and action.[48]

> I will feel this way; my sister wife may feel this way. And you need to think very carefully about the choice you're going to make, because it's going to have a very real consequence. . . . He's been pretty good about just being thoughtful. Sometimes he does stupid stuff. I've done stupid stuff. Everybody does stupid stuff, but a little listening goes a long way.

This kind of emotion work focuses on "interpersonal emotion-management," requiring men to effectively deal with the emotional climate in which wives may disagree on fundamental issues.[49] It can also mean acting as a mediator to smooth out the rough edges of multiple sexual and familial relationships. Avery, an independent who was in a plural marriage that dissolved when the first wife left, described what it takes for a husband to be exemplary. She said, "It is the ability to have a successful relationship, balance that relationship with multiple women, and actually have it work." Amy, a young mother in Centennial Park and one of two wives, explained the necessity of men's emotion work to ensure family harmony.

> My heart goes out to the men living this, because it really does take a big person and a man to honestly put his own feelings aside about a lot of things, and just must look for the benefit of the whole. . . . Instead of having it going in three crazy directions, to kind of bring it together and figure out what would be best for all. And a lot of times that means putting his own agenda aside.

Men's selflessness and consideration were offered as necessary for successful plural marriages.

Self-sacrifice was also important for women who described performing a homosocial femininity that complemented and shaped conciliatory masculinity to balance power relations. Homosocial femininity entails building social bonds among the wives as friendships and/or practices of sharing household responsibilities, such as deciding on a child care schedule. On the surface, the fact that wives must share a husband would seem to severely circumscribe the choices they can make about their family and work lives, and in some cases this is true. When wives do not nurture emotional bonds, it becomes difficult to function as a family. Women formerly and currently in plural families discussed dealing with feelings of jealousy, rivalry, and anger that can arise between wives and toward the husbands. Wives discussed their strategies to deal with this competition and rivalry, a strategy that focuses on building strong relationships between the wives and requires the husband's performance of conciliatory masculinity to manage jealousies. Elizabeth recounted how she seldom experienced jealousy and offered her advice on how to deal with it: "And what I usually say to people is, 'Get your feelings out of the bedroom and into the living room and kitchen, and not worry about the bedroom.' Well, that's easier said than done, I realize that. But this is a long-term, eternal thing." Her words highlight how wives in some religious traditions focus on religious belief to enable them to overcome feelings of jealousy and competition, pointing to how labyrinthine love is structured within specific social contexts.

Wives discussed the ways that plural families provided them with choices about work and family life. Sandra, in her 30s, married at 18 years of age, and the second of two wives, recounted how relations with other wives served as a system of support.

> One of the main things that a sister wife will see, that she is never alone. . . . If she needs somebody to talk to, if she needs somebody to lean on to take her children for a while, while she goes to work. I can't think of how many times I've come home late from work and find dinner sitting there waiting for me.

Overall, respondents felt that this support system was an advantage in their everyday lives. Sister wives described dividing tasks based on career trajectories and personal preferences. Megan, one of five wives in her mid-30s, explained how women must juggle so many roles and that living in plural families opened possibilities for finding work-family balance.

> Not every woman wants to be a homemaker, but lots of women, still, they would like to be a mother, and it's really hard for a woman to have it all. She is trying to fulfill like four or five roles all at once when it's a monog-

amous situation. But in a polygamous situation, I kind of feel like it does open it up for a woman that wants to have it all to do that.

Choice means negotiating roles in the family, which can change over time. For many, a sister wife provides support in meeting family needs. Emma, in a plural family with Matt, Charlotte, and Evelyn, described how important it was to have someone committed to the children at home.

> Evelyn works a lot from home, so she'll also stay most of the time with the younger children that are not in school. . . . And I am seeing that in a lot of families, where it's been a real benefit. I've got a sister, and she and her sister wife, they already made the agreement when they got married that she would stay at home with the children, and the other one would go get her career, because that's how they wanted it.

Rapport and teamwork are essential in offering choices to women in plural marriages, as Tammy explained.

> Much is gained by having another wife in your husband's family. And to have the relationship of a sister wife, it's like a mother-daughter relationship—only not, and it's like a sister relationship—only not, and it's like a best friend relationship—only not. It's kind of . . . to be on the same team with your husband, and yet to have a woman who thinks like a woman, and to be able to share and be a support system to each other.

Tammy's perspective underscores the relationship between wives and husband: While the husband is head, the wives are a team, and they view things similarly and can support each other. She described making choices together that did not involve the husband, thereby attenuating his power.

In plural marriages that are successful, husbands perform conciliatory masculinity to nurture homosocial bonds between wives, giving them the space to work out their feelings about the husband-wife relationship. Matt explained that when one of his wives was angry with him, she would often go to the other two wives to talk about it. He said, "Sometimes they will agree, but a lot of times it's just a safe place to listen. It's more objective." This also meant that, at times, all three would unite against him, underscoring the importance of social bonds between wives that can enable them to curb their husband's patriarchal power. Likewise, these bonds can facilitate resistance to men's bad decisions or behavior. Jack, who is in his 50s and whose plural family broke down when the first wife could not get along with the second, described the advantages in his friend's family of three sister wives: "You have three monitors, so to speak, of bad behavior."

Homosocial femininity thus offers a form of power that allows wives to balance work and family and resist men's bad decisions. When sister wives are not rivals, they relate in ways that enable emotional expression and support. Julie explained the challenges of nurturing a relationship between wives and husband.

> It's just like if you were in a relationship, and then all of a sudden, you add somebody else. So, it's not just you two trying to work things out. It's you three trying to understand and communicate with each other. And honestly though, I think Ellie and I have an easier time communicating than we do with Benjamin, because he's a man and we're both women. So, we understand that you're emotional and you cry.

The bonds between wives can prevent relations of domination that might characterize patriarchal family situations. Instead, women can work together to ensure the patriarch does not overreach his power.

The issue of patriarchy and the gender inegalitarianism of polygyny that permits a man to marry multiple wives and not vice versa allows governments to treat women's agency as suspect. Governments seek to "save" women who are willing to take on the victim role and leave their plural marriages. Otherwise, wives are criminalized, just as husbands are. This racial project others those in plural families and makes women more vulnerable. Women in plural marriages have resisted having their agency made suspect by explaining the benefits of plural marriage. For many of these women, it is a choice to share a husband that society should accept. Still, the ability to choose is limited by the social context and structural conditions under which polygyny is lived. The idea of women's choice is central to the ways that governments regulate the forbidden intimacy of polygyny. The administrative ambivalence that allows governments to condemn polygyny while tacitly supporting its existence becomes even more stark when faced with the question of polygynous women's sexual agency. The consequences of this regulation, addressed in the next chapter, are to push polygynous families, and especially women, underground.

5 | PUSHING POLYGYNOUS FAMILIES UNDERGROUND

It was very hard for these people because they were people who do not live. In fact, they were always living in secrecy . . . especially for [their residency] papers. So how can they live? I do not know. How can you be comfortable when you always must lie, hide? And that wasn't because they were dishonest people! It was because it was the system that made them do this.
—Agna, association director, France

In fact, polygamy continues in Mayotte! Polygamy continues, but people do not report it, because officially you cannot declare a civil marriage with three people. But a lot of people continue to practice it.
—Combo Abdallah Combo, sociologist, Mayotte

And frankly, part of the reason why the men are reluctant to be out is being identified as a polygamist could cost them economically, could cost them legally, could cost them socially, and it was just not something people shared. And frankly tried to hide . . . keep secret.
—Brooke Adams, journalist, United States

We think [criminalization] affects Bountiful. It forces people to hide their identities, to conceal their intimate relationships, and we think those are very harmful effects. We also think that criminalization forces polygamous families to be more secretive, to be less likely to reach out, to access social services and other resources.
—Grace Pastine, litigation director, British Columbia Civil Liberties Association

THUS FAR, STUDYING MULTIPLE POLYGAMIES has uncovered the importance of social context for how polygyny is lived. At the structural level government regulation of polygamies is based on a racial project that coalesces around a shared definition of polygyny as other. The four epigraphs reflect the social consequences of this racial project based on secrecy and hiding. In France Agna created an association in 2000 to help African families, especially women, with administrative assistance, literacy courses, and educational support. As a Malian immigrant herself, she worked with many polygynous families in her community to support their decohabitation. She described that many had been forced to live in secrecy, with one wife recognized officially in the administrative paperwork and the other wife or wives forced to use the identity of the official one to gain access to medical and social benefits. Emphatically, Agna expressed the negative consequences of the French system, which forces otherwise honest people "to lie, to hide." France's move to make polygamy illegal in Mayotte also introduced secrecy. Combo Abdallah Combo, a sociologist in Mayotte who studies family relations, explained that the French administration provided the option of being recognized as polygynous to polygynous families that had been formed before polygamy became illegal. However, most families chose not to make an official record of their marriages. Thus, in the eyes of the law, polygynous wives are not recognized and their marriages are invisible.

In the United States, Brooke Adams, a reporter for the *Salt Lake Tribune* from 1999 to 2014, described how she came to cover the issue of plural marriage when it began to heat up after Warren Jeffs became the FLDS prophet in 2002. She told me, "People within the polygamist communities were very shut down, and it was very difficult to get them to speak to you to hear their point of view or to try and get inside the community to know what was happening and what was going on." Eventually, she was able to gain the trust of many and listen to their stories. In her epigraph she points to the fact that "men are reluctant to be out" as polygamists because of the economic, legal, and social costs that could result, drawing on language of "the closet" to describe the historical need for many LGBTQ+ people to hide their sexual identity or orientation or face economic and/or social consequences. Likewise, lawyer Grace Pastine, who argued the case for the British Columbia

Civil Liberties Association in the polygamy reference case in Canada, noted that polygamy's ban pushes families underground and creates a climate of fear. For her, the ban has "harmful effects," circumscribing "people's ability to fundamental life choices."

What are the connections between "poly stigma"—the shared knowledge that devalues and stigmatizes polygamous relationships relative to monogamous ones—and the structural factors that push polygynous families into clandestinity? To answer this question, I examine how the racial project of regulating polygyny fuels the stigma and fear that drive families to hide. This includes a moral dimension linked to ideals of monogamy as *the* superior family structure. Sociological approaches to conceptualizing stigma uncover how processes of labeling human differences can fuel negative stereotypes and demarcate "us" and "them." These micro- and meso-processes then take on structural aspects of discrimination and social, economic, and political power.[1] Stigmatizing polygyny is a way to displace anxieties about the current changing structures of intimacy onto a marginalized family form marked as outside the realm of Western ideals. This stigma pushes families to hide and maintain secrecy. Across country contexts, racial projects of regulating polygyny produce different outcomes based on race and citizenship. In the following sections I consider the consequences of polygyny's stigmatization in the Western world.

RACIAL PROJECTS, POLY STIGMA, AND CLANDESTINITY: FRANCE AND MAYOTTE

Forbidding intimacies that are stigmatized as harmful and retrograde has been a key racial project of Western governments to uphold whiteness and belonging by repudiating a "backward" family form. In France the government's focus on polygyny has marked nonwhite citizens and noncitizens alike as uncivilized and not French. This racial project has stigmatized racialized populations in France as patriarchal and nonprogressive by joining together Islam and race in a manner that allows polygamy to be a surrogate for racism. Although the government has sought to abolish polygyny in metropolitan France, it has had to deal with territories such as Mayotte where polygamy has been traditionally practiced. The conversations about transforming Mayotte from a territory to a department, enabling the Mahorais to become French citizens, centered on banning polygyny and repudiation. Thus prohibiting polygyny for anyone who turned 18 after January 1, 2005, became a way to eventually abolish its practice in Mayotte. The rationale was to bring the Mahorais closer to respecting "the fundamental principles of our Republic," as the French Senate informational report of 2008 declared.[2] In this way, polygyny has served as a litmus test for republican values that automatically marks anyone who can be associated with it as a racialized other.

Institutionalizing Racialized Stigma in France

Many of the individuals I interviewed discussed how the French government used the issue of polygyny to stigmatize nonwhite populations in France. Lawyer Christophe Daadouche referred to Jacques Chirac's infamous speech on polygynous families when he was mayor of Paris in 1991. Chirac stated:

> How do you expect the French worker who lives in the Goutte d'Or [in Paris] and who works with his wife and who, between them, earn around 15,000 francs and who has, on the same floor, next to his council flat, crammed in, a family with the head of the household, three or four wives and 20 kids, and who earns 50,000 francs in social security payments, naturally without working? If you add to that the noise and the smell, well! The French worker on the same floor is driven mad and we must understand him. . . . And it is not being racist to say this.[3]

According to Daadouche, "This speech [that Chirac gave] from Orleans was absolutely disgusting. Absolutely disgusting! And Chirac gave it during the moment of urban violence, stating that urban violence was perpetrated by polygamist children." The acceptance in France of discourses that link racialized populations with polygyny is evident in Chirac's case. His speech, which has highly polemic and became known as the "noise and smell" comment, did not have any negative political ramifications. Instead, Chirac's political career flourished, and he became president in 1995.

In 2005 politicians and intellectuals blamed polygamy as a primary cause for the urban violence that took place in Parisian suburbs after the death of two teenage boys as a result of police neglect.[4] Although systemic racism, high unemployment rates in the suburbs, and tensions with the police that led to the electrocution of the two boys ignited and spread the unrest, the conservative UMP Party (Union pour un Mouvement Populaire) and public intellectuals pointed to polygamy as creating the conditions of delinquency among urban youth that fed the flames of revolt. Académie Française historian Hélène Carrère d'Encausse, a prominent public figure, claimed that African immigrant polygynous families were the source: "Many of these Africans, I tell you, are polygamous. In an apartment, there are three or four wives and 25 children."[5] Employment Minister Gérard Larcher argued that polygamy was the root cause of the inability of immigrant parents to control their children. In an interview with the *Financial Times*, he linked the antisocial behavior of youth to the lack of a father figure in families with multiple wives and numerous children. UMP parliamentarian Bernard Accoyer echoed these comments when he publicly blamed polygamy as "certainly one of the causes, though not the only one" for the riots.[6] He decried the "fact" that polygamous families are "nonnormative, uneducated, and disorganized."[7]

Using polygamy to scapegoat North and West African immigrant families is a key element of the overall racial project that relies on the demonization of forbidden intimacies to taint marginalized populations in France. Social scientist Pauline Gaullier commented:

> Polygamous families embody a great otherness compared to the model of the family as it commonly appears. . . . Immigrant populations very quickly become repulsive, and it becomes necessary to target certain people in this way to blame and not question the real issues which immigrants face [in French society].

Relying on polygamy to stigmatize Muslim immigrants as not *really* French has been a strategy since the 1990s. Sociologist Christian Poiret explained that the issue of polygamy "comes up regularly . . . a bit like a sea serpent, about every five years." He noted, "We saw the question reappear in 2005 at the time of the revolt in the suburbs." Social scientists have identified the concept of political homophobia as perpetuating homophobia and the public denigration of same-gender sexualities as a political strategy.[8] In this case one can point to "political polyphobia," which permits French government officials to perpetuate the stereotype that North and West African immigrants are polygamists, a political strategy to deflect attention away from the structural racism that these populations experience.[9]

Following Poiret's timeline, the issue arose again in 2010 when Interior Minister Brice Hortefeux accused Liès Hebbadj of polygamy and threatened to strip him of his French passport. On April 2 French police pulled over Sandrine Moulères in Nantes, France, and fined her 22 euros for driving while wearing a niqab that they claimed obstructed her peripheral vision. She wrote a memoir about the incident, describing how the police officer declared, "I don't know how it is in your country, but here we don't dress like that." She responded, "Your country is also mine, because I am French by birth."[10] After hiring a lawyer and supported by her partner, Liès Hebbadj, an Algerian-born French citizen, Sandrine Moulères filed an appeal, setting off a maelstrom of government investigations and media coverage over the issue of polygyny. The French government scrutinized the history of the family to find that Hebbadj had four wives and fifteen children.[11] Hortefeux threatened to revoke Hebbadj's citizenship, but Hebbadj had married only one of his wives legally. He tried to turn his case against his accusers by stating that "if one is stripped of French nationality because one has mistresses, then many Frenchmen could be."[12] Christophe Daadouche described the situation: "He's a guy in Nantes, a bearded man with four wives, and [the one who was pulled over by the police for driving while wearing a niqab] was a blond woman. So, that was worse than anything, these polygamists are not just Africans, they are *our* women." He noted that Hebbadj was the perfect caricature: "Opening the evening newspaper, he was the absolute figure of what we wanted to present as *the* polygamist."

This political polyphobia illuminates how the French government uses polygamy as a symbol of separatism and nonintegration in France. Most recently, in 2021 polygamy again became a way to signal racial otherness when the government passed a controversial bill with the goal of combatting the dangers of what it called "Islamist separatism," a term used by French president Emmanuel Macron to represent Muslims who participate in a form of sectarianism that results in what he sees as an unwillingness to integrate. To fight against this separatism, the bill states that no residence permits can be issued to foreign nationals who are living in a state of polygamy in France and that all offenders will be expelled. However, critics have pointed out that these provisions already exist in current laws.[13] Why include a provision that already exists, and why put it in a bill that purportedly seeks to fight Islamist extremism? The answer lies in the ways that the law connects polygamy, immigration, and separatism to legitimize the view that Islam is backward and patriarchal.

Laws in France that regulate the entry of immigrants and their rights have consistently used polygamy to mark otherness and nonassimilation. Both the French Civil Code and the Code of Entry and Residence of Foreigners and Right of Asylum (CESEDA) state that the government can "oppose the acquisition of French nationality by the foreign spouse" on the "grounds of indignity or lack of assimilation other than linguistic." The next paragraph states that a proof of lack of assimilation consists of "the polygamous status of the foreign spouse or a sentence pronounced against him on account of the offense defined in Article 222-9 of the Penal Code."[14] The offense consists of acts of violence against a person under 15 years of age. Daadouche exclaimed, "It's in the same section of the law. There is not even a comma. There are 150 articles, one could have put [these two offenses] in different articles. It is in the same legislative provision!" He described the outrage of linking polygamy with the abuse of a minor. According to him, there is "no connection [between the two], but we feel obligated to make the child abuser and the polygamist coexist in the same sentence!" It is not unusual to stigmatize polygamy by presenting it alongside other controversial or illegal practices, such as female genital cutting.

Restrictions against polygamy have been highly visible in French immigrant law. Danièle Lochak, a professor of law and former president of GISTI (Groupe d'Information et de Soutien des Immigrés), castigated the CESEDA for the way it connects polygamy and immigration. She stated in a 2012 article:

> One might wonder about the relevance of this hunt for polygamists. . . . If we stick to the effects of this discourse, this way of always putting polygamy in the foreground when it comes to immigration, as if the two phenomena were necessarily linked—whereas polygamy concerns only a very small fraction of foreigners residing in France and remains confined

to certain communities—is neither innocent nor indifferent. . . . [It gives] credence to the idea that immigrants are decidedly not integrable.[15]

Tying immigration and polygamy together, the word *polygamy* appears forty-four times in the CESEDA. Daadouche exclaimed, "We feel obliged in each article to say, 'except for polygamists.' It is too much! It could be put in one article regarding polygamy, but no, we put it over and over, not polyga-mists, not polygamists . . . !" Consequently, polygamy is highly visible in the legal structure as a central problem of immigration, when it in fact involves a small percentage of the immigrant population.

The stigma of polygamy acts to taint the Muslim population, especially immigrants and people of color. Anthropologist Catherine Quiminal dis-cussed with me the moral distinction that France creates between good and bad immigrants: "Many [politicians and policymakers] intervened by saying, 'These African families, polygamists, who are not able to raise their children, are barbarians, etc.' So, there are the good immigrants and the bad immigrants, and the Africans were among the bad immigrants." The fact that polygamy could be attributed to African immigrants provided an easy way to cast doubt on the entire population. Sakou, a Malian commu-nity leader in Paris, explained that politicians on the right "make it a po-litical phenomenon." He continued, "It is a form of propaganda, a form of stigmatization—whether true or false—to ensure that a certain population is seen as all being polygamist." They "make it a slogan, always talk about it, and ensure that the French are afraid of these populations that are sup-posed to practice polygamy." In his view, being Black and/or Muslim carries assumptions about certain practices, such as polygamy. According to Fatou, who is a Muslim from Mali and works with immigrant populations, "On many official [documents for immigrant men], they don't even ask the ques-tion. Straight away they put 'polygamist,' because these men belong to the Muslim religion where polygamy is authorized in their countries. So [the authorities] say to themselves that, at one point or another, they will have to find a second wife." These kinds of assumptions fuel stereotypes that put all Muslim men of color in question. Association leader Isabelle Gillette-Faye pointed to the concrete discrimination that takes place, such as for hous-ing: "Some municipalities clearly say, 'We refuse to provide [government-sponsored] family housing, because these men are going to take a second wife.' So, real discrimination." The idea that all Muslim men are potential polygamists becomes a way to deny basic services.

Several participants pointed to the hypocrisy in France of the way that the dominant culture stigmatizes polygyny while simultaneously tolerating what has been called the double life of a husband with his mistress and children. Legal scholar Michel Farge discussed this "provocation" with me.

> You can try to reflect on the extent to which French law accommodates situations of polygamy in France, which are purely internal. That is to say that French law offers a paradox between the complete rejection of polygamy when it is consecrated by foreign law—a person simultaneously married to two women—and the treatment of French law for a man who has a wife and a mistress. . . . One can say either that French law is hypocritical or that it tolerates situations of de facto polygamy.

He explained that the child of a mistress has the same status and rights as the child of the "rightful wife." Many cited François Mitterand as the most infamous example. He led a double life for thirty-two years. While married to his wife, Danielle, with whom he had three children, at the age of 47 he met Anne Pingeot, who was 20 at the time, and had a daughter with her— Mazarine, born in 1974. They were together for thirty years; she even lived in a wing of the Elysée for a time. However, the public knew nothing of Mitterrand's double life until near his death, as he was able to manipulate the release of information about his private life.[16]

For immigrants who are denied permanent residency because of polygamy, Mitterrand's de facto polygamy was a revelation of the racial project that demonized them while turning a blind eye to the "polygamy" practiced by many white men. Christian Poiret stated, "We like to give moral lessons to others, but look at François Mitterrand with Mazarine, look at many famous men who have disjointed love and family lives. So, in France it is always a bit like 'do as I say but above all don't do what I do'! That annoys me a bit." According to community leader Sakou, "When we talk about polygamy today in France, we think of Africans, Muslims, while these same Africans say that Europeans, whites, are polygamists, they have mistresses!" The boundary work that situates polygamy as the denigrated practice of "Africans, Muslims" in contrast to having a mistress—what is viewed as a perhaps unfortunate but normalized aspect of mainstream French culture—points to the racial project that stigmatizes this forbidden intimacy and deflects attention from problematic aspects of society. Reminiscent of Arlene Stein's findings in *The Stranger Next Door*, in which LGB populations in small-town Oregon became scapegoats to focus attention away from broader social and economic problems, polygamists are scapegoats to ease anxieties over the white French family that is beset by its own problems of infidelity and heteropatriarchy.[17]

The situation in Mayotte also revealed hypocrisy. Mansour Kamardine was a member of Parliament for Mayotte from 2002 to 2007 and helped to bring about the abolition of polygamy that allowed a referendum on whether or not Mayotte should become a department of France. He recognized the contradictions in the position of France toward polygamy.

> It is accepted by the Court of Cassation. Here is a couple, the gentleman has extramarital relations and has a child. The gentleman died in a traffic accident. The legitimate woman comes to ask for reparation, but the unofficial, clandestine companion also comes to seek reparation. And when the Court of Cassation says, "Yes, she too deserves compensation because she suffered, and so on," it is also a way of recognizing the de facto existence of polygamy. So, we can be criticized, but I often said to my colleagues, "We, at least, have the advantage of courage, of transparency. We make it clear to everyone, 'I am a polygamist, I have several wives. You are the same, but you hide and reproach me.'" So, this is not normal.

Men of color who take responsibility for their wives are outlaws, whereas white husbands who hide their adulterous affairs and often do not take responsibility for children born outside marriage are just citizens. The racial project of using polygamy to demonize immigrants and people of color is evident. In metropolitan France this racial project has consequently led to many families becoming clandestine and women being made invisible in the eyes of the law.

Pushing Polygamy Underground in France

We have learned that, after the passage of the 1993 Pasqua law, France no longer recognized polygynous families, and those who entered the territory before 1993 had to regularize their situation or lose their ten-year residence permits. Also, as discussed earlier, the policy of decohabitation was instituted to regulate the problem of overcrowding in the small apartments of polygynous families. The goal was to put an end to polygyny. However, my interviews underscored over and over how little information exists on the prevalence of polygyny in France. Christophe Daadouche told me that there was no way to quantify how many polygynous families existed before or after the policy of decohabitation: "Anyone who gives you numbers is a liar! . . . All the politicians gave us figures, and I don't know how they come up with these." Part of the difficulty is that so many polygynous families live underground. Djénabou, who left her polygynous marriage and started an association, explained that still in 2015, many years after the policy of decohabitation began, a large number of polygynous families existed: "I know lots and lots of them. The numbers that are given are completely wrong. Because there are plenty of families of Malians, Guineans, West Africans, who are in polygamy in France, except that no one knows." Many polygynous families remained hidden even before the 1993 law, but, as one government worker told me, after 1993, "it still exists, but in forms that are no longer visible. That is, before polygamy was visible, but after the law came into effect it became invisible." Association leader Agna agreed that polygyny "is hidden. For example, polygamy is often lived in seclusion, in lies, in 'it's not right.'" The need to hide becomes a survival mechanism.

The clandestinity of polygyny is fueled by the fact that anyone identified as living in a state of polygyny in France could lose their residence permit, which breeds conditions of hiding. Fatou explained the serious consequences for polygynous families: "They are obliged to lie, they are obliged to hide, they are obliged to say this, to say that, but none of it is true!" Even more troubling, second or third wives often have no existence in the eyes of French law. Association director Aissata told me that before 1993 wives would often remain underground until they had their first child, at which point they could apply for status as the parent of a French child and their "clandestinity could stop." However, sometimes "husbands held them back" to avoid losing benefits. This reticence worsened once the policy of decohabitation was put into place. Younger wives with children would receive benefits as single women once they had their own residence. Because the children of the first wives were often adults or nearly adults, this meant that the husband and first wife were no longer eligible to receive benefits. Thus husbands would try to block the process.

The most extreme cases of hiding completely erased the identity of secondary wives. Often, they would have to use the legal documentation of the official wife. Sekou, who heads an organization for immigrant African men, explained:

> [The second wife's] children will not be in her name. When a woman in France is undocumented, when she goes to the hospital, when she is pregnant, she uses the residence permit of the first wife. In most cases, she is not the mother of the children [in the eyes of the law]. So, for her to get out of hiding, she must have a residence permit. A residence permit frees her!

Stories of women who had no identity in France were prevalent. Simone, who works with an association to help immigrant women, told me about a woman who had been married in Côte d'Ivoire. This woman was illiterate and did not know that there was already a first wife. When her husband brought her to France, he took care of the administrative procedures, and she had a ten-year residence permit. Later, a neighbor saw that the name on the permit was not hers. Instead, it was the name of the first wife, who had given birth to three children in France with their husband. So, the second wife had given birth to her children using the other's residence permit. The children belonged to the first wife in the eyes of French law. It took years of going through the process of decohabitation and completing paperwork to finally gain her own identity and register her children in her own name.

Likewise, Djénabou, who left her polygynous marriage, discussed families that she knew where the second wives lived completely underground. According to her, although the law banning polygamy is important because it sets limits, it also gets in the way of helping many women.

> I met five different families in different contexts where the young girls from immigrant backgrounds were immersed in polygamy and had to

live underground. These women who are here have no identity. It is the first wife who is declared, the one who is known at the administrative level. The second or the third are completely erased from society. For them, they cannot go and say, "I no longer want to be in polygamy," because if they do, the husband will lose his residence permit.

One young girl lived in Paris and slept in the kitchen because the two wives had ten children in a small apartment with three rooms. The girl had to use the identification card of the first wife, which meant that "she can't do anything, she can't leave the apartment, she can't find a job, she's completely erased, even though she speaks French very well!" Anti-polygamist activist Awa Ba explained the fear that this perpetuates: "It happens that these women have no papers, because the second wife comes to France clandestinely. This makes these women afraid. They are afraid to go see the authorities, even if there is violence, etc." Thus secondary wives are put into extremely vulnerable positions to survive in France when living in a state of polygyny.

Polygamy's Continued, Somewhat Undercover Presence in Mayotte

Whereas many who practice polygamy are being pushed underground in metropolitan France, in Mayotte polygamy is hidden from the authorities but continues to be practiced openly. Although polygamy is banned, many told me that polygyny is still practiced and recognized in the population. Faycal Maliki, a teacher and president of an association that works with families in Mayotte, explained that efforts to eradicate polygamy and punish those who practice it are more aggressive in metropolitan France than in Mayotte: "Already, those who are in metropolitan France, from the start, they are hiding from the institutions—whether it is the Malians, the Comorians, even the Mahorais who are there—they know that polygamy is against the law." Accordingly, there is more legal surveillance. In Mayotte, however, the situation is different. Maliki explained that even the first president of the General Council of Mayotte from 1977 to 2004, Younoussa Bamana, was polygynous. According to Malik, if someone had said to Bamana that polygamy must be prohibited for Mayotte to become a department, he would have said, "No, no, no, in that case, it's better to become independent [as the Comoros Islands did]." For him, polygyny has strong roots in Mayotte that are not easily deracinated. Actoibi Laza, a teacher who instructs native languages in Mayotte, said that the law had changed little: "When one is polygamous, one lives a polygamous life as one would have lived before the law."

It became clear that polygamy continues in Mayotte but is now under the radar of French authorities. Daourina Romouli-Zouhair, economic and social environmental adviser for Mayotte, emphatically told me that polygamy had *not* decreased since becoming illegal: "No, it's not a minority practice!" Combo Abdallah Combo, a sociologist at the Regional Institute of Social Work, offered his analysis of how polygamy persists but has changed in Mahorais society, explaining that a polygynous relationship often begins with an extramarital affair that must be regularized in the eyes of society, especially if the woman becomes pregnant. He gave the case of his own father, who was married and lived in a village with his family. After he began working in the city of Mamoudzou, he decided that he did not want to be alone and began an extramarital affair. The woman became pregnant. Abdallah told me, "One cannot get someone pregnant outside of marriage. It becomes known, and so one has to formalize the relationship religiously."

After polygamy became illegal, some men still felt it necessary to conduct a religious ceremony to make the relationship official, but others did not. Mohamed Sidi, councilor for Mamoudzou and the sixth vice-president of the Departmental Council of Mayotte, explained to me that polygamy "must no longer exist" in Mayotte. Yet, "in practice, that's not what is happening, and what is funny is that it is not the old people. There are young people who are still doing polygamy, but in an informal way. It's not official." Abdallah also acknowledged that polygamy has become less official. He stated that many say, "Well, we are Muslims, we can do polygamy." But according to him, "It's unofficial now" and religion is used to justify it. Romouli-Zouhair also spoke of an unofficial polygamy that she called a hypocrisy: "Polygamy is disappearing, but I fear that it will give way to great hypocrisy. Why? The polygamy that was known before, that was accepted, we are entering [what has become] an unofficial polygamy, thus a hidden polygamy. So, I call it hypocrisy." The mores and customs that once regulated polygamy are disappearing, according to many of the people I interviewed. This means that polygamy persists but in a more informal way than it did in the past.

In recent years this unofficial polygamy takes a form called daytime marriages, in which the husband stays with his wife at night and sees the second wife only during the day. Chayma, a Mahoraise official, explained these daytime marriages: One husband said, "I stay with my first wife, the mother of my children—we spent thirty years of life together—and the other wife, I'll see her in the morning. And in the evening, I sleep at my first wife's house. And it's like that every day." Chayma described the situation.

> Before, when there was polygamy, you have a wife in Mtsamboro, and another wife in Mamoudzou, but this woman knows that her husband has a wife in Mtsamboro. The women respected each other, and the children saw each other during the holidays and played together. Now that's not the case, men hide women on the right, on the left. There is the official wife, but then there are several wives because of illegal immigration.

Askandari Allaoui, head of a division of the Delegation of Mayotte in Paris, also described how illegal immigration makes it easier to have unofficial polygamy. He told the story of Kawéni, a village where many undocumented women from the Comoros and Madagascar live.

> At one point, the mayor wanted to clean it up. The neighborhood is very hot. They brought in the CRS [the general reserve of the French National Police], except once they got there, they couldn't pick up anyone, because everyone they met had papers that allowed them to stay. What happened? These women were able to have children with Mahorais men who do daily polygamy—daytime marriages. And so, they are no longer deportable.

He further explained, "This is a form of polygamy, maybe less responsible but that has remained hidden." This informal, daily polygamy is much harder to regulate, an unintended consequence of Mayotte's departmentalization where many seek to benefit from French nationality.

Informal polygamy is also practiced more easily because the French government removed the function of the *cadis*, Muslim judges who had been appointed by France to conduct religious, often polygynous marriages. I

interviewed a group of *cadis*, including the "Grand Cadi," whose main mission is to represent the Muslim religion in Mayotte. He said, "There is no
hiding. First, the law is being imposed on us, so there is a conflict. . . . There
is what we believe and what is customary." Another *cadi* further clarified,
"Even though the law prohibits it, there is also another law that shows that
it is doable." According to these religious leaders, individuals who want to
practice polygyny should not hide, because they are following the laws of
a higher power—the Muslim religion. Mohamed Nassur El-Mamouni, the
representative of the Grand Cadi, provided his perspective that, although
it is not possible to go back to what existed before—because two civil marriages are not allowed in France—the government should find a solution
that does not push people to conceal their marriages. One Mahorais citizen
explained this resistance to polygyny's ban: "There is not a single *cadi* who
will accept that polygamy is prohibited. The *cadis* themselves are polygamous!" Although France did recognize polygynous marriages for those
born before 1987, prohibition makes it illegal for *cadis* to participate in or to
consecrate any polygynous unions after 2011.

French law makes it mandatory to perform a civil marriage at the local
city hall before an optional religious ceremony. However, in Mayotte most
marriages, some being polygynous, are celebrated only religiously and are
never recorded civilly. El-Mamouni elaborated that France should have
acted in a similar way to the Ivory Coast, where it is possible to enter the
names of two or three wives into the family registry: "All the women therefore receive their social rights in an equitable manner, and the man is controlled." In other words, the recognition of polygynous unions diminishes
men's power to abuse their position. Soifaouya, who was in a polygynous
marriage when I interviewed her, told me, "With a little hindsight, we say to
ourselves, 'Wouldn't formalizing things be a good thing?' " For her, the fact
that polygyny has become more unregulated has made women vulnerable.
This argument parallels that made by fundamentalist Mormons and those
who worked with these families. Even as most acknowledged that some
men abused their power, most agreed that the need for families to hide from
the law created conditions for abuse to persist without being reported. The
racial project of regulating polygyny is expressed quite differently among
the fundamentalist Mormon population, however.

RACIAL PROJECTS, POLY STIGMA, AND THE CLOSET:
THE UNITED STATES AND CANADA

In the United States the racial project of regulating polygyny has focused on wiping out polygyny's stain on whiteness. Historically, the practice of polygyny justified "the demotion of Mormons from full citizenship on the grounds of racial inferiority."[18] Today, fundamentalist Mormons argue that they still are not able to act as full citizens in a society that makes it illegal to cohabit with more than one person when acknowledging them as spouses. Being citizens and white means that racialization is much more subtle and allows polygynists to escape some of the more negative prejudices and consequences of the state's racial project. The open secret of plural marriage in Canada seems also to have benefited from the community's whiteness, allowing the community to exist for many years without prosecutions, which have occurred only recently.

At the same time, recent politics, such as calling polygamy a "barbaric" practice, highlight how the stigma of polygamy is linked to the state's racial project.

Stigmatizing White Polygamists as Other in the United States

Fundamentalist Mormon plural families in Utah and norther Arizona have sought to hide in plain sight. Harper, from Centennial Park, described the emotional challenge of being together as a family when they were outside the community. "My husband and one of his other ladies, it was openly obvious that they were together but not married. Because none of us are legally married. And so, for years, she was his mistress. And I was right there, but, no, in no way having any sort of a relationship with him, openly." When they would go to conferences, they would have multiple hotel rooms and her husband was "trying not to run into people in the hallways [laughs]. You know, because no one knows about me, and everybody knows about her." When I interviewed Terry, Nancy, and Esther, who are independents and have eight children together, they recounted the prejudice they experienced in Utah compared with other places they had lived and visited. Nancy stated, "People just really don't care that much. And, I mean, maybe there's more tolerance in other places. More like a 'live and let live.'" Matt, Emma, Charlotte, and Evelyn, also independents, described the types of discrimination that occur. Matt stated, "People think Utah is the friendliest area, and it's the most discriminatory area I've been to—against polygamists. When I would show up with three wives and a couple of babies, you know, people just spot you because they know more what [plural families] look like. And they treat you worse." Given that the dominant religion in Utah is Mormon, one might expect more toleration of plural families who practice it as part of their faith. However, several people explained to me that the opposite occurs. Mormons are more prejudiced against polygamist fundamentalists because Mormons often feel stigmatized by its historical practice. Nancy explained, "It's the Mormons that have this huge issue about overcoming the stigma. So, they're like, stomp it out, stomp it out, stomp it out. It never happened! And in other places, a lot of people are like, 'Well, isn't that interesting.'" Even though the stigma of polygamy might be lessened in other states, general disapprobation toward the practice means that it is likely still experienced.

Many fundamentalist Mormons experienced being an outsider when they were growing up because of their plural families. Nancy talked about not being allowed to play with the non–plural family children at her school: "I had a couple of friends in elementary school that were like, 'My parents said I can't play with you.' So, I lost some friends over that." Joan discussed her upbringing as difficult but not as bad as what her own mother had experienced.

> Joan: The stigma at school was severe sometimes. . . . And my sixth-grade year was the only year really that I dealt with a lot of what I felt like was . . . I think it wasn't really persecution, but there was a lot of meanness from some of the other kids. They picked on me a lot. In private, they would just ask mean questions. Anyway, so I didn't like that at all. That was hard. [*laughs*].
>
> Melanie: They called you names?
>
> Joan: Yeah. Yeah, they called us names. It was nothing compared to what my mom grew up with up in Salt Lake.

The stigma was something many carried with them for their entire lives. Matt talked about the fact that society is constantly "frowning on you, making fun of you, and trying to tear your family apart." He experienced people refusing to provide services and giving dirty looks, especially for his children: "It's particularly the hardest on the kids because adults have these nicety filters. Their prejudice is under the radar. The adult neighbors are supernice and friendly to us, but the kids won't even come over. They will tell our kids, 'Oh, we can't go to your house. Our parents won't let us.'" The experience of stigmatization continues for those being raised in plural families today.

As is true of many stigmatized groups, those raised in plural families discussed having epithets hurled at them when they were young and even as adults, in this case *polyg*, to mark them as being from polygamist families. Samantha talked about the early 1980s and how it "kind of struck me when we had the 'polyg' thing called to us. I mean, we were mistreated when we went out." Harper a decade later also experienced being called a polyg: "I didn't like being called a polyg when I went out. I didn't like this hostility and this having to live a life in secret just so I could be accepted socially. Because I wanted to live this way, I didn't see anything wrong with it. I saw a number of benefits." In 2015 Matt said that his son got into a fight and was suspended after he defended himself for being called a polyg. Paul Murphy, the director of communications and policy for the attorney general's office from 2000 to 2013, heard many stories from people living in plural families who discussed verbal abuse.

> Basically, they were "the others." People did not know them; they did not understand them. They were demonized. Some of the stories they tell about how they are treated by the public are horrifying. We had one woman speak at one of our conferences, and she was a basketball coach for the girl's high school. They played a game in a different city, and the kids were screaming, "Kill the polygs, kill the polygs."

This verbal abuse creates fear and trauma for children growing up in plural families. Charlotte, who was raised in a plural family and then entered her own, talked about the way that polygamy's ban perpetuates stigma: "Since it's been criminalized for such a long time, and the dynamics that that creates, it enables people to go ahead and be prejudiced, and use that, and throw it off to the side. Just to go ahead and have those biases and not check it." In the eyes of the public, being a "polyg" is unsavory.

Many felt that the media played a strong role in perpetuating stereotypes, especially the news organizations owned by the Mormon church. Terry, the husband of a plural family, explained that the local news would always take the opportunity to "blow up" any problem in a polygynous family: "That stigmatizes it big time." His wife Nancy recounted a headline she had seen just a few days before: "It says, 'Polygamist ninjas arrested for something.' And I'm like, 'Okay, so how is the fact they are polygamists have anything to do with the story?'" Using the word *polygamist* sensationalizes the story and perpetuates stereotypes about polygamy and crime. Avery explained that fundamentalist Mormons who practice plural marriage are treated as second-class citizens in the media and other institutions: "If the definition of a second-class citizen is someone who can be harmed in the workplace, harmed in the public square, harmed in the media, harmed in the schools, and just generally burdened because of his or her lifestyle, then we are still second-class citizens." These accounts point to discrimination and status loss that occur as a result of participating in a disparaged forbidden intimacy.[19]

Fundamentalist Mormons who practice polygyny are almost exclusively white, but discrimination and stigma can be traced to racial dynamics that have long considered polygyny a practice of the "backward races."[20] This perspective feeds the stigma of being in a plural family. Emma, herself in a polygynous family, explained that stereotypes shaped people's judgments that precede any thought: "I mean, obviously some of the bigger stereotypes really is that all of the men are perverts, and all the women are really brainwashed or oppressed, and the children are abused, and that polygamy itself creates abuse." Focusing on polygamous men's sexual perversion participates in broader racialized stereotypes of violence and perversion attributed to heterosexual Black and other men of color.[21]

Racialized understandings of polygamy are evident in the stereotypes over welfare abuse. Many pointed to the fact that polygamy is equated with welfare dependency, a stereotype often attributed to African American single-mother families.[22] Matt exclaimed, "I mean, comments all the time I get is, 'You're on welfare. We are paying for all of their kids.' People can't let go because they can't compute in their mind how they afford two kids, and I can afford twenty-five. You know, I get it, but it's not off welfare. We've been fortunate never to use it." A dominant narrative says that those living in polygamy are not responsible for their children. For Terry, the secrecy builds stigma and nurtures stereotypes such as welfare fraud.

> And when something is a secret, people assume the worst, right? They make monsters out of the darkness, and that builds on the stigma. And builds that support for it's bad and it's wrong. Whenever there's any welfare fraud, it's filtered out by the media. And almost always, you hear this comment of, "Well, I wouldn't care if they just live their life, if they weren't abusing the welfare system."

Participants were quick to admit that welfare fraud did happen but rarely. For example, in 2017 Lyle Jeffs, the brother of Warren Jeffs and a former FLDS bishop, was convicted of food stamp fraud that diverted about $11 million in food stamp benefits to a communal storehouse. Speaking to the power of the leadership over FLDS members, many families had experienced food insecurity even as the leadership accumulated wealth. Even in this case, however, investigators ultimately dropped their investigation against rank-and-file members, determining that members who did receive benefits were eligible.[23]

Journalist Brooke Adams examined the claims of welfare overuse among the FLDS in the 2000s. In the Hildale and Colorado City communities, where the FLDS is predominantly located, the numbers include outlying areas. She stated, "Not just in the FLDS community there, but some of the surrounding areas are low-income people, right? When I talked to the authorities in Arizona, when I did my story on that, they told me that the rate was not any higher than they would expect from an area like that. I think, as I recall, they said it was lower." Matt described the stereotype that you "show up in your prairie dress getting welfare, everybody's going to see that. And so, I think there are reasons behind the stereotype, but I just don't know that it necessarily holds up." Stereotypes contribute to the necessity of being clandestine, especially among closed communities like the FLDS.

Hiding in Plain Sight

Polygamy's ban and the stigma attached to living in a forbidden family have led to secrecy and hiding. This common theme was repeated throughout my interviews with those living in polygyny and those who have worked with these families. Evelyn, who was raised in a plural family and then entered her own, described the fear and judgment that dominated her upbringing.

> And so, we were taught from a young age to just kind of keep your mouth shut about it, and just try not to bring attention to that, and so it made it hard to be yourself. You know, it's like, "Okay, I've got to be careful what I say and not get too close to people this way." So, it was scary because there were a lot of judgments, and things like, you know, so negative any time any story came out in the news, it was just like you want to bury your face in case somebody knew about it.

Her family home was vandalized years later, with slurs painted on the driveway and car. Matt explained that Evelyn's parents "[didn't] call the cops." It was "a regular neighborhood," and according to Emma, her sister wife, Evelyn's dad "knew it was related to polygamy because it said 'polygamous bitches.' Yeah, and so he has that historical, 'You know, we don't call the police, we just deal with thing. Let's clean it up.'" Mike explained the logic, "We don't call the police . . . just hush-hush. And that's how the kids are raised. And that's how we are taught. It's just, 'Keep your head down and take it.'" They explained the negative impact of this secrecy on their psyches and sense of well-being. Terry also was raised to be quiet: "And speaking of the stigma, because of the law we try to keep it quiet. We were always told, 'Don't ever deny that I was [in a polygamist family], but don't tell anybody.' Now that takes us all into where we hide, where people don't talk about it. I know families that change their kids last names, so the people don't pick up on it." He described a vicious cycle where the need to keep quiet led others to view them as "weird and secretive."

Many described childhoods that were loving and positive. At the same time, there was always an underlying fear based on the idea that the government could intervene, prosecute polygynous husbands, and take away the children, which occurred in the 1953 raid. Olivia was just 3 years old during the 1953 Short Creek raid, and she described how it shaped her life. Her immediate family was living outside Salt Lake City, but they had family members living in Short Creek. Olivia explained that there was a raid "pretty much every decade." In 1953 the government of Arizona "experimented with removing the children. And one of the women that we knew lost ten of her children, and they adopted them out. So, the big fear for my parents was losing their children." Her father had been arrested before she was born and charged with practicing polygamy, and then he was arrested again after the raid. Olivia said that her dad fought the charges in the courts as part of his constitutional rights but ended up going to prison in the late 1950s for several years. This fear followed her into adulthood. She stated, "When I was old enough to go to school, I kind of kept to myself and didn't say much. Just thought if I was a real good girl and stayed out of sight, I would be safe." It Olivia took many years to find her voice.

Experiences of the raid affected even those who were born after it occurred, such as Hannah, who was born several years after 1953. Her mother (the second wife) and her children had been taken from the community and made wards of the state. She recounted:

> For the state to release my mother and children to my father, she had to sign a consent form with the state that she would no longer practice polygamy and that she would have nothing to do with my father. Well, three years later when I was conceived, it was obvious she had something to do with my father, and so she had to quit her job and go into hiding. So, she always tells me I was her baby that was born in hiding.

Hannah's mother was in the late stages of a pregnancy with Hannah's older sister when the raid occurred (she already had three children). She was dropped off at a woman's doorstep and told that this would be her new home: "The woman had cleaned out a toolshed in her back yard and put out a couple of cots in there for my mother and her children." When her mother's water broke and she went into labor, the woman dropped her off on the hospital steps: "So, she walked into that hospital, never having been in a hospital before, and when she told them she was from Short Creek, they of course immediately turned cold and icy to her, and she said the next thing she knew, when she woke up, she had delivered the baby, and there was no baby." They had taken the baby, and for 48 hours "she pleaded with every nurse that came in the room and every doctor to please tell her whether the baby was dead or alive, and what the baby was, and she said she got no answers." They finally gave the baby to her. Hannah explained that her father was alone for a couple of years before any of his wives and children were able to return. Some were gone up to seven years.

Growing up with those fears of law enforcement, and, you know, just every time you turned around you were afraid that whatever you said or did might get your father in trouble. And so, you lived in secrecy. And they say, "Well why do you isolate yourselves? And why are you so secretive about your lives?" Well, those experiences forced us into secrecy, and so we learned to distrust government, and law enforcement, and all those things.

The fear was so great that if a truck went by that could be a sheriff, all the neighborhood kids would hit the ground and hide. Still, Hannah chose a plural family for herself: "I loved being from a plural family and to this day, I knew I wanted it for my own children. I knew that there were just so many benefits of being raised in a large family that that's what I wanted for my own children." Although less secretive than her parents about her plural family, feeling the need to hide her family background had left psychological scars.

Many described how it can be impossible to remain hidden. Plural families are often recognizable. Harper discussed her childhood in terms of the 1953 raid, even though she was born in the 1980s. Her parents instilled the need to be careful, but the discrimination she experienced provided further evidence of the need to be cautious.

We were constantly being reminded by our parents, even years after the 1953 raid, because we grew up with parents who experienced that firsthand. We dealt with discrimination, a lot of discrimination in places like Hurricane and St. George. Very hostile. People knew where you're from, and it's obvious where we're from. The way that we dress, our mannerisms, things we participate in. It's kind of you get in the car and you go outside of this bubble that you live in out here [laughs], where you can live openly and freely. And you put on . . . a cloak of caution.

The need to hide in plain sight often had impactful consequences. Nancy described how her mother found out, when she was putting several of her children into kindergarten, that "my dad was never put on the birth certificate, because I think that the doctor really doesn't like the fact that she is a plural wife, and they knew it." Terry emphasized that these things happen; "it's not just bogeymen." Esther, the second wife who was not raised in a plural family, emphasized, "It is scary!" Being in a plural family could have negative emotional consequences.

The trauma of the 1953 raid was reignited when the Texas government carried out a raid on the YFZ Ranch. Journalist Brooke Adams had covered the issue of polygamy and the FLDS for many years. She stated that historically, before Warren Jeffs, "the FLDS community was actually really kind of open." She continued, "If you go back to the time of the '50s and the '53 raid, the community had a different—they didn't have a name—but they were in *Life* magazine and *Look* magazine and did a lot of media stories. So, they've sort of gone through evolutions too, about their openness." The group became more secretive after a schism occurred in 1984 in which a small group split off in protest over the "one-man rule" doctrine that altered the leadership of the church implemented by Rulon Jeffs, Warren's father. Many people I interviewed were critical of Warren Jeffs and his iron grip over the FLDS. At the same time, the raid was seen as another example of the government separating mothers from their children and traumatizing families. A social worker described how people "just fell off the face of the earth" out of fear after the raid, making it extremely difficult to provide the help people needed. Amy, who was raised in a plural family and later entered her own plural marriage, stated:

> After the raid on the FLDS community in Texas, I was a little bit worried, because I know that there's a lot of things wrong with the FLDS. I honestly do believe Warren Jeffs is a bad guy, but what they did is they went in and blanketed an entire community because of his guilt. And so, it made me worry that what if they found someone in my community to be guilty of some awful things and come and take my children away because someone in my community was guilty? . . . To think of that in your own situation, it's scary.

Amy's assessment that the government could decide to separate dozens of families and take the children away because of the guilt of a few was a point that terrified many.

The fact that polygamy was illegal made people feel vulnerable. Nancy told me that she was pregnant at the time of the Texas raid, and "I just like cried all day for two or three days after that happened just because it's so terrifying." She said that people in her community had felt somewhat safe before the 2008 raid because it was unusual to be arrested for polygamy. "Just mind our own business; keep your head down. You know, if your kids get sick, try not to go to the hospital, but just play it cool and everything should be okay." After the Texas raid, she described how no one felt safe anymore. "It's not that hard for the government to just say, 'Okay now these ones too.'" When the raid happened, Samantha was in a leadership position in Centennial Park and feared for her own children and all those that she felt responsible for under her direction. She described asking herself, "What do I tell my kids? How do I help them find each other and get home? And if they take me out of the picture, how do I help my kids if they take the kids?" She was in tears as she described how one of the men in the neighborhood who was not in a plural family handed her a paper with his number on it, telling her to have the kids memorize it, and he would get them wherever they were to keep them safe.

There was agreement among my interviewees that banning polygamy forced people underground and that the need for secrecy made it easier for exploitation to occur. Brian, who was raised in a plural family in Centennial Park, told me that the consequences of the ban on polygamy could be seen with the FLDS.

> I think that's just a good example of what happens. People had to go underground, and that's kind of been the irony of the conversation. It's like, "Why are you scared of government?" And it's like, "Well . . . because you're going to put my dad in jail, so we're just going to hide from you." It's in the hiding that some of the stuff that Warren was able to do happened.

Brian pointed to evidence that Warren Jeffs was able to feed on people's fears of the government to control them, even after he was sent to prison in Texas. Ivy, one of five wives, explained that historically it was the polygamy ban and government regulation that created the conditions that enabled the rise of prophets such as Warren Jeffs: "They created the society, they created the law, they created the closed society." Likewise, Joan iterated the idea that fear of the legal system kept polygamy "very hidden. And when bad stuff is hidden, it tends to get worse [laughs]. So, I think that's why you see so much corruption." She argued that banning polygamy made it easy to associate it "with abuse and incest." Jack also pointed to the fact that after a hundred years of the government seeking to "hunt you down, and throw you in prison, many cowered and hid in little compounds in far off corners of the state and surrounding states." For him, this history has shaped communities to become secretive: "And so, it got all a little bit weird. And whose fault? Where do you point the finger of blame for it going a little bit weird?" In his view, the government has to bear some responsibility. The need for secrecy was also perpetuated in Canada where the media and stereotypes shaped how the small community lived.

Stigma and Open Secrets in Canada

The small community of fundamentalist Mormons in Bountiful has received ample negative media attention in the past thirty years. In her memoir, Mary Jayne Blackmore, the daughter of the community's former bishop, Winston Blackmore, discussed the impact of the media frenzy she grew up surrounded by: "Being a kind of visible minority [a Canadian designation for those who self-identify as someone who feels racially marked by others] and living life in the glare of the media is just part of life for fundamentalist Mormon women."[24] Her statement recognizes the racial project that the media perpetuates of fundamentalist Mormons as the other. As Mormon fundamentalists, women in the community stand outside the mainstream, white Canadian society.

Daphne Bramham, who has been a columnist at the *Vancouver Sun* since 2000, is the most renowned journalist to write about this issue, including her 2008 national bestseller, *The Secret Lives of Saints: Child Brides and Lost Boys in Canada's Polygamous Mormon Sect*. She reported on the polygamy reference case, and her name came up often during my interviews with lawyers and interveners. Several discussed her journalism as perpetuating biases. One woman who served as a witness for the amicus stated, "You know, there are Christian biases, there are Daphne Bramham's biases of let's say the Bountiful women. And I understand where she's coming from and how she feels about that, but her journalism is very biased [against these women]." Several on the amicus side pointed to the ways that Bramham's writing influenced the case. George Macintosh, the amicus curiae who argued against the attorneys general of British Columbia and

Canada, described going into the case with some concern about possible bias: "I knew that Daphne Bramham's writings had probably influenced the thinking over the last ten years of a lot of people in British Columbia. So, I was apprehensive of a bias having been established through that writing." On the side of the attorneys general, lawyers described Bramham's work as important. One intervener stated, "The first thing I read was Daphne's book." The book does not mince words, calling the community of Bountiful "Canada's dirty secret for more than sixty years" and "the polygamy capital of Canada."[25] The language is meant to provoke, because Bramham charges that Bountiful consists of extortionists, misogynists, racists, child abusers, and pedophiles who are perpetrating crimes that need to be prosecuted. Although the polygamy reference case did uncover numerous crimes committed in the community, Bramham treats polygamy as so many others do: as something that itself breeds these ills rather than the more complex interplay that results from hierarchical and male-dominated religious sects.

The prairie dresses that the FLDS women wear in Bountiful played a big role in how they were perceived in the media and in the polygamy reference case. Describing the dress of FLDS women, Bramham stated, "They dress in long sleeves with ankle-length skirts that barely conceal the full-length temple garments—holy underwear—and sneakers. The women are like Stepford wives with bad hair and clothes."[26] In the reference case an intervener on the amicus's side pointed to the negative perception that the attire of the women made.

> I think it would have been nice to see a group that isn't as governed by the dress code, which is a shocking thing to see. I think that's tremendously important, because . . . maybe it's too much to attribute to the clothes, but I think if you do see someone who is dressed in a certain way among others who are dressed in a certain way, you do tend to assume that their thoughts, including about marriage, are governed by an external and not very choice-giving force. And so, in that respect, I think it would've been good as well to see that people can live in polygamy without being governed by or associated with—at least anymore—somebody like Warren Jeffs.

Her allusion to people not governed by the dress code refers to the side of the community that is no longer FLDS. The otherness of the FLDS is apparent in their conservative dress. The overall bias in the courtroom against the group was remarked on by other lawyers. One lawyer who was on the side of the amicus elucidated: "I think that in the chattering classes—most of the lawyers in the courtroom and expert witnesses and myself—I would say that within our liberally educated, one- or two-university-degree kind of people, we tend to have a bias against people in the dark end of the valley." According to him, this conventional thinking fueled an argument or a viewpoint against polygamy: "I think the bulk of the expert evidence would be likely to be found on the government side [arguing in favor of the ban against polygamy]." He was not surprised by the outcome of the case.

The bias against polygamy was so strong that it bled into what many saw as "progressive" polygamy. One lawyer arguing as an intervener on the side of the attorneys general exclaimed, "To me, what is the really shocking part of the story is that governments, both the federal and provincial government, have advocated the criminalization of polyamory. And this is huge news. And yet it's been almost ignored [by the media]. She noted that the argument of the attorneys general depended on the meaning of *ceremony*.

> And the ceremony includes consent. So, if you said, if you and me and another guy said, "Should we live together as lovers? Is it agreed? Yes. You consent? Yes." That could be criminal. So literally, the law says, "A ceremony, a rite, a contract or a consent." And they quoted that. So, de facto, the federal government is virtually prohibiting all cohabitative polyamory. And to me, this is deeply shocking. And the fact that the media has not paid attention to it is indicative of a possible normalization of that prohibition, which could then give rise to blowback, a moral panic against those who want to resist that.

This lawyer found it disturbing that the government would seek to ban what some call good polygamy, which she saw as a "prejudice perpetuated by the state." Yet she does not express any concern that normalizing polygamy's prohibition could also hurt other plural families, particularly women and children, who are polygynous for religious reasons. Because these families are seen as constituting harm, they exist outside what Gayle Rubin has called the "charmed circle" of acceptable sexual practices or, for our purposes, acceptable sexual family forms.[27]

The distinction between good and bad polygamy was highlighted in the words of another lawyer intervening on the side of the attorneys general: "Some people are happy in one kind of relationship, and other people are happy in another. It's not for me to judge whether something should make someone else happy." For him, polygamy could be okay when "a whole bunch of conditions" are met, including "no children involved, no coercion, and it's at such a small scale that it doesn't contribute to the lost boys problem, and on and on." His first criteria—that no children be involved—is reminiscent of how the custody rights of lesbian and gay parents have been regulated over time. For him, the conditions were too long to make it conceivable that a good kind of polygamy could really exist.

In a similar vein to Grace Pastine, who is quoted at the beginning of this chapter, several participants described how banning polygamy contributed to Bountiful's isolation. One intervener on the amicus side provided an analysis of the ways that being "closeted" creates harms: "And there are harms that are shown when sexual populations are closeted, so that's something that needs to be considered. And this law [that bans polygamy] never considered any of those things when it was incorporated in the 1890s. It was just incorporating the previous morality." She presented evidence that it is harder to help women and children in Bountiful, because "if dad is abusing mom, mom is not going to complain against dad, because now she could be criminal because she's in a polygamist situation." She noted that decriminalization would also mean "destigmatization, which means that people would be more accepting. But if they think it's criminal to do that, then there's going to be a lot of judgments, blame, and negative attitudes." Her words are reminiscent of the interviews I conducted in the United States in which plural families discussed the harms of being in the closet. Janis Porter-Hirsche is one of the few researchers to conduct in-depth interviews with individuals from the FLDS side of Bountiful since the community split in 2002.[28] Her research attests to the fact that the FLDS has become more insular over time. Two young women she interviewed suggested that the government's persecution of the group by banning polygamy helped to create the isolationism that serves Warren Jeffs, which then exacerbated public discrimination against FLDS women. One of the women stated, "If someone's lifestyle is illegal, why would they go to the law for help?" A vicious cycle occurs in which outside agencies do not understand the FLDS and then this ignorance reinforces FLDS's distrust of outsiders.

Participants in the three countries and Mayotte pointed to the fact that secretive communities create conditions for social ills to flourish. Some polygynist groups are secretive and self-isolated, such as the FLDS. Other secretive new religious movements—a religious or spiritual group that has modern origins but is peripheral to its society's dominant religious culture—also reflect some of the dynamics seen in Bountiful and the FLDS. For example, in the United States the government has inflicted raids on the Twelve Tribes, the Family International, the Branch Davidians, Scientology, and the Nuwaubians.[29] The Branch Davidians practiced polygamy, and both the Branch Davidians and the Family International were accused of child sexual abuse. These groups came to be defined as cultlike and secretive. However, neither of them was defined by a specific stigmatized practice, perpetuated by the media's focus on polygamy, as the FLDS has been. A Google search for FLDS brings up such titles as "The Woman Who Escaped a Polygamous Cult,"[30] "19 Things You Probably Don't Know About FLDS Polygamists,"[31] and "Ex-FLDS Members Who Broke with Secretive Polygamous Sect Buy Former Compound."[32] As Nancy emphasized earlier, the media uses the term *polygamy* to mark individuals or groups as outsiders or bizarre, adding the term as though the involvement of polygamy explains why crimes are committed.

Fear and stigma have pushed people living in polygamous families underground in France, the United States, and Canada. In Mayotte most who practice polygamy do so by evading the law. The consequences in all cases have been to make women in these relationships more vulnerable, particularly when it comes to having access to social services. Benefits or help that might be accessed is often avoided because of the fear of prosecution, especially for husbands who are seen as exploiters of women and children. Although the racial project of being marked as polygamous is explicit in France, it is more subtle in the United States and Canada, where a predominantly white population participates in a practice that is seen as barbaric and inegalitarian. In the next chapter, I consider how whiteness enabled a social movement in the United States that has successfully sought to decriminalize polygamy in Utah.

6 | RECOGNIZING POLYGAMIES

> Why can't I have the right to live my life? Why do they
> want to stop me [from having a polygynous family]? If this
> is really a democracy, why don't we let people choose
> the life they want? Before France arrived [in Mayotte],
> there were already these traditions and customs that
> they respected until 2000. Why from 2000 onwards
> does it become an obstacle? This needs to be explained.
> —*Haïdar Attoumani, former second duty*
> *mayor, M'tsangamouji, Mayotte*

> I know that there are many men who find it scandalous
> that they are prohibited from living in a situation
> of polygamy [in France]. In general, these men rely
> on the fact that they are not of French nationality,
> that they do not apply for French nationality, that
> they keep their nationality of origin, and that this
> should allow them the right to live according to the
> customs of those countries, but for the moment
> these are rather individual reactions which, to my
> knowledge, have not led them to organize networks.
> —*Jacques Barou, researcher, CNRS*

> These ladies are just giants to me! Giants in their
> example, giants in their testimony, in sticking up for what
> they believe [about polygamy]. And being living examples
> for decades of what they believe. They are now standing
> up and saying, "Look, I might look like this, and you might
> not respect the way I look, but I have a right to speak for
> myself and say what I feel and live the way I choose to."
> —*Harper, Mormon fundamentalist, United States*

THE RACIAL PROJECT OF REGULATING polygamies, which is
linked to national identity and citizenship as markers of belonging, has
shaped the possibilities for movements for and against polygamy in each

of the study countries. As the words of Haïdar Attoumani and Jacques Barou make clear, there is no organized social movement for recognizing polygynous relationships in either Mayotte or France. In Mayotte, a former French colony, the ban on polygamy developed over time, as Haïdar Attoumani pointed out in his comments about France's current intolerance of Mayotte's culture and traditions. He was one of the few public officials who openly professed to having more than one wife, even though many of my interviewees described public officials as having multiple wives. As detailed previously, polygyny in Mayotte has become mostly invisible to French authorities even though it is still widely practiced, sometimes openly and sometimes not. The Mahorais have embraced counterpractices in which people decline to declare their marriages to the state and instead choose to follow local customs. These counterpractices are often due to a mistrust of the French government, and the Mahorais establish their families of choice without worrying about the French legal system. In metropolitan France the populations practicing polygyny are generally not citizens and are vulnerable to losing their residence permits, pushing many underground. Although polygyny continues, the anger many feel over polygamy's prohibition does not translate into protest. According to Jacques Barou, who has extensively studied African immigrants in France, individual rather than collective responses to polygamy's ban are the norm. On the other hand, a few women-led associations have fought against polygamy in France.

In contrast, the United States has witnessed more recognizable social movements for and against polygamy's prohibition since the 1990s, when activists called for more enforcement and fueled debate over how best to deal with abuse.[1] As an anti-polygamist movement grew, numerous women in plural marriages began to fight against what they claimed were misconceptions of polygamy, seeking its decriminalization. Other movements have also gained traction, such as the movement for Christian polygamy, which seeks to make legalization a broader conversation in American society. Mark Henkel, the National Polygamy Advocate and founder of the Christian evangelical polygamy organization TruthBearer.org, described how the media always focused on fundamentalist Mormon polygamy. In 2005 Henkel appeared on the *700 Club* with Pat Robertson, a show once watched by millions of evangelical Christians. The expectation was that the woman who interviewed Henkel would be able to discredit him, but she "found herself completely surprised at the compassion for women that I had," and "the basis that I was using in the Bible, the argumentation was flawless." According to Henkel, "In that moment, for the first time in history, the two words *Christian* and *polygamy* were no longer a contradiction in terms." His movement subsequently took off. Harper, whom we have heard from in previous chapters, detailed her admiration for the women who stood up to defend their choice to live in a plural family. Based on this prior activism, she made a difficult decision to also stand up as a member of a plural family, consenting to participate in a television series on plural marriage.

Researchers have demonstrated the ways that gender, race, and nationality and citizenship have shaped responses to prohibitions against same-gender sexuality and marriage.[2] In the fight to legalize same-gender marriage, scholars such as Kathleen Hull and Rosie Harding built on the concept of "legal consciousness" to consider the ways that "people understand and use the law" through ceremonies to celebrate their same-gender unions when these unions were not recognized under the law and/or were illegal.[3] This body of scholarship has shown the importance of understanding how people use the law in their everyday lives to bolster their activism. For example, Verta Taylor and her colleagues found that people participated in same-gender weddings with the intention of making claims about their right to marry and that the initial protest in 2004 in which individuals participated in a month-long protest in San Francisco sparked other forms of political activism that initiated a statewide campaign for marriage equality in California.[4] Race, nationality, and citizenship are key in developing legal consciousness.[5] A recent example examines how negotiating citizenship and being undocumented in the United States forms a legal consciousness that motivates social action. For U.S. citizen children whose family members are undocumented, there is a sense of privilege, responsibility, and guilt as they seek to help undocumented family members.[6] This body of research, to my knowledge, has not compared the national and transnational contexts in the development of legal consciousness, particularly concerning the fight against laws that ban forbidden intimacies.

Whether and why groups fight for or against polygamy is the focus of this chapter. In what follows I examine the ways that national identities shape the ability for counterpractices or social movements to flourish. Why have self-proclaimed social movements that seek to criminalize or decriminalize polygamy grown so much in one national context—the United States? How has polygamy been confronted in other national and postcolonial contexts—France and Mayotte? In the following sections I uncover the ways that whiteness and citizenship status allow some polygynous populations to draw on dominant cultural repertoires of "coming out" to successfully fight for decriminalization. We begin in Mayotte, where many criticize the French government's hypocritical manner of implementing polygamy's prohibition as a condition for becoming an overseas department. This discontent is manifested more as counterpractices where people live their lives outside the purview of the state. In France the main activism has arisen out of associations that work with African populations to provide better living conditions. Some seek to abolish polygyny, but most remain neutral. Finally, we turn to the United States, which has witnessed movements for and against polygamy that draw on other movements as a framing mechanism. Legal consciousness is enabled by the conditions of belonging as white citizens. These cases illuminate how the law, race, citizenship, and regulation work together to create the social conditions that make contesting forbidden intimacies desirable.

FRENCH INTOLERANCE AND DISCONTENT IN MAYOTTE

In 2012 Christiane Taubira, then minister of justice, put forward a bill to open marriage and adoption to same-gender couples to comply with François Hollande's campaign promises to permit "marriage for all," embracing the idea that the new law would finally make the institution of marriage universal and republican.[7] A few days later, an organization calling itself Manif pour Tous (Protest for All, an ironic take on "marriage for all") called for demonstrations in cities across France, igniting massive street protests that continued throughout the fall of 2012 and the spring of 2013.

In Mayotte there were no massive protests against what became known as the Taubira law. One protest did occur in May 2013, bringing together a small gathering of *cadis* and other religious men who stood in front of the prefecture with a banner asking, "Pourquoi non à la polygamie, oui au mariage gay?" (Why no to polygamy, yes to gay marriage?).[8] The protest was covered by a conservative magazine, which stated that in Mayotte the debate over same-gender marriage and polygamy is "reopened by unexpected supporters of the Taubira law."[9] It became part of the right-wing political rhetoric when in 2016, the niece of Marine Le Pen, leader of the extreme right National Front Party, tweeted the article to support her claims that the legalization of gay marriage has opened the door to "many abuses. Other minorities will seek to have their form of love recognized; I am thinking of polygamy."[10] Le Pen's niece explicitly embraced the racial project of using polygamy as a racializing strategy. Her tweet of the article and its photo of Mahorais men with their banners not only cautioned her constituency against a slippery slope between the legalization of same-gender marriage and polygamy but also advanced the idea that the slippery slope would empower postcolonial minorities (who are also French citizens) to demand their rights to have their "form" of *abusive* love recognized.

Unlike in metropolitan France, there were no protests against same-gender marriage in Mayotte except the one asking, "Why not polygamy?" The political climate in Mayotte did not express concern over this culture war issue as it did in metropolitan France. According to Jean Veron, the general director of Caisse de Sécurité Sociale de Mayotte (the social security system) from 2012 to 2016 and a white man from metropolitan France, "There was no demonstration [here] as there was in metropolitan France. The gay marriage law has not been a problem here." He noted that a same-gender marriage—for a white gay male couple living in Mamoudzou—was officiated shortly after the law passed. According to the local paper, *Le Journal De Mayotte*, Mayotte is the first Muslim-dominated territory in the world to allow same-gender unions and to officiate a gay wedding. According to Veron, "While there is a very strong tradition here on a lot of things, there is also a kind of tolerance, which is quite surprising sometimes." He commented on the small demonstrations that did take place, which he summed up as, "Once you accept gay marriage, why are you bothering us about polygamy?" For him, "They are not wrong in their reasoning, on that point of view!" However, he noted that only men had demonstrated for polygamy, not women. For him, "Women don't aspire to polygamy, women aspire to something else. And therefore inevitably, it will come to an end." Veron was hopeful that polygamy would become obsolete as Mahoraise women continue to be more educated and independent.

The question of polygyny's decline, however, is more complicated, and as noted previously, I found evidence that it is continuing and may even be increasing, especially among the younger population. The quote of Haïdar Attoumani presented at the opening of this chapter was used to help explain why he, a man in his late 30s at the time of the interview, had chosen polygyny: "Me personally, I'm in it, and I did it right after [the law was passed to prohibit it]." When I asked whether he saw his choice to enter a polygynous marriage as a form of resistance, he replied, "Of course! Of course! It should have been made clear why it is an obstacle because I see no obstacle. On the contrary, it is I who must be able to satisfy both my households." He explained, "And in our family, we are five brothers. All five of us are polygamists, even though our father isn't." For Attoumani the prohibition of polygyny created a shock wave throughout Mahorais society. Several Mahorais leaders told me that the law made no sense for their society. One government official stated, "We are forced to [prohibit polygamy]. Now the law says it is prohibited, so we consent." Attoumani stated that the *cadis* demonstrated on several occasions and that debates on the radio and television took place for "months and months."

> There has been quite a bit of reporting on this, young women saying they are fed up with their celibate life. They will gladly agree to live with co-wives. There is even an association called Femmes Leaders [Women Leaders], which advocates that instead of women remaining without a husband they agree to be co-wives.

The activism of Femmes Leaders, which is more complicated than Attoumani's portrayal, is discussed later in this chapter. However, the idea that some Mahoraise women were unhappy about polygamy's prohibition was repeated in several of my interviews.

Several professional women told me that they had friends and acquaintances who thought it would be beneficial for polygamy to be recognized. A French government official who asked to remain anonymous told me that after polygamy was repealed in Mayotte, women rallied against the law, saying that polygamy was protecting them. A Mahoraise feminist lawyer explained that the issue of polygamy is complex: "There were no demonstrations in the streets to say, 'Let's proscribe polygamy!'" Instead, many women perceived "that polygamy ensured rights, it preserved certain guarantees for children, for women." Other participants said that some Mahoraise women did not agree with polygamy's prohibition. When I interviewed Mohammed Abaine, the delegate for associations of the General Council of Mayotte, and Hamida Maliki, a policy officer for Population Services, they discussed the fact that polygamy's prohibition was not something the population advocated for and that women were some of the first to protest it.

> Abaine: But this is not a law that came directly from the population. Besides, the first demonstrations were by women. When the polygamy law was passed, it was the women who were the first to stand up and say, "This law is going to prevent us who do not yet have a husband from getting one. We prefer the wrong door to no door at all!"
> Maliki: That's an expression: "It is better to have a house with a door that does not close well than a house without a door."
> Abaine: People say, "I'd rather share the apple than not have any at all."

Being a single woman is stigmatized in Mayotte, and some women preferred to enter polygynous relationships rather than live without a husband. Soifaouya, who was in this situation, stated, "In the end, between polygamy and being rejected by society, one prefers polygamy." She made the difficult choice to become the second wife after the man she married broke his promise to divorce his first wife. She explained, "It is very difficult when you feel that you are not accepted by the group or society." Although she expressed mixed feelings about her polygynous marriage, she preferred it to the other option.

Scholars who have conducted research in Mayotte also did not find women organizing against polygamy. Élise Lemercier, who was part of a team studying the departmentalization of Mayotte, told me that women were wary of the French government: "The French state is not the defender of women." She said the issue was not a priority for the Mahorais population, and because the government was satisfied to make it illegal, there was little concern that it was practiced under the radar. The women's association Femmes Leaders explained that the issue of polygamy was not a priority. I interviewed the president and four members who described the association's founders, the *chatouilleuses* (the ticklers). In the fight for Mayotte to maintain its ties to France from 1970 to 1975, the *chatouilleuses* conducted collective actions that involved surrounding government officials and "tickling" them to the point of making it difficult to breathe. They were protesting the island's integration into the Comoros archipelago, which would have led to an independence they did not want. For them, this change of status would have meant greater insecurity.[11] Because tickling could be portrayed as innocuous, the women adopted this method to scare away important visitors, such as the Comorian minister Mohamed Dahalane during his first visit to the island. The word *tickle* put a pacifist face on these actions, which could become violent. For example, in 1969 Zakia Madi, a *chatouilleuse*, died in a clash between supporters and opponents of independence. Thus there is a history of women's activism and leadership in Mayotte.

This activism did not concern polygyny, and the women presented mixed opinions on the topic. President Moinaïcha Aniki described Femmes Leaders as "rebels," about fifty members "who will never accept to be with polygamous husbands." She explained that few women in Mayotte choose polygamy; instead, they find themselves in a polygamous marriage against their will. However, all agreed that polygamy's prohibition has not helped women. In fact, Faouzia Cordji, president of an association that supports women victims of violence, explained that polygamy's ban is "on paper only" and was just a way to make Mayotte appear ready to integrate into France's mainstream society. She pointed to the fact that the very Mahorais men who helped prohibit polygamy are themselves polygamists: "We ask ourselves why [these men] prohibited polygamy while they practice it?" She described a deteriorating situation for women in polygyny after the law, in which "people don't talk about polygamy anymore as if it doesn't matter." According to her:

> Today, it's every person for themselves. Social issues, they don't interest a lot of people. It's complicated to mobilize, in fact. Everyone denounces [polygamy], especially when we get together. . . . Still, it is complicated to really provoke public debate, because everyone is busy in their little life. We are there, we commit, we demand, we denounce, but it is true that for the moment, it is an inconvenient problem—polygamy—but even if it bothers, mobilization [is difficult].

Polygamy might be an inconvenient problem, but for many, including this group of women leaders, it was not the most important aspect of their lives. In fact, as they explained, prohibition has weakened traditional rules that were put in place to ensure that polygynous wives were recognized and cared for. Today, it is more common for husbands to take another wife in secret, without the first wife's knowledge. According to them, this new way of doing polygamy was also important to address.

Several argued that the goal should not be to eradicate polygyny but to support women. Soifaouya stated that polygyny was something no one discussed: "We don't really discuss it in depth. But me, I put the subject on the table . . . , but it's like I'm ashamed to talk about it. Even though I know everyone knows it, and everything, but at the same time, I'm ashamed." She felt it would be easier to live if polygyny were something not to feel ashamed about. Hamina Ibrahima, who chose to become a second wife and was very happy in her marriage, described what needed to happen for the women who suffer in polygamy.

> It is not to say that we eradicate it. We will never be able to do that, but for all the women who suffer, there needs to be a place where they can go to have fun, to identify things, to say things. It's to recognize this po-lygamy—not on the legislative level. One is not going to say, "It is recognized, now, we can have two wives, three wives." No, but to recognize that it is a scourge that exists.

Maliki thought education was key: "The law didn't settle things, we all agree! So rather than adopting a law, perhaps we should have had a campaign [to educate women]." Likewise, Daourina Romouli-Zouhair, a retired government official, explained that many women suffer in polygamy but that it "is not going to end tomorrow or the day after. You know, as a joke, I say that polygamy exists in Mayotte as it exists in mainland France, but over there, it's called having a 'mistress.'" According to Romouli-Zouhair, one must nurture women's associations: "So, it's making moms work to be independent and no longer depend on their husbands. . . . Women's associations lead the fight. We also include the young men, because you can't just take the women aside and leave the men out." The key, according to many of my participants such as Romouli-Zouhair, is recognizing that polygyny will continue and supporting women in plural unions so that they can have better lives. Rather than organizing to fight for or against polygamy, my participants described counterpractices that would allow the Mahorais to choose the families they desire regardless of French law. Many in Mayotte accepted polygyny's persistence, either as a family form they preferred or as something that would likely not disappear. Likewise, the fact that polygyny persists in metropolitan France was also tolerated, even if it no longer existed on paper. In metropolitan France some seek to eradicate polygamy's de facto forms and others say, like the Mahorais men who protested at the prefecture, "Why not polygamy?"

"ENDING" POLYGAMY IN FRANCE

As discussed in previous chapters, many of the participants in France described the violence of the Pasqua law that made it illegal to live in a polygynous family, especially given that France had allowed family reunification of polygynous wives in the 1970s and 1980s. When I interviewed Aissata, an association director, one of her colleagues who was present stated, "We find that they are violent, these laws. I do not know if elsewhere polygamy is treated under the same conditions. . . . Here, we only see polygamy, but there is worse than that." In her view the issue of polygamy has often garnered too much focus, and general violence has a much worse impact on immigrant women, including anti-immigrant sentiment in French society.

Although the law was described by many as draconian, some African women led the way in rallying for a law to end polygamy in France. Claudette Bodin, co-founder of Afrique Partenaire Service, explained that several women came to her saying, "Claudette, we don't want our husbands bringing second wives here." She replied, "Yes, but what do you want me to do?" Their response: "Ah, but you have to do something and . . . everything." For Bodin, this was not an issue that she initially wanted to take on: "These women really made me act, because before I tended to say that you shouldn't interfere too much with the cultural systems of other people." Her strategy was to organize around the idea of not having two wives in the same dwelling. She explained that they "did a whole campaign on polygamy issues." Agence France-Presse, an international news agency headquartered in Paris, picked up the story and passed it on. Claudette stated,

"We had a whole media campaign—radio, television, the BBC in England, in Germany, etc."

Bodin personally did not judge whether polygyny was good or bad. "I think that all customs relate to the environment in which we live." She felt that there were conditions in which polygyny made sense. However, she came to understand that living it in France was difficult.

> And, even if the people were very poor, [there were] never two women in the same house [in Africa], because including in the village, a man takes a second wife, and first builds her a hut in the ground—a detached house. Never two wives in the same house. That was the custom. Then, well, in the Qur'an, [a man can marry] up to four women. But you still must read the rest: "Provided you can give them the same living conditions for everyone." That was not possible here [in France]. So, we started campaigning at the request of the African women against polygamy in France. Not against polygamy but against polygamy in France.

The idea of never two wives in the same house and the religious requirement to treat all wives equally helped to distinguish the campaign as one that was not targeting polygyny in general but instead the way it was lived in France.

Bodin recounted how at a meeting in Seine-Saint-Denis, a suburb of Paris where many immigrants live, she had a conversation with the prefect, who reproached her and her co-founder. He told her, "It looks like basically you don't condemn polygamy." She confirmed, "Indeed, we do not condemn polygamy. It's people's own business. If a woman prefers to have a bond with the father of her children, even though she doesn't live with him, it might even be positive." Anthropologist Catherine Quiminal, who had worked with Bodin on the issue, stated, "There were quite a few African women who called for the ban." She described how many of the women had lived in France for several years, "and suddenly they had a concubine arriving. So, that for them was horrible. . . . Moreover, it was done in secret. They weren't warned." For Quiminal, it was not a problem to ban polygamy in France, "but it's more how you do it. What are the terms of this ban?" According to Quiminal, the fact that the ban focused on denying residence permits benefited no one and cut off resources, especially to second wives.

As Jacques Barou recounted in the quote at the beginning of this chapter, men were upset by the fact that their polygynous families were banned in France when they were legally married in their country of origin. However, they did not organize to fight against the law. Association director Aissata recounted how many polygynous husbands resisted the policy of decohabitation and especially the requirement of divorcing all wives but one. Over time, some men changed their perspective when they realized that despite the divorce on paper, they could continue to maintain their families in different residences. She described one man as follows: "I still remember, he was very old. He said 'I, at the beginning, refused to move out, but today we are happy.'" Her colleague explained that this trajectory was followed by other men.

> You should know that we work in a neighborhood where there were a lot of polygamists. Initially, many came to say that it was [our association] that trained their wives to divorce. Today, these same people are the ones who come and say, "Oh, thank you! We didn't know at first how much better it would be. Before, everyone together. The ladies in the house were not talking to each other. There were conflicts between the children."

For many families the arduous process of undertaking the decohabitation paid off. And women's associations were key in helping these families.

Other interviewees spoke to the ways that men adapted to rather than fought the law. For example, Tandia Bakari, a man in his 60s from Mauritania who has one wife there and one in France, explained that neither of his marriages were official in France. From the perspective of French law, his wives are "concubines" or "mistresses": "What is marriage here in Europe? It's when you get married in the town hall, but if you have a relationship with another woman, you are not married. So that is why there is a difference in understanding of the term *marriage* between the two communities." He explained that the law creates tensions.

> When one carves out a law for a category of society, knowing that what they practice may be practiced in [their] country without it being prohibited by a law, one only creates tensions between people. Because someone can be like, "This is a law that only concerns me." I think it must

be phrased differently. Because today, if the Pasqua law bans polygamy, Muslims can say they banned it just for us Muslims. And that is not good.

Bakari told me that he was involved with men's associations in France and that, even though he did not agree with the law, he encouraged men to follow it: "As much as you say that I can marry four or five wives, it has to be done according to the laws here." The law says that you are only married if you register your wives at the town hall. "Since you, traditionally or religiously, are allowed to get married without paperwork, you can live in cohabitation." This ability to twist the law to meet men's needs infuriates some activists who are fighting against polygamy in France.

Although some African women rallied in the 1990s to ban polygamy in France, a few associations led by women of color began organizing much later to end polygamy. One concern is the de facto polygamy that Bakari described in which men married multiple wives religiously, in unions that were not recognized by the state. Awa Ba is an activist born in Senegal and raised in a polygynous family. She recounted that her family worked well overall as she grew up, although jealousies and some verbal abuse did arise. Her opinion of polygamy changed when Aby, her older sister who lived in Senegal, found out that her husband of almost twenty years had married another woman in Gambia and had a child with her. He had kept his second wife secret for five years, until the day that this woman called Aby's house demanding to speak to her husband. Aby was devastated, according to Ba. After Aby died, years later, Awa Ba wrote a book, *Polygamie: La douleur des femmes* (Polygamy: The Suffering of Women), and began an association in 2013, En Finir avec la Polygamie (End Polygamy). She stated:

> What I would like above all through this association is to make known and recognize the pain of women locked in polygamous marriages. In France, little is said about it because polygamy is only practiced among foreigners; in Senegal, and everywhere else where it is common, polygamous marriages are not mentioned since they are the norm.

Ba's goal is to work in countries where polygamy is the norm to end the practice but also to shine light on the problems in France. For her, the French law is not efficacious because it still allows men to marry multiple wives religiously: "They must come up with a law that fights against these religious marriages. If they don't take care of these marriages, they won't be able to fight polygamy." For her, the policy of decohabitation still allows the men to shuttle to each wife's residence, continuing the practice that on paper has ended. She would like to see these men receive a penalty or a fine. Ba advocates for a law that would be similar to the current law in Utah, which makes bigamy an infraction (not a felony) to *purport* to marry another individual when a person is legally married to another individual. However, in Utah, as we have seen, this law was not effective in ending the practice, even when it was a felony.

Ba's association as well as associations such as Ni Putes Ni Soumises (Neither Whores nor Submissives) have been the most vocal proponents to end polygamy in France and elsewhere. In contrast, no movements have been organized to fight against prohibiting it. When the debate over same-gender marriage occurred, there were no protests speaking in favor of polygamy like those that occurred in Mayotte. Neither have there been protests over the policy of decohabitation. In many ways this lack of activism is not surprising. Most of the population that practices polygyny consists of immigrants and people of color who are vulnerable to having their papers retracted or who could be deported. The fact that polygyny in France is not homegrown but migratory makes it easy to view it as marginal and problematic. Most people I interviewed expressed that polygamy should be illegal in France. Many pointed to the hypocritical acceptance of French men's mistresses as acceptable even if frowned on, but this criticism did not lead to any engagement with the idea that polygamy might be a type of family that some prefer. Because many African women rallied against it, as well as evidence that it is often thrust upon women without their knowledge or choice, polygamy became a hard sell.

In France the debate over monogamy has just begun. Whereas movements in favor of nonmonogamies have flourished in many parts of the world, such movements have been slow to take root in France. I interviewed Catherine Ternaux, who wrote *La polygamie, pourquoi pas* (Polygamy, Why Not?) in 2012. She told me that she decided to write a book on polygamy because it is a forbidden topic: "It is still very taboo in France!" The reason for this is partly polygamy's association with Islam and partly the way the subject has been politicized. She stated, "Sometimes, we [my partner and

I] talked about it with friends, and I noticed that there was immediately a tension, a difficulty, because my point was to say, 'Well, finally, why would polygamy be reprehensible? Why monogamy?'" She recounted her childhood experience of her parents' divorce when she was small and the fact that her father later explained that "when he left my mother for another woman, he still loved my mother." According to Ternaux, in our society you must choose: "That made me wonder about this divorce requirement." In addition, she had a friend who lived in a situation of "hidden polygamy," moving between two homes for the past ten years. This woman's husband was either unaware or did not want to know.

Ternaux was particularly interested in questioning the norm of marriage. As she was writing her book, people open to the idea of nonmonogamy would ask her, "But why marriage? Polyamory can be experienced outside of marriage." Ternaux explained, "What interested me, precisely, was to question marriage, the institution, the society." There are blended families now, and the landscape of marriage and family has changed. Based on this, she asked, "Well, why not? . . . Why, ultimately, are people forced to experience these situations in a hidden, very unofficial way?" She recounted, "I was surprised to find that this subject was discussed in the eighteenth century, a very long time ago. . . . And then, it was not addressed again for over a hundred years." Her research and contemplation led her to conclude: "I haven't come up with an argument that would make polygamy impossible." In terms of the current law, she explained, "The immigrants who are in a polygamous situation, I find it repressive for them. I think it's quite terrible." Ternaux was one of the few people I interviewed in France who provided an expansive critique of the institution of marriage in connection to polygamy. For her, part of the problem has been the conflation of polygamy with Islam in France. She stated that the goal should be to fight against gender inegalitarianism and not polygamy itself. In France and Mayotte the question of polygamy is connected to African populations. It is an issue automatically racialized and connected to France's colonialist past in complicated ways, making the simple question "Why not?" inconceivable. In the United States, among a population that is mostly white, the idea of why not has not only been posed but also become a full-fledged social movement.

COMING OUT OF THE POLYGAMY CLOSET IN THE UNITED STATES

In Utah activists on both sides of the issue have turned to the state to argue for either stricter prosecution of polygamy or decriminalization. Over time a legal consciousness developed among those who were for and against its practice; activists on both sides turned to the law as a solution to the problem of polygyny. In the late 1990s an anti-polygamy movement, Tapestry of Polygamy (later Tapestry Against Polygamy), started. Vicky Prunty and Rowenna Erickson were two of the prominent founders. Their stories appear in a book by Andrea Moore-Emmett, an award-winning journalist who wrote *God's Brothel* (2004) about the lives of women who left polygamy. Prunty was raised Mormon and married Gary Batchelor at age 18 at the Mormon Temple in Salt Lake City, abandoning her plans to attend Brigham Young University.[12] The couple became involved in fundamentalist Mormonism, and Gary eventually married Mary when Prunty was pregnant with their fourth child. In her account in *God's Brothel*, Prunty states that she "deeply loved" her sister wife but found it increasingly difficult to share her husband. After leaving the marriage, Prunty made it a goal to start an organization to help women who leave polygamy. For her, "Women have no safety net and no control over the poverty and homelessness waiting if they leave."[13]

Rowenna Erickson was raised in the Kingston group, or the Latter-Day Church of Christ. In her account in *God's Brothel*, she recounts stories of incest and misery that she experienced while growing up and marrying the son of the group's founder, Charles Eldon Kingston. Her husband also married her sister. She finally left her plural family at age 57, describing the sexual abuse she had experienced during her thirty-seven years of marriage. Erickson died in 2018. When I interviewed Prunty, she described creating Tapestry with Erickson.

> We started it as Tapestry of Polygamy—Carole King's "Tapestry." And just because there were so many similarities in stories that we would hear and share. And yet, the patterns were different too. It was like we were unraveling this tapestry of polygamy and kind of creating a new life. So, later we realized that it was kind of ambiguous, the name, because I would get calls from polygamists, saying, "Can you help me?" "No, we can't." So, we decided to put "against" instead of "of."

Prunty talked about her activism to educate senators and other public officials in Utah on the consequences of polygamy. According to her, "We helped many people, and it's really hard to get people to go public with their stories when they are so humiliated." Tapestry commissioned *God's Brothel* and helped identify women to share their stories. According to Prunty, Tapestry was able to help many women who left polygamy and to shift the conversation about polygamy in Utah to recognize the abuses that were taking place. Prunty and Erickson's activism later spurred other groups to take up the mantel, such as Sound Choices Coalition, founded by Kristyn Decker, the daughter of the late prophet of the Apostolic United Brethren. In 2003 she ended her 33-year marriage and left polygamy. She authored *Fifty Years in Polygamy: Big Secrets and Little White Lies.*[14]

I interviewed Mary and Gary Batchelor, who recognized that the activism of Tapestry pushed polygamists to "step up publicly." Gary stated:

> Because [Tapestry] did that, that became the impetus for us to say, "Enough is enough," and it really did a lot in terms of getting polygamists from all walks to come out of the shadows and say, "Look, this is who we are. We're good people, we have good children, we believe in education, we don't believe in abuse, we don't believe in underage marriages, and we want people to be aware of that." So, I think Mary [Batchelor] in a way was the vanguard of that. She and some other ladies—Anne Wilde, Linda Kelsch, Marianne Watson—they wrote a book [*Voices in Harmony* (2000)], and they created an organization called Principle Voices. So, in a way, it parried a lot of the dark, invective.

Many of the pro-polygamy advocates I interviewed acknowledged that Tapestry's activism was the basis for the emergence of the pro-polygamy movement. Moreover, according to Mary, Tapestry shed light on the crimes that needed to be prosecuted: "I think there was good that came out of Tapestry because there were abuses." She described the case of Tom Green, who was convicted in 2001 of bigamy and child rape. "None of us knew that he had married Linda at 13, got her pregnant. We didn't know that. That came out in court, you know, so there are things that you had no idea it's going on, unfortunately." Those I interviewed were unanimous in their support of fighting against abuses, and this became one of the central themes that the pro-polygamy movement embraced: to end abuse but not polygamy itself.

A number of researchers have examined the ways that opposing movements shape and sustain one other.[15] The foundational and organizational structures of movements are important in their ability to fight against their opposition, and legislation can be a significant factor in shaping the ability to acquire resources and affect public opinion.[16] Tapestry turned to the Utah legislature to educate public officials on polygamy's harms, but Principle Voices sought to provide a different perspective on polygyny other than the idea that it is synonymous with abuse. This meant organizing the various fundamentalist groups to work together. One of the leaders described the first meeting in her house, organized by the women leaders of Principle Voices.

> Women unified the diverse polygamous groups in Utah. We had the first meeting here. Principle Voices sponsored it, the four of us. And we invited the leaders or key people from each of the groups. We had twenty-four people in my living room. When they walked in to see people from—I don't know how to explain that—it's just like if you had a family that had been separated and were antagonistic and hadn't got together and didn't want anything to do with each other, and all of a sudden, they are walking into a room and hugging each other and so glad to see each other.... Would you believe women brought these priesthood leaders together? That's a switch! Because these priesthood leaders, they are macho men, and they don't want to be told what to do by women.

Mary Batchelor, Linda Kelsch, Marianne Watson, and Anne Wilde were educated and independent, and they began to lobby politicians to decriminalize polygamy. Mary told me about how David Zolman, a member of the Utah House of Representatives from 2001 to 2003, provided a roadmap for their activism: "We held a meeting with David Zolman to come and talk, and we invited a ton of polygamists to come. He told us, 'If you people want rights, you have to fight for them. And you can't commit incest, you can't mess with underage girls.'" This began a campaign to ensure that different groups did not break the law and practice underage marriage.

Several participants discussed the importance of activism in the face of what appeared to be a crackdown on plural families as a result of the trial of Tom Green and concern over polygamy's stain on the reputation of Utah in hosting the Winter Olympics in 2002. Anne Wilde recounted how twelve women went to the capitol to protest a new bill that would have made it a third-degree felony for parents to permit a minor child to enter an unlawful marriage or for someone to solemnize a union between a woman and a man who was already married. Then Democratic Utah senator Ron Allen sponsored the bill, declaring the need to fight human rights violations in closed polygamist communities.[17] The women met with legislators to "explain the reasons why this was not a good thing, taking away our rights in our own home," Anne Wilde recounted.

Mary Batchelor was invited to debate Ron Allen by the Women's Legislative Study Group. She related her words during the debate: "I can speak to this from the perspective of a woman, and [Ron Allen] is not a woman. I can tell you the impact it will have on me, as a consenting adult. At my age, I should have the right to choose the person that I want to live with, and how to construct my own family." When the bill was presented at a judiciary committee meeting, over a hundred people attended to protest. Anne Wilde stated, "It was the most people that had ever come before a judiciary committee in the history of Utah politics for or against a bill. It was very impressive!" According to Mary Batchelor, the debate pushed Allen to offer a friendly amendment that "gave us everything we asked for." She described that the women decided to support the amended bill, which reduced the penalty for performing illegal marriages from a felony to a misdemeanor. The amended bill passed. Mary discussed the media's astonishment that the women supported it: "They are hailing victory, but we don't really understand why because this is an anti-polygamy bill!" For Mary, the bill was not anti-polygamy but anti-abuse. She stated, "Look, I can't say we got everything we wanted. They modified the existing statute and made it a misdemeanor for someone to perform a void marriage." The bill designated that a third-degree felony applied only if one performed a polygamist marriage with a minor. "And frankly, we held that as a victory because that's the first improvement in any law applying to polygamy since the laws were passed against polygamy in this country. This was the first improvement." Passage of the bill helped to reinforce their message that polygamy and abuse are not synonymous.

Protesting the bill provided the first opportunity for polygamists to present themselves to the media. Mary Batchelor described how a local TV journalist asked her, "Are all these guys polygamists?" When she told him they were, he exclaimed, "I have never seen so many polygamists in one place." The activism of these women motivated others to act. Randy, a religious leader in Centennial Park, told me about how his community came to support activism for plural marriage. He recounted seeing women on TV protesting the proposed law.

> One day I was watching the news, Salt Lake channel, and there's, I think, three or four ladies up at the capital with paper sacks over their head and little eye slits, with their banners, you know? And they were campaigning for freedom of choice to live plural marriage. And we looked at that, and we said, "You brave women. We want to be brave with you."

Their chance came in 2003. The increasing debate over polygamy led Mark Shurtleff to organize a "polygamy summit" in southern Utah with then Arizona governor Terry Goddard to address the question of how to help women who want to leave abusive polygamous households. The summit was criticized because it invited anti-polygamy activists without inviting practitioners of plural marriage from the surrounding communities in Hildale, Utah, and Colorado City and Centennial Park, Arizona.[18] Paul Murphy, then director of communications and policy, explained, "And so, they invited people like Tapestry and social services, everybody that supposedly had a say about polygamy, but they didn't invite any polygamists. And so, they had a law enforcement meeting and a broad social issues meeting. And more than 100 women from Centennial Park showed up at the meeting, uninvited!" Hannah, one of the plural wives who attended, described the experience.

> Well, we packed the room so full that they decided they better adjourn and get a bigger room. . . . I remember one lady. She wasn't born and raised here, and she had converted at the age of 24 and was a plural wife. And she was not going to take this sitting down. And she wanted to speak, and so she went up to the mic when they gave us an opportunity to speak, and she just gave it to them. She said, "This is America, and I chose to marry the man I married because I love the man I married." She said, "And no one can tell me who I should marry. You don't have the right to tell me who I can love."

This first summit was transformational according to the Centennial Park members I interviewed. Randy stated that the summit began the Centennial Park Action Committee (CPAC), whose goal is to "deliver to the public a correct view of the polygamous lifestyle . . . with the objectives of dispelling popular stereotypes commonly held by people at large, [and] of defeating unjust laws which currently exist aimed at the polygamous minority."[19] CPAC has worked closely with other groups to get its message out.

Members of polygamist communities felt empowered to protest laws they felt were discriminatory. The fact that most of these individuals are white allowed them to easily organize and make their case that "we are not very different from you." To do this, they drew on the ideas and language of the LGBTQ movement, espousing the idea of a right to sexual and familial privacy. When I interviewed Harper, she told me how she admired the activism of LGBTQ people to fight for their right to marry: "I appreciate anyone in an alternative lifestyle that stands up and says, 'We have the right to live this way.' Because they do. And we do. And I am just full of gratitude for everyone that stands up for their rights." She described having "very dear friends" who were lesbians and gay men and that, for her, the slippery slope "is not so slippery." She said, "I don't know if they like to be lumped into the same boat with me as much as I like to be lumped into it with them. But I appreciate it." Hannah recounted her use of what became a well-known phrase after the polygamy summit: "Don't talk about us without us." She further elaborated: "Don't go in there behind closed doors and try to figure out our problems."

Protesting closed doors and encouraging people to come out of the closet became a way to describe polygamists' decision to be public.[20] Linda Kelsch discussed the fact that prohibition has kept people in the closet: "If you decriminalize polygamy, people will come out! The only reason they must hide is because they're afraid they will be arrested. So, if you decriminalize it, you can regulate it." Likewise, Hannah said, "I think it's time for us to open our doors and get our head out of the sand and stand up and say, 'This is the life we have chosen, and this is how we live, and it's really not that much different than yours.'" Randy explained, "We're standing up and we're saying what we believe, we're defending our position openly, and we're more or less out of the closet." Even public officials referred to the need for polygamists to come out of the closet. Mark Shurtleff described the need for polygamists to be public.

> But then, these polygamists said they wanted to change things. And my advice to them, "You either got to do it in court, or you have to get the legislature to do it. The biggest problem Warren Jeffs has is the secrecy, is the isolation, is doing things behind closed doors. That not only allows him to abuse people's rights but also breeds distrust and fear in everybody else. Come out of the closet, so to speak. Get out in public, go to the legislature.

This quote is remarkable coming from someone whose main duty had been to enforce the law that banned polygamy. However, he understood the importance of working with polygamist communities to fight against abuses. David Zolman explained that many wanted to keep the polygamy door shut: "Ohhhh! So, this society, which has been closed for a hundred years, I am starting to open the door to this closed closet, and there's a little odor coming from the room." He recounted how others cried, "Don't open that door! It stinks in there!" His response, "No, open the door so we can get it aired out. Let's get them back in society." The closet serves as a helpful metaphor to leave behind secrecy, just as it was for the LGBTQ movement.

As citizens who adhere to a contested form of Christianity, fundamentalist Mormon polygamists in the United States may be family outlaws, but they have more power to "come out" and fight for their rights. Joe Darger, who chairs the Principle Rights Coalition, a group that grew out of Principle Voices to fight for decriminalization, explained that it was "just educating people both within the culture and out. It's really bridging what's been an underground secretive culture and bridging that communication and empowering people and understanding." As white American citizens, fundamentalist Mormons were able to challenge dominant cultural norms of monogamy, even after the state reinstituted stricter laws that made participating in a plural marriage a felony in 2017. One Utah senator who I interviewed discussed the idea that "the polygamists are us."

> Yeah, these people are us! The way that Utah looks at the polygamist communities is the way the whole rest of the world looks at Mormons. So, what the hell? Why don't you lead by example? How would you like to be

treated? Because it will come down to that someday, maybe. So, maybe growing up inside the Mormon state, Utah community, they didn't really see that.

His words point to the fact that mainstream Mormons who are not fundamentalists and do not practice plural marriage also experience stigma and discrimination. After the polygamy summit in 2003 Mark Shurtleff began the Safety Net Committee. The goal was to prioritize the special needs and concerns of those living in fundamentalist communities, such as safety, collaboration, education, and outreach. Even though anti-polygamist groups protested, the meetings included polygamist representatives from different communities.

These efforts helped many polygamists to come out publicly, but others discussed the fear they still felt, even during the short period when polygamy was essentially decriminalized in 2015 and 2016. Matt described how—even after the *Waddoups* decision that decriminalized polygamy—the practice may never become as socially accepted as LGBTQ rights.

> The analogy I use is, we're like the dog that has been chained up and beaten for so long in the yard, that we finally have the chain unleashed, and we're not going anywhere, and we're still afraid we're going to get beaten. We didn't realize the chain has been unleashed. As a people, we are very, very cautious. You didn't see us marching in the streets with that decision. You didn't see people out there like, "This is okay." Because we don't have the social acceptance. The gay marriage movement, even if it was only half [of the population], they still had enough support. We're not going to get that.

Charlotte elaborated: "No polygamy parade!" Still, as more and more people come out, there is hope that one day there will be social acceptance. The Williams family participated in a reality TV show, *My Five Wives*. They described their decision to come out on national television. According to Brady, "Yeah, we decided to do this as an important enough thing that we should take that risk for the sake of our children." Nonie added, "Not just for our children, I think, for the sake of society. I think my choice came to not just for my family, but for all those polygamist families that are out there, that are oppressed by the stupid laws [*laughs*]." In response to my question about how they would answer people who think that polygamy needs to be illegal because of what goes on in closed societies, she stated, "They created the society, they created the law, they created the closed society." Michael Cawley and his three wives were one of the families who participated in the documentary *Polygamy, USA*. For him, "The more we can share, and the more people can see, and understand, they can make their own judgment about [polygamy]. But what they don't know, it's left up to the imagination and people's imaginations get filled in with whatever craziness or reality they have experienced." Terry and his two wives discussed their hope for a better future: "I am very, very interested in decriminalization because it's going to change the stigma over time, right? Before too long, you'll have a sitcom with a polygamist family as neighbors." This hope motivated many to take risks that felt scary, because being public could mean more scrutiny of their parenting and family lives. However, the hard work to make it known that "a lot of polygamists are just normal people in mainstream society" ultimately led to polygamy's decriminalization in the state of Utah in 2020.

In examining the ways that people in different countries have organized to fight for or against polygamy, we must return to the multiple ways that polygamies are lived. For vulnerable immigrant populations of color, organizing to fight for a forbidden intimacy that marks their otherness was not feasible. When polygyny is lived as homegrown in Mayotte, people participate in counterpractices that ignore the law and form their own families of choice. For women who have suffered in polygynous relationships or who ended up in a polygynous marriage against their will, there is broader support among feminist groups and mainstream society to hear their voices. However, as a racial project in the United States, the prohibition of polygamy enables people who "look like us"—white and citizens—to form a legal consciousness concerning what they view to be unjust laws that prohibit their family. Just as same-gender couples fought for their right to have their families recognized legally, polygamists in Utah formed their collective identity on the idea of rights and drew self-consciously from the LGBTQ movement to frame their discourses in ways that can resonate in mainstream society. *Sister Wives* features Kody Brown telling us why they chose plural marriage: "Love should be multiplied not divided." These simple words reflect the concerns of many of my interviewees, who focused on the importance of seeing polygyny as an opportunity for more love (and sometimes more strife too). The series also shed light on the evolution of the Brown family's legal consciousness, as they fled Utah to avoid possible prosecution for coming out on public television, to the moment when Kody and Robyn announced to their children in episode 6 of the fifteenth season that Utah had essentially decriminalized polygamy for consenting adults. This legal consciousness became key to motivating polygamists to fight for their right to live polygyny.

CONCLUSION
IF YES TO SAME-GENDER MARRIAGE, WHY NO TO POLYGAMY?

I think a lot of these issues are very much about bias and discrimination, and about tolerance. I think the issue of polygamy is very much about tolerance, or that's what we think it should be about. That being accepting of social arrangements that may seem very different or very contrary to the Canadian norm, but nonetheless, making room in society so people can pursue what they feel is the good life.
—*Grace Pastine, litigation director, British Columbia Civil Liberties Association*

It may be true that the mild form of polygamy still has these bad mathematical effects, so polyamory will still have these bad mathematical effects. But [polygamy] doesn't perpetuate and spread and get traction until it relies on some authority and purports to be binding. And then it seems to just take and spin out of control. And then the authority just becomes more authoritarian, the binding becomes more iron clad, and you get [pauses] . . . You know what we said in the argument that Bountiful didn't invent polygamy, polygamy invented Bountiful.
—*Craig Jones, lead counsel for the attorney general of British Columbia in the polygamy reference case*

THE POLYGAMY REFERENCE CASE IN British Columbia, Canada, crystallizes the debate over polygamy and the regulation of forbidden intimacies. Putting polygamy on trial pitted those who view it as an acceptable "social arrangement" when it does not involve harmful practices, such as underage or forced marriage, against those who view it as fundamentally and unquestionably "objectionable," harmful not only to those involved but to society itself. One longtime anti-polygamy advocate summed up the latter perspective: "Monogamy supports a democratic society. Polygamy does not support a democratic society!" The argument that polygamy is inherently anti-democratic was a dominant theme throughout the trial, and there was little recognition of the problematic ways that purported Western ideals of superior monogamy tainted this perspective. In his decision Justice Bauman sided with the attorneys general in confirming that prohibiting polygamy "has been linked, both temporally and philosophically, with the rise of democracy and its attendant values of liberty and equality."[1] This revisionist history, which elevates monogamy as a causal factor in the emergence of the democratic state, rests on an imperial gaze that neglects the hierarchical and gender inegalitarian history and structure of monogamous marriage. It also exemplifies the racial project of governing forbidden intimacies that enables states to define themselves against a repudiated, racialized other.

Considering this racial project, the decriminalization perspective did not stand much chance of succeeding in the polygamy reference case. How and why should one accept tyranny and anti-democratic practices such as polygamy in "enlightened" societies such as Canada? Certainly, some may have asked similar questions when reading some of the stories I have recounted in this book. Polygamy, as it is broadly practiced as polygyny, is largely patriarchal and appears to offend feminist ideals of gender egalitarianism in family life. The goal of my research has been to complicate this narrative by presenting the ways that *polygamies* are lived according to labyrinthine love and in different social and structural contexts. This allows for polygyny to be included in a spectrum of practices of nonmonogamies rather than singled out as something that "seems to just take and spin out of control" and become "iron clad," as lawyer Craig Jones characterizes it. When male domination flourishes unchecked in polygynous households and/or groups, women and children can be forced to submit to polygyny in ways that are disempowering and harmful. The leadership of Warren Jeffs offers a good example of a hierarchical community that demands nondeviating devotion to a prophet who perpetrated many crimes—underage and forced marriages and sexual assault, among others. As argued previously, such abuses are not necessarily tied to polygynous communities but can be found in other groups that demand obedience, especially in the context of religious belief. Even in hierarchal groups that perpetrate abuse, polygyny can be lived in a nonabusive manner. The interviews I conducted with people who helped the FLDS and the time I spent volunteering to distribute food and clothes to FLDS women and children confirmed for me these women's commitment to their families and their desire to nurture close bonds among wives, even as Warren Jeffs sowed seeds of discord. In all three countries and Mayotte, I found strong evidence of families who made polygyny work, even under extreme government regulation and challenges of housing and space.

By way of conclusion, in this chapter I return to considering how polygyny as a forbidden intimacy is regulated in the context of other "progressive" intimacies that have become more accepted: same-gender marriage and polyamory. I reflect on the racial projects I have outlined in this book and the ways that racialized mononormativity enables states to outlaw polygamy and solidify a national identity of enlightened "Western" values. Next, I turn to the question of women's rights, suspect agency, and legal jeopardy. On the one hand is the argument that prohibiting polygamy is necessary to protect women's rights against the kinds of exploitative practices that can accompany it: taking another wife without the consent of the first, underage and forced marriages, abuses children may experience at the hands of other wives. In addition, some argue that polygyny offends gender equality in general by allowing men to marry multiple wives but not providing the same option to women to marry multiple partners. On the other side is the argument that some women prefer polygyny, that some children benefit from having more than one mother, that criminalizing polygamy makes it harder to report abuse, and that people should have the ability to live in their families of choice. This section considers the consequences of this debate that equates gender egalitarianism with progress and polygyny with regression. Finally, I consider the question of decriminalization, arguing that we need to incorporate intersectionality to better formulate our reasoning behind polygamy's prohibition.

RACIAL PROJECTS IN GOVERNING FORBIDDEN INTIMACIES

France, the United States, and Canada have pursued different racial projects to define their national identities based on a conception of forbidden intimacies, often understood as "barbaric" and "uncivilized." At times, these pursuits have been explicit, at other times implicit. In each case the subtext is grounded in notions of superior Western values that enable each country to turn attention away from their own problematic and inegalitarian histories and laws. We cannot understand the current ways that forbidden intimacies are racialized and regulated without looking to the past. In the mid-nineteenth century monogamous conjugal norms provided the context for "imperial consolidation of the nation-state."[2] A range of scholars have demonstrated that discourses from this period rely on a "cult of domesticity," which is grounded in imperialist and racialized understandings of family and nation.[3] These discourses "not only monitor[ed] the borders between the civilized and the savage but also regulat[ed] traces of the savage within."[4] Regulating forbidden intimacies in the context of an imperialist logic brought together domestic, national, and imperial ideals of the nuclear family that were important in the "making of racial categories and in the management of imperial rule."[5] At the time, nation-states easily justified laws and policies to circumscribe forbidden intimacies such as polygyny by relying on the idea of its savagery.

I was surprised to find extensive racialized discourses and justifications concerning polygyny persisting in the twenty-first century, even in the context of important theoretical developments of the past fifty years that have succinctly analyzed the racism that propels such projects, such as Edward Said's concept of orientalism, a way of seeing that imagines and distorts differences of Arab peoples and cultures compared with Western cultures.[6] All three countries rely on similar discourses that point to the "savagery" of polygyny. However, the most striking example is the polygamy reference case in British Columbia, in which lawyers and the Supreme Court justice argued for the importance of monogamy to uphold democracy. Often, these ideas migrate across borders. Former Utah attorney general Mark Shurtleff called the FLDS the American Taliban, referring to women's "subjugation" that takes place because of polygamy. This idea crossed the border to Canada when Daphne Bramham equated the Taliban and the FLDS in her book. She described a 2001 speech by George W. Bush that referred to the Taliban imprisoning Afghanistan women in their homes and denying them access to health care and education: "The Bushes were referring to the Taliban in Afghanistan, but they might as well have been talking about women and children in the United States and Canada living under the tyranny of the Fundamentalist Church of Jesus Christ of Latter Day Saints (FLDS), the largest polygamous sect in North America."[7] What are the consequences of these racial projects, and how does each country rely on the others to bolster these projects?

France's racial project of regulating polygyny is connected to its history of colonialism in North and West Africa. In Europe in general, understandings of polygyny have been shaped by the Western obsession with the harem. In the eighteenth and nineteenth centuries in France, cultural representations in art and literature were dominated by images of the Orient as other, exciting the male gaze and offering a counterpart to France's own national and political identity.[8] Western literature has portrayed harem women as passive objects and depicts the harem's physical and social spaces in phantasmic terms. The image of secluded harem women fueled the state's desire to defend native women who became the *"object* of protection,"* justifying a nation-building project to bring the "superior system of Christian marriage to the uncivilized natives."[9] Polygyny was one of the reasons for France's civilizing mission of its colonies in the late nineteenth and early twentieth centuries.[10] It came to shape the meaning of Muslimness, representing the ultimate difficulty of applying French law to Muslim subjects. The solution was to provide colonial subjects with some rights while denying the possibility for citizenship.[11] Thus polygyny enabled the French government to regulate citizenship based on racialized forbidden intimacies that condemned colonial subjects for their "barbaric" culture and family organization.

I have documented how this racial project persists in present-day France in policies used to regulate polygynous populations. In early years France had a more liberal approach that allowed polygynous family reunification, even if subsequent wives were not entitled to all social benefits. With rising anti-immigrant sentiment, France's then interior minister Charles Pasqua created and passed laws with the goal, as he expressed in an interview, of attaining "zero immigration."[12] Given the colonial history of France's focus on polygyny as a method to define national belonging, it is perhaps not surprising that that the Pasqua law had a focus on polygamy. With the passage of that statute, only one spouse of a French immigrant would be issued a spousal and work visa and the family would be subject to deportation unless they legally divorced and physically separated, with each wife living separately (decohabitation). Long-standing French law protects immigrants with children born in France from deportation, but many immigrants lost work permits and/or had to renew temporary visas every year. In this schema polygyny was a strategy to control citizenship and belonging. Past histories of colonialism also set the terms for contemporary discourses that marked nonwhite populations as other when associated with polygamy. Participants working with immigrant populations discussed the problematic way that officials would automatically mark "polygamous" on immigration forms for African men, even if they were not. In France's eyes, immigrants from Africa are seen as always potentially polygamous.

Although its racial project has determined national belonging and citizenship status based on being or potentially being polygynous, France has demonstrated administrative ambivalence in its regulation of polygyny. Its compromise to allow polygynous women to remain on the territory, rehousing them to live apart from their husbands, might be seen as a combination of punishment and reward. On the one hand, they must divorce their husbands, at least on paper, or lose their residence permits. On the other hand, they are aided in finding a more spacious apartment. Unfortunately, these policies have been applied unevenly and inconsistently, with some families suffering more than others. In some cases wives have been moved close by to allow the families to continue to see each other with ease. In others cases the wives are relocated far away, making it more difficult for the husband to shuttle between wives. Decohabitation is often arduous, and families that are unable or decide not to do it have been pushed into hiding, particularly the secondary wives, who sometimes have no legal presence in France.

France's racial project also focused on polygyny in Mayotte as a condition for it to become an overseas department and for the Mahorais to become French citizens. Polygamy was progressively banned in Mayotte beginning in 2005. Even though France did recognize former polygynous unions performed before 2005 if they were registered, I heard from many Mahorais that they were not interested in state recognition of their polygynous households. Before 2010, the *cadis* (Muslim notaries and magistrates) oversaw the local laws that were governed by custom and the rules of Sunni Islam, including performing polygynous unions. After 2010 France removed the *cadis'* official functions and made them nothing more than mediators; however, imams performed polygynous unions. Thus most of the participants I interviewed confirmed that new polygynous unions continued, especially among the younger generation. France's administrative ambivalence in dealing with polygyny in metropolitan France is reflected in Mayotte as well. Although polygamy is prohibited, little effort has been made to end the practice. Instead, France treats polygyny as if it were no longer a problem to be addressed, except in ancient cases that have been registered. The small group of *cadis* and religious men who protested outside the prefecture to ask, "If yes to gay marriage, why no to polygamy?" raised a question that asks us to carefully consider the racial project that embraces same-gender marriage as mainstream and marks polygamy as other.

France's administrative ambivalence works to stigmatize people of color of the Muslim faith—by creating moral and political panic over polygamy to represent racial otherness—while simultaneously acting as though it has rooted it out, pushing polygynous families underground. Different branches of the government deal with the issue in different ways. The family allowance system has no official way to recognize polygamy after the 1993 law came into effect. It seeks to implement the provisions of decohabitation while keeping the interests of children in the foreground. In other words, families with children who meet the income standards for support will receive that support whether or not in polygynous unions. In contrast to this more liberal policy, French immigration services use polygyny to deny access to citizenship and to permanent residency. I found that even when polygynous families followed all the rules, including divorce and decohabitation, secondary wives were still not able to renew their ten-year residence permit. Polygyny is a minority practice among a minority population in France, but the racial project focusing on polygamy uses this forbidden intimacy to cast doubt on the Muslim population's ability to integrate.

Thus regulating polygyny allows France to reinforce whiteness and non-Muslimness as integral to what it means to be French.

The racial project in the United States differs substantially from that in France. The issue in France concerns mostly people of color of Muslim faith, often from former colonies, where racialization takes place explicitly. In the United States the most visible people who practice polygyny are fundamentalist Mormons and Christians who are white and mostly share Judeo-Christian values with the (now slight) majority population of white Americans. Much less known and/or studied are Muslim African Americans who practice polygyny[13] and immigrants to the United States from countries where polygamy is legal and who quietly practice it, ranging from African immigrants in New York City to Hmong immigrants from Vietnam in Minneapolis.[14] A growing body of legal literature considers the impact of polygamy's prohibition on immigrants and how they live their lives in the United States.[15] These populations appear to live in ways that are more underground than the populations in France, an issue that social scientists must address in future research. For this study I focused on fundamentalist Mormons because they are the population practicing polygyny with the strongest legal and political presence and history in the United States.

The populations that motivate racial projects differ in France and the United States, but some important similarities in the historical roots of their racial projects have influenced the ways that polygyny is understood today. France's civilizing mission to Christianize colonial subjects parallels the United States, which imposed Judeo-Christian marital and work standards on Native populations. In the nineteenth century some U.S. states recognized Native plural marriages.[16] Still, American officials pursued ways to reform kinship systems, which could involve several wives living in different towns, representing "an unintelligible foreignness."[17] The goal of the federal government was to inspire or even force Indians to adopt Christian-model monogamy because it was viewed as important to civilization and morality. This focus on a civilizing mission is not surprising, given European thinkers' writing on the importance of monogamy for civilization. For example, Montesquieu's *Persian Letters* stimulated other Enlightenment thinkers to associate monogamy with political liberty and polygamy with despotism.

The historical similarities between France and the United States in their racial projects diverged as the American federal government had to deal with polygyny among its own white population. Polygamy in the territory of Utah rapidly became a national embarrassment. Popular novels on Mormons of the time equated it with tyranny and abuse of women. The institutions of slavery and polygamy were linked together in the newly formed Republican Party platform, which decried the "twin relics of barbarism—polygamy and slavery."[18] As legal scholar Martha Ertman argues, on the surface the rhetoric of abolitionists and anti-polygamists appears similar in arguing to end tyranny, but these two were diametrically opposed in their relationship to white supremacy. Abolitionists worked to decrease racial hierarchy by emancipating slaves, whereas anti-polygamists sought to "reinstate white supremacy" by "associating racial hierarchy with domestic political order" and by using polygamy as a key threat to the political system.[19] Thus, according to Ertman, race was at the center of anti-polygamy laws passed at the federal and state level.

The racial project that motivated anti-polygamy laws in the United States continues; however, the federalist nature of family law, in which each state has its own laws against bigamy, has fueled administrative ambivalence that is moving more in the direction of legalization than prohibition. As of 2021, polygamy is banned in every state through various laws that are not directed at any religious or cultural group.[20] Some states also prohibit cohabitating in a polygamous relationship. Utah is the state where most of the legal battles have taken place, although in Texas after the YFZ Ranch raid, criminal charges of bigamy and sexual assault put eleven FLDS men in prison. Whereas polygamy is now effectively decriminalized in Utah, in Arizona, where Centennial Park is located, polygamous cohabitation is still a felony, making it possible to receive a sentence of two and a half years and be fined up to $150,000. Challenges to this law may be likely in the future.

My research in Utah and Arizona has shown that whiteness matters for racial projects and for how polygamy is lived. Although participants shared with me their fears of prosecution and the need they felt to stay underground, many came out as polygamists in their communities to join a movement to decriminalize it. Women tended to be the leaders in this movement, vocalizing the reasons that plural marriage was important to them. Government officials, such as former attorney general Mark Shurtleff, approached the issue with administrative ambivalence: on the one hand, calling the FLDS the "American Taliban" for the ways they treat women; on the other, not pursuing prosecutions of plural families unless other crimes were involved. Taking such a position appears much easier when dealing with a population of white American citizens who "look like us." TV shows such as *Big Love* and *Sister Wives* have also helped to destigmatize the practice. Nearly all the dozen TV shows on polygamy feature white families. This public attention has meant a fourfold increase in polygamy's moral acceptability according to the Gallup Values and Beliefs poll; in 2003, acceptability was 7%, and in 2020 it reached 20%.[21]

Fundamentalist Mormons, who are white citizens, have been able to cultivate a collective identity and a movement to fight against unjust laws in a way not possible in France, where the population of polygamists consists of racialized immigrants. In France individuals recounted the injustices of the way that polygamy is regulated, but there was no collective movement to fight these. This is perhaps not surprising, given that those living in polygyny are a small percentage of the population of immigrants in France. Moreover, organizing to fight against injustices for polygynous families would feed into stereotypes that all Muslim families are polygynous or potentially so. In Mayotte, although some individuals protested polygamy's prohibition, the Mahorais mostly adopted counterpractices that focused on choosing their families without involving the French state, a decision that, although not recognized as a formal type of activism, can be seen as a form of resistance to the French ban on polygamy. In the United States several hundred protesters gathered at the Utah state capitol in February 2017, one of several protests to fight the passage of the draconian law against polygamy in which children held signs stating, "I love all my moms."[22] An organized social movement made such protests possible and likely helped to pave the way for polygamy's decriminalization in 2020.

Canada's public face of polygamy also consists of white fundamentalist Mormons. However, the population is miniscule, about a thousand people living in Bountiful, British Columbia, not all of them in plural marriages. The history of polygamy in Canada parallels that of the United States; both have similar nation-building projects that condemned polygamy as evil and despotic in contrast to the virtues of monogamous marriage. In the case of Canada marriage was a "fortress" to guard its way of life.[23] Interestingly, Canada viewed its southern neighbor as much too liberal in instituting "demoralizing and degrading" marriage and divorce laws, and the goal of Canada's nation-building project was to maintain marriage's "purity" against such threatening trends.[24] This meant that Canada's racial project not only attended to the "threat" of polygamy among Indigenous populations but also elevated this concern even more with the immigration of Mormons from the United States to southern Alberta in the 1880s. Government officials viewed the United States as exporting its lax morals to Canada, and they closely surveilled the Mormon population, passing an anti-polygamy law in 1890.

The constitutionality of the law was tested in the polygamy reference case in the Supreme Court of British Columbia in 2010 and 2011. Justice Bauman decided in favor of the law's constitutionality, focusing not only on the harms of polygamy to women and children but also on the harms to the institution of monogamous marriage. What is the state's interest in protecting it? The court portrayed monogamous marriage as *the* dividing line between the evolution of Western civilization and the "'barbarian' custom" and "tyranny" that polygamy represents.[25] This language clearly articulates the problematic orientalist understandings of *other* practices that were prevalent in North America in the nineteenth century. This is best represented by the court decision's focus not just on the white men living in plural marriages in Bountiful but on immigrants living in Canada who are "from cultures and faiths" that allow polygyny and might practice it if it were decriminalized.[26] The court cited France specifically as the worst-case scenario. It drew on evidence presented by the attorneys general, stating, "France's experience with immigration-based polygyny is instructive."[27] After detailing the immigration policies that allowed polygynous wives to join their husbands in France, Justice Bauman summarized, "What happened in France is acutely relevant because it belies any suggestion that the social or economic conditions that may make polygyny attractive elsewhere in the world simply do not exist here, and that the practice would therefore not take hold."[28] The strong implication is that the government must protect monogamous marriage as a central feature of Canadian society to ensure that immigrants from cultures with "barbarian customs" will not practice polygyny in Canada.

Canada's racial project to regulate forbidden intimacies was again ignited to rehearse what it means to be Canadian when it passed the Zero Tolerance for Barbaric Cultural Practices Act in 2015. Among other provisions, the government distinguished polygamy as a new ground for inadmissibility of the right to stay in Canada. After the Conservative government left office, the Liberal government removed the reference to "barbaric cultural practices," pointing to the insult of using the word "barbaric" to describe diverse cultures in Canada.[29] Still, all provisions of the law remain in effect in 2022. Accordingly, the law treats a permanent resident or foreign national who applies to enter Canada (or who is already in Canada) with even one of their polygynous spouses to be practicing polygyny, making them potentially inadmissible.[30] No evidence is required of a criminal conviction or misrepresentation of status. Could someone in a polygynous union who is visiting Canada by themselves be expelled for practicing polygamy? This is an open question asked by the Canadian Bar Association. This far-reaching amendment to immigration law points to Canada's racialized history of using forbidden intimacies to define belonging and citizenship.

Canada's overt racial project inciting Islamophobia is perhaps most astonishing when we consider the Canadian Multiculturalism Act. The *Canadian Encyclopedia* sums up the act's legacy: "The Act affirmed Canada's status as a multicultural nation. . . . It laid the groundwork for the eventual creation of the Department of Multiculturalism and Citizenship, which worked more specifically to address barriers to equal opportunity and integration."[31] Neither France nor the United States shares such a broad-based policy to support cultural diversity and equality. The concept of multiculturalism and its perceived global failure has been debated at length, but this policy has been key to shaping Canadian law and identity.[32] The Canadian government is also exceptional in commissioning a report in 2001, *Beyond Conjugality: Recognizing and Supporting Close Adult Relationships*.[33] The report's authors sought to rethink the ways that the government regulates conjugality, specifically identifying the importance of tailoring laws to better capture the realities and changing nature of personal relationships. This embrace of family diversity was influential in legalizing same-gender marriage in Canada. Ultimately, Canada's progressive policies have created a backlash that seeks to draw strict boundaries to outlaw "anti-democratic" plural families.

The comparison of France, the United States, and Canada suggests that political polyphobia is behind Canada's continuing support for the anti-polygamy law and legislation such as the ban on "barbaric" cultural practices. Fear of the consequences of liberal policies may push this reaction. More broadly, Canada draws on its racist and colonialist past to reclaim the white supremacist perspective on monogamous marriage as the progenitor of civilization and democracy. This finding demonstrates how regulating forbidden intimacies allows countries to consolidate a national identity based on racial othering. Canada's history of supporting cultural diversity may give it more power to support anti-polygamy initiatives without being criticized for xenophobia. Overall, the racial projects outlined in this book demonstrate how fears over the practice of polygamy are deeply intertwined with profound uneasiness over racial, sexual, religious, and cultural difference.

Analyzing the configurations of racial projects in these countries sheds light on how governments solidify national values by protecting the polity from sexual and familial others. All three countries—Canada most explicitly—rely on racialized mononormativity to justify prohibition. In this view white monogamous values are central to democracy and civilization. Once, Western states relied on forbidding same-gender relations to decide who belongs; in recent years polygamy has increasingly become the focus of forbidden intimacies that mark the other who is not worthy of inclusion.

Although racial projects might be undertaken that cast doubt on government objectives in prohibiting polygamy, I have outlined social conditions that might merit such prohibition. One of the strongest arguments is the potential of polygyny to disempower women. In the next section I consider the question of polygyny's impact on gender equality. What do the findings of this book tell us about forbidden intimacies and gender equality?

GENDER EQUALITY, INTERSECTIONALITY, AND THE LEGAL CONUNDRUM

As I spent time with women who had suffered in their polygynous unions—especially those who were compelled or forced to marry, some underage—I found myself thinking, "Of course, polygamy needs to be prohibited. If it were decriminalized or legalized, wouldn't that provide a green light for men to form polygynous unions, forcing some women to be in polygynous marriages whether they want to or not?" Then, I would interview women in plural marriages who described the social consequences of criminalization on their families and lives. Fear and the need to hide were major themes. Many women described the benefits of being in a polygynous union, including opportunities to share household labor and child care among wives. After these interviews my reasoning would do a one-eighty: "Polygamy needs to be decriminalized to end fear of prosecution and in some cases deportation. Decriminalizing polygamy could benefit many of these families and could allow for greater inclusion in society." As my mind seesawed between these two positions, it was clear that broader issues concerning how we understand agency, family, and sexuality were at play.

Polygyny is often treated as a singularly harmful category that is bad for women. According to economist Shoshana Grossbard, who testified as an expert witness in the polygamy reference case in Canada, "Far from polygamy being beneficial to women, it usually is anathema to women's economic, social and emotional well-being."[34] My comparative project resists these universal assessments, examining how polygamies are lived in different social contexts and places—some homegrown, some migratory. I have argued that polygyny is not intrinsically good or bad but that it is structured and embedded within various social locations that shape the way it is lived. Migratory polygamies in France, where polygynous families of up to twenty members are often squeezed into tiny apartments, are difficult and challenging. Overcrowding in small apartments in the Parisian suburbs is not just a problem for polygynous families. Large immigrant families pack many family members into small apartments.[35] The tight quarters can be disastrous for polygynous families in which wives have little space to themselves and where jealousies can flare. Even under these conditions, I interviewed children and wives who described happy childhoods and harmonious family dynamics.

The different ways that polygamies are lived is captured by the concept of labyrinthine love. Understanding the emotion work that is done in multipartnered relationships moves us away from the binary thinking that has motivated the distinction between monogamy (good, supports democracy) and nonmonogamy (bad, supports tyranny), or the distinction that many have made, including in the polygamy reference case, between polyamory (good, supports gender equality) and polygyny (bad, exploits women). The Canadian court went so far as to carve off "bad" polyamory as banned—one man and more than one woman in a polyamorous relationship is captured by the law. In contrast to this good-bad dichotomy, the concept of labyrinthine love emphasizes the structure of intimacies that are shaped by government regulation, resisting the idea that love and sexuality are solely personal phenomena that can be labeled good or bad, healthy or harmful. It complicates social theorist Anthony Gidden's conceptualization of confluent love, grounded in equal emotional exchange.[36] This concept is also useful in considering other types of disfavored intimacies, such as arranged marriage, which can similarly reinforce "Western notions of rights and neoliberal concepts of choice."[37] The complexities of love in arranged marriages points to their structure in different social contexts and different forms of love other than the dominant Western fixation on eros (passionate and romantic love).

Although the concept of labyrinthine love seeks to complicate the good-bad dichotomy, some feminists and their strange bedfellows would argue that no good can come out of polygyny's patriarchal structure.[38] As Martha Bradley-Evans expressed, polygyny is patriarchy on steroids.[39] It can provide justification for men to have complete control in relationships with multiple wives, especially when religious belief upholds men's authority. By ignoring the multiple ways of living polygamies, government officials and detractors point to the gender inegalitarianism of polygyny to condemn its practice. I have sought to consider more carefully what gender inegalitarianism means. Often, same-gender marriage is advocated as the more progressive form of family because the gender dynamics rooted in patriarchy do not apply.[40] This perspective on "progressive" forms of family also applies to polyamory. In the polygamy reference case the closing argument of the Canadian Polyamory Advocacy Association made this association explicit.

> If polyamory is post-modern and monogamy is modern, then polygamy in the form that has been overwhelmingly dominant within the written record of history—patriarchal polygyny—is pre-modern. The inequality

that entitles only the male partner to non-monogamy is contrary to both the modern norms of gender equality and monogamy.[41]

This discourse of modern or postmodern monogamy and polyamory fails to consider the unequal gender relations that persist in heterosexual unions. Consider what sociologist Jane Ward calls the "tragedy of heterosexuality," in which straight women and some men try to fix a fraught patriarchal system in which intimacy and sexual pleasure exist beside durable forms of inequality and violence in straight relationships.[42] Or consider my article with colleagues Nicole Andrejek and Tina Fetner on the ways that men and women understand "regular sex" to exclude women's orgasms, making them something extra, perpetuating the gender gap in orgasms.[43] In this light, the focus on polygyny as gender inegalitarian and premodern turns attention away from the unequal gender relations that continue to structure all relationships, even in cases of polyamory and same-gender relations.[44] Does polygyny differ from other forms of intimacy in being *only* about gender inegalitarianism? I have sought to challenge this assertion.

If polygyny is patriarchy on steroids, is this due to a multiplication of one bad thing? My findings demonstrate that multiplication can also challenge the power dynamics in patriarchy. Like research on conservative religious families that explores the ways women hold power in relationships that adhere to patriarchal principles,[45] my research challenges the idea of a universal patriarchy that subjugates women in polygyny. To make plural marriage work, I found that many men perform a conciliatory masculinity that blends normative masculine standards of leadership with nonnormative ideals of emotional labor and conciliation.[46] Complimenting this, women perform a homosocial femininity that shapes conciliatory masculinity to balance power relations. Wives build social bonds as friendships and/or practices of sharing household responsibilities, deciding who works inside and outside the home. Patriarchy does not just mean male dominance in this approach. According to Samantha, "You say I subscribe to a 'patriarchal' lifestyle, and I do, but we have two different connotations— evident by the fact that, for you—the word equates to the appeasement of male ego; for me—it is the way of living that contains the ideals necessary to become the person my God expects me to be."[47] She goes on to describe a "cultural imperialism" that reduces women like her to an "inferior other," reasoning that for their own good, "these poor women and children need to be rescued and shown the errors of their ways."

Samantha's words reflect critiques of efforts to "save" women—often poor and/or women of color—from cultural practices that are viewed as oppressive in Western cultures, such as wearing the headscarf. Anthropologist Lila Abu-Lughod sums up the argument concisely: "We should want justice and rights for women, but can we accept that there might be different ideas about justice and that different women might want, or even choose, different futures from ones that we envision as best?"[48] For some women, living in a plural marriage allows them to express their godliness; others embrace it for helping balance work and life responsibilities. Justice and rights will look different for these women. Samantha also points to the ways that women's agency is suspect under the law. The cultural imperialism that Samantha refers to connects to racial projects that use women's rights and equality to justify various kinds of government interventions, including war and criminalizing cultural practices in ways that racialize and other non-Western populations.[49] Even though fundamentalist Mormons are almost exclusively white, their practice of polygyny troubles whiteness as a family form that governments and courts call barbarian.

In this book I have shown how, in all three countries and Mayotte, prohibiting polygamy ultimately makes women more vulnerable. France's approach has erased the existence of polygyny in both metropolitan France and overseas departments such as Mayotte, where it continues outside the purview of government regulation. On the one hand, prohibiting the act of living with multiple wives in France may discourage men from migrating or bringing over multiple wives. On the other hand, secondary wives may be left in their country of origin to fend for themselves, only getting to see their husbands during visits. For migrants living in France, prohibiting polygamy has sometimes meant the complete erasure of a woman's identity. Her husband may register her under the legal wife's name and identity. In some cases children born to the secondary wife are also registered as the children of the legal wife. In the United States women in plural marriages are also pushed underground and are less willing to report abuse in the context of criminalization for fear that the husband will go to prison. The same findings were reported in Canada in the research of legal scholar Angela Campbell.[50] However, for some participants, prohibition is necessary because these women in plural marriages are beyond saving. In this perspective polygyny is a threat to gender equality and to society in general, not to the specific women who consent to these relationships.

What does this debate over women in polygamy mean for its prohibition? How does it resolve the dilemma of recognizing the voices of those who have been hurt in polygynous relationships and of those in polygynous relationships who are harmed by its prohibition? The past couple of decades have seen numerous legal arguments for either criminalizing or legalizing polygamy. Legal scholars such as Martha Strassberg and John Witte have argued that "polygamous marriage contributes to the development of despotic states and monogamous marriage contributes to the development of the modern liberal state."[51] These scholars tend to defend prohibition by pointing to the abuses in cases "where religion dominates public life" and where "becoming polygynous opens the doors to the acquisition [for men] of even greater religious, economic and political power."[52] Ultimately, these kinds of arguments rest on the idea that polygyny is backward and produces extreme forms of patriarchy.

In this book I have analyzed these kinds of claims as participating in racial projects. At the same time, it is important to take seriously the ways that polygynous relationships can constrain choices and increase the reach of patriarchy. Other legal scholars, such as Mark Goldfeder and Donald C. Den Otter, have provided arguments to think about the possibilities of legalizing plural marriage. For them, legalization will allow governments to more successfully regulate and investigate the abuses that have been identified in some polygynous families.[53] These scholars attend to the future of *polygamies*, dealing with the complexity of "multiplying everything that is good in a traditional dyadic marriage: love, responsibility, selflessness."[54]

Several conclusions follow from this study of forbidden intimacies. First, it is important to listen to the voices of the women who live in different kinds of polygamies and those who have left. Treating women as criminals does little to regulate the problems that animate much of the debate over polygyny, such as patriarchy on steroids. Regarding women's agency as suspect does not take seriously why some women might desire a plural marriage. After listening to the diverse perspectives of the participants in this study—ranging from those in polygynous unions to those who police them—I believe that decriminalization of polygamy is necessary to support women's rights. This may seem like a betrayal of feminist principles, but it makes little sense to outlaw families, including wives, and push them underground in ways that makes it more difficult to help women and children when things go wrong. Social context matters, and laws need to reflect how best to regulate potential harm while supporting what some see as the multiplication of love. In other words, the law must reckon with labyrinthine love—intimacies that are always complex and are not narrowly determined by culture. Mayotte provides the clearest example of the negative outcomes of prohibition. Prohibiting polygyny has made women perhaps even more vulnerable, because polygyny no longer exists in the eyes of the state and has become less regulated by local religious governance.

In lieu of prohibiting polygamy, the intersectional feminist approach I have suggested by thinking about labyrinthine love—which attends to structural locations based on race, class, gender, sexuality, and colonialist histories—would build on the multiple ways that polygamies are lived and move away from racial projects that use forbidden intimacy to create and mark the other. Social justice movements must fight against patriarchal relations, sexual, gender-based, and racial violence, colonialist legacies, racism, and heterosexism—and we can add monogamism—to create a more just society. In sum, governments must no longer rely on the condemnation of forbidden intimacies to brandish their progressive credentials when so much work needs to be done to end the kinds of violence that the polygynous imaginary has come to represent.

APPENDIX
METHODOLOGY

For much of my career, and for this book in particular, I have studied conservative families and politics, particularly those driven by the religious right. To do so, I drew on my upbringing in a conservative Baptist family in California to make sense of the worldviews that inspired conservative movements and initiatives, such as the Promise Keepers[1] and the marriage movement that promoted heterosexual marriage and worked to continue the ban against marriage for LGBTQ+ populations.[2] Polygamy was not on my radar as a topic of interest. However, in 2006 my curiosity was piqued by the *Newsweek* article "Polygamists, Unite!"[3] It described Marlyne Hammon, whose father was arrested in the 1953 Short Creek raid in Arizona, along with dozens of other men, and sent to jail on charges of polygamy. Hammon stated in the article that this experience had taught her community to live quietly and keep their heads down. But no longer! Now in a polygamous relationship herself, she is a founding member of the Centennial Park Action Committee, one of the groups I studied that is fighting for decriminalization. The *Newsweek* article described the emergence of polygamy activists who were drawing on the increasingly successful activism of the marriage equality movement. I knew a little about fundamentalist Mormons, but I was surprised to learn that a Christian evangelical polygamy movement had also arisen in the early 2000s. The article quoted Mark Henkel of TruthBearer.org as stating, "Polygamy rights is the next civil-rights battle."[4]

During this time, I also began to obsessively watch the HBO television series *Big Love*, created by Mark V. Olsen and Will Scheffer, a writing team who are in a monogamous same-gender relationship. I was fascinated by the conceit of the series, using polygamy to explore the American family and to subvert ideas about marriage. In an interview with Terry Gross on *Fresh Air*, Scheffer and Olsen described how Olsen came up with the idea while driving back to New York from a family trip in Nebraska.[5] Scheffer's response: "Yuck." This is a common reaction, and I must admit it was also mine before I began studying it. Olsen explained that the series pushes back on the Republican Party's embrace of family values that upholds the nuclear, heterosexual family as the only moral option. Terry Gross exclaimed that this was "a strange response, because . . . well, for a lot of obvious reasons."[6] They go on to discuss the problem of patriarchy that defines these relationships. In another interview Olsen addressed whether polygamy is inherently abusive: "Some feminists argued back in the '60s and '70s that marriage was inherently abusive and patriarchal—that it was not a good deal for women. As the feminist movement has matured, there has been an evolution in that thinking. Polygamy can grow into a healthier model for some women."[7] Thinking about polygamy as a form of subversion was fascinating, and I put this idea in my list of possibilities for future research.

In 2008 I took a job outside Toronto, Canada, at McMaster University. A year later, the issue of polygamy began to make headlines when two fundamentalist Mormon leaders were charged in Bountiful, British Columbia, with practicing polygamy. This began my pursuit to study polygamy as a form of forbidden intimacy. As I researched the topic, I became fascinated by the question of how Western governments regulate a family form that they ban. These families exist, everyone knows they exist, and the law forbids it. How do governments justify this ban and regulate families viewed as retrograde and outlawed? After being awarded a one-year Social Sciences and Humanities Research Council (SSHRC) grant and with permission from the McMaster Research Ethics Board for research with human subjects, I traveled to Vancouver to conduct research on the British Columbia Supreme Court case in 2010 and in 2011. The trial began on November 11, 2010, and I attended the proceedings until December 16. The proceedings recommenced on January 5, 2011, but I couldn't return until the closing arguments began on April 1 and ended on April 15. I took extensive field notes while I was there, and I was able to meet and have informal conversations with many of the lawyers and interveners, allowing me to set up times for in-depth interviews. Although I had to miss several weeks of the trial, I obtained transcripts for the entire case, which I read and coded. I began interviewing lawyers and interveners in late November and completed the interviews at the end of April.

The reference case alerted me to possible challenges in conducting research on polygamy. At the start of the trial, I had read Angela Campbell's research based on interviews with women in Bountiful, which offered a window into their lives.[8] Drawing on these accounts and her time spent in Bountiful, Campbell found that prohibiting polygamy led to isolation and made it difficult for some to access social and health services outside the community, even as the FLDS created distrust of such services. In my view, a feminist approach would prioritize women's voices and recognize the problems of banning plural marriage. I didn't expect those on the side of the attorneys general to take this approach, but even so, I was surprised when at the beginning of the trial the attorneys general and the lawyers for Stop Polygamy in Canada took issue with Campbell's qualifications, initiating a voir dire to determine her competence as an expert witness. The questioning focused on her lack of official training in qualitative methods. I wrote in my field notes:

> It is infuriating to sit in the audience as a sociologist with expertise in qualitative methodologies and listen to misrepresentations of what counts as "good" qualitative research. The lawyers on the attorney generals' side are grilling Angela Campbell concerning her knowledge of methods, such as whether she knows the expression "investigative discourse analysis," which they cite as being a technique "well understood" by qualitative sociological researchers. Being unfamiliar with the term, I looked it up. It is a seemingly arcane term used in law enforcement for a type of content

analysis to examine "the statements of suspects and alleged victims."[9] In other words, *not* a term often used by qualitative sociologists!

The irony of lawyers with limited knowledge of sociological qualitative methods accusing a legal scholar of inadequate knowledge was not lost on me.[10] I felt vulnerable to such attacks, even with my expertise and background.

Thus, early on, I realized that I was in a difficult position as a feminist qualitative sociologist who wanted to understand the social consequences of polygamy's prohibition and regulation. The confrontational nature of the court case drew clear lines between the two sides. Moreover, I found that some who were in favor of prohibition were quite virulent against anyone who would consider otherwise. As I outlined with my co-authors Jessica Braimoh and Julie Gouweloos in our *Signs* article, "Judging Women's Sexual Agency: Contemporary Sex Wars in the Legal Terrain of Prostitution and Polygamy," the case made some strange bedfellows between feminist and conservative Christian groups, participating in what we argued was a new era of the sex wars.[11] Some actors even denounced expert witnesses for the amicus on their blogs, such as the research of Angela Campbell.

Politicization made it difficult to approach various actors in public for fear of being seen as favoring one side or the other. I tried to remain discreet in approaching people to interview, finding the situation quite stressful. I often felt that I had to be more reticent than I would normally be. I was relieved to find that the lawyers and interveners who agreed to be interviewed were overall quite open, and I was able to gain insights into the various perspectives on each side. At the same time, the highly politicized atmosphere of the trial shaped my strategy to studying polygamy, pushing me to consider even more carefully the research design and methods of the broader project. At this time, I decided not to conduct in-depth interviews with individuals in Bountiful, because Angela Campbell had already conducted twenty in-depth interviews in the 2000s. I realized that it would be difficult to gauge whether my interviews would overlap with hers, and I did not see the need to replicate them. To close out my research in Canada, I traveled to Montreal in 2016 to interview the French-speaking population about polygamy.

Research in Canada pointed to the need to study the consequences of generalizing polygamy as a singular, harmful phenomenon and to the need for comparative research to provide stronger evidence of the social consequences of government regulation of polygamy. In planning the broader project, I saw the United States as an obvious choice because of its transnational relations with Canada that would allow me to consider state-level and transnational movement of ideas of law and regulation. I decided on France to study the consequences of governing polygamy among racialized populations from former colonies, a quite different dynamic than the most visible white populations in North America. Given the close ties between Canada and the United States, I thought it important to include a population with close ties to France—such as a former colony—where polygamy was prohibited, ruling out such countries as Mali, Senegal, and Mauritania. I proposed Benin, a French colony from the nineteenth century until 1960 that outlawed polygamy in 2004. I modified my plan after conducting my initial research in France in 2013, when I learned about Mayotte, which had become a French department in 2011 and had outlawed polygamy in 2005. Making this change provided an opportunity to study France's regulation of polygamy as a banned practice in its metropole and in an overseas department with French citizens.

This study is not an ethnography in the traditional sense of the term. I did not seek to immerse myself in a community or communities of people living in polygyny or plural marriage. Whereas scholars such as Janet Bennion lived in polygynous communities—in her case, the Allred Group in a village at the base of the Rocky Mountains—I sought to understand more broadly how polygamies are shaped in social contexts and in different cultures.[12] Bennion's ethnography allowed her to point to the ways that broader society misconstrues women living in plural marriages. In this book I build on her insights to study how polygyny as a forbidden practice shapes how it is lived and how states are themselves shaped by banning and regulating these families and practices. Although comparative in nature—examining government regulation in Canada, France, Mayotte, and the United States—I have sought to understand the relations between laws, practices, and people, a relational ethnography that moves beyond bounded places and groups.[13] My commitment to thinking about the ways that laws and ideas move transnationally across borders helped illuminate the nuanced ways that polygamies are regulated. My proposed project was awarded a five-year SSHRC Insight Grant and received permission from the McMaster Research Ethics Board. Thus the broader journey began.

CROSSING THE GLOBE: THE PERILS OF ETHNOGRAPHY ON FORBIDDEN INTIMACIES

Being White and Fitting In

On a cloudy afternoon in April 2011, I entered a restaurant in Creston, British Columbia, to meet a woman in a plural marriage and two of her daughters. I had flown to Creston after the end of the polygamy reference case trial to visit Bountiful, located just north of Washington State. One of the women who attended the trial had connections with the community in Bountiful, and she put me in touch with Mary Jayne Blackmore (the fifth child of Winston Blackmore), who was the principal of the school for Winston Blackmore's side. She invited me to present information on applying and attending university to the high school students.

Arriving at the restaurant that first afternoon, I was nervous, not sure what to expect. On the one hand, my religious background gave me confidence that I would feel an affinity with this family. On the other, I had just spent months listening to and reading testimony from the polygamy reference case that focused on the otherness of the people in Bountiful. What would it be like to chat with members of this community, who dress in the recognizable conservative style—prairie dresses and long braids? As I walked in, I passed a woman and her two daughters who were dressed in modern clothing. I searched the restaurant before realizing that I had just walked past them. I was embarrassed that I had prejudged their appearance. After we sat down, I quickly realized how wrong my stereotypes were. I wrote in my field notes: "The mother is dressed in pants, low-key, like most moms in their forties. The two daughters are both beautiful, one in her early twenties and the other in her teens. Both are dressed stylishly in jeans and girlie tops. The older one has a nose piercing!!!" The next day, I arrived in Bountiful, and there I did see many in the traditional FLDS attire. Because the community had been divided since the excommunication of Winston Blackmore, there was a vast difference in the ways that one side dressed and interacted. I was able to meet people only on the Blackmore side, who mostly wore contemporary clothing. After my presentation to the high school students, Mary Jayne invited me, along with another community member, to go horseback riding to see the community. During the tour, I had several informal conversations with women we met. They expressed hope that the British Columbia reference case might lead to decriminalization. However, if the court ruled in favor of keeping the current law, they felt it would have little impact. They would go on living their lives as they always had under conditions of prohibition. This experience set me on the path to examining the existence of polygamies and the varied social contexts in which they are lived.

My fieldwork in Bountiful made it clear to me that being a white woman who could fit into conservative religious environments was a plus for conducting research among fundamentalist Mormons in Canada and the United States. In Utah the movement against the decriminalization of polygamy was in full swing, and I found that many individuals living in plural marriages were eager to share with me their experiences and reasons for why polygamy should be banned or decriminalized. When I arrived in Utah in 2014, I met Elizabeth, whom a colleague had put me in touch with, at her home outside Salt Lake City. She was in her 60s, white, and in a plural marriage. The house belonged to her, and her sister wives lived in their own residences. Elizabeth reminded me of my mother, wearing a pantsuit and her hair in a bouffant. She served tea and cookies, and we had a nice conversation about living in a plural marriage. She agreed to be interviewed and put me in touch with other individuals in plural families. This first experience mirrored subsequent interviews, which were generally easy to schedule and in which people were willing to discuss their opinions and experiences, whatever their perspective on polygamy.

I spent roughly three months in Utah attending various events, visiting different communities of fundamentalist Mormons, and interviewing individuals who were in polygynous marriages, individuals who worked with these populations, and government officials and lawyers who dealt with polygamy's criminalization. I asked those I interviewed whether they knew of others who they thought would consider participating in the study. I was able to interview a range of people living in plural marriages who were independents and those who belonged to various fundamentalist Mormon groups, including the Centennial Park group, the Apostolic United Brethren, and the Davis County Co-op. I also interviewed government officials, social workers, scholars, and journalists who had written stories on various polygynous communities. I traveled to southern Utah to visit the two communities there, the FLDS and Centennial Park. In Hildale I stayed in America's Most Wanted Bed and Breakfast, the former compound of Warren Jeffs surrounded by high white walls and few windows. Willie Jessop, who was once Jeffs's bodyguard, purchased the compound and turned it into a hotel. It hadn't been open for long when I stayed there, and I wrote in my field notes that it felt more like a bunker where people lived in fear than a bed and breakfast. I had trouble sleeping the first night. Yet the area was surrounded by beautiful canyons, and by the end of my stay I had acclimated. Again, I was constantly aware that everyone I met was white and that I fit in—except in Hildale and Colorado City, where I clearly did not belong because of my contemporary clothes. Still, I was able to volunteer at a food and clothing drive in Hildale for the FLDS, which gave me the opportunity to chat with FLDS women and young people. Some clearly did not want to be approached, but others were more open. This ease of access to various populations in North America did not apply to conducting research in France and Mayotte.

Conducting Research as a Foreigner

I knew there would be challenges when I decided to include France as a case, both in terms of my lack of language skills and the racialized and vulnerable population that was in question. As to the first challenge, I had spent five months in Paris when I was 20 and took some rudimentary French classes. So many years later, I could speak French but far from fluently. I began taking French classes and brushed up on my skills. My hope was to hire a research assistant when I arrived in France to help conduct interviews and transcribe them. I traveled to Paris in 2013 and spent five months conducting initial research and making contacts. I considered hiring two potential research assistants, but neither worked out because of their own personal and professional complications, so I began conducting interviews myself. By that time, I was able to converse more easily in French. When

I was able to return in 2015 for four months, I began searching again for a research assistant while continuing to conduct interviews on my own. I attended various meetings in Parisian suburbs that brought people together to support immigrant populations, and I contacted individuals who worked with polygynous populations to interview them and get referrals. Finally, I was able to hire a research assistant who did conduct some interviews and another who worked with the first to transcribe them. The first assistant had a Senegalese colleague who led an immigrant men's group in Paris, many of whom were from West Africa. She interviewed five of these men who had multiple wives but who were not currently living in plural families in France. Either all their wives lived in the country of origin, or one wife was in France and the others were in the country of origin. Two of these men had multiple wives in France before the Pasqua law was enacted, but after it passed, for various reasons, each decided to send all his wives back to the country of origin. It wasn't clear from the interviews how much say the wives had in these decisions.

Many interviews required travel to the Parisian suburbs, and this was not feasible for my research assistant because of safety reasons and the time required to take public transportation. I was able to travel by motor scooter, which made getting to various suburbs much easier and relatively safe. There were also challenges. One day, I had to get to a suburb in the rain, which meant that I was soaked to the skin during the interview. Still, I made it work, and in the end, I conducted most of the interviews myself with the support of my French-speaking partner, who helped whenever there was a translation problem. I interviewed association leaders who worked directly with polygynous populations, social workers and scholars who had studied the policy of decohabitation, and government officials who were responsible for applying the laws.

Another major consideration in my research was the racialized population in France at the heart of this study. Identifying people living in polygyny and willing to do an interview proved challenging, as many were either living in the shadows or were not interested in discussing their family situation, which was seen as stigmatizing. This became a central concern, as I considered whether my focus on polygyny in France might further stigmatize the populations I was studying. Many of those in polygynous relationships, as well as those who worked with them, remarked that people of color in France can be seen as potentially polygynous because of the tendency to equate people of color with immigrants who are seen as other for practices such as polygyny or wearing a headscarf. From the beginning, my focus on how racialization leaves whiteness unmarked in regulating forbidden intimacies has sought to challenge such stigmatizing images.

Not being French (and having an American accent when speaking French), I was able to avoid some of the racial dynamics specific to white French citizens who are seen as discriminating against people of color for not being "really French." Over time, I built relationships of trust with people who worked with polygynous populations and interviewed those who were in situations of polygyny or had decohabited. I explained that I wanted to understand their experiences in the context of polygamy's prohibition. There were instances of misunderstanding. In one case, one of the social workers I interviewed helped me set up an interview with a woman who had decohabited but was still in a plural marriage. When I arrived to do the interview, she thought I was a social worker there to interview her about the problems she was having with her apartment. When I explained that the interview was for a sociological study to understand the consequences of regulating polygynous families, she agreed to participate but did not want to be audiorecorded. She was quite mistrustful at first, but as the interview continued, she openly shared with me the challenges she faced in the years she had lived in France as a result of the law changing in 1993. In some cases my religious background worked in my favor. One interview I had with a mother in a plural marriage and her three daughters became an interesting conversation about family and belief. When I told them about my background growing up in a very religious family, this opened a door to discuss what it meant to be Muslim and the importance of faith in making decisions about entering a polygynous relationship. This interview lasted almost two hours and was incredibly informative.

Before traveling to Mayotte in the summer of 2015, I was fortunate that one of the scholars I interviewed in Paris put me in touch with his student from Mayotte, Askandari Allaoui, who agreed to an interview. Allaoui is a religious and political leader in Mayotte, and he helped set up interviews with numerous government officials and leaders of associations in Mayotte. I spent six weeks conducting interviews and participating in cultural activities. A highlight was the opportunity to attend the preparations for a great marriage, which I describe in Chapter 2. As I had limited time in Mayotte, I often conducted more than one interview a day, keeping a busy schedule, which was exhausting but enabled me to become familiar with the culture. As much as possible, I attended events and worked in places that allowed me to meet people, and, in several cases, people in polygynous relationships. The fact that polygyny is now prohibited in Mayotte meant that most people, especially politicians, were unlikely to claim this status. Even so, I was able to interview people in polygynous relationships. For example, four interviews started off being with individuals who were in government positions or who worked with polygynous populations, only to lead to self-disclosure of a polygynous relationship. In these cases I was able to ask questions related to their polygynous relationship. I interviewed officials who others said were in polygynous relationships, but this was not information they shared.

My presence as a white foreigner in Mayotte complicated the research. For example, after interviewing a government official, pseudonymously named Faissoil, we walked out of the government building together and passed another official, who I call Yazidou Ben. Faissoil introduced me, described my research about government regulation of polygamy, and said that Yazidou Ben should consider doing an interview with me. At this point, Yazidou Ben became agitated, declaring that he wasn't a polygamist and that Faissoil should do the interview, as he was! They spent several minutes calling each other polygamists before we all went our separate ways. This exchange alerted me to the fact that many Mahorais were unwilling to share their family status with an outsider doing research. On another occasion, a young businessman I had interviewed set up an interview with one of his friends who was in a plural marriage and agreed to be interviewed. When I arrived, I waited for twenty minutes after texting him to say that I had arrived. I was just losing hope that he would come when he arrived and led me into an empty office building. He was clearly nervous, and I was concerned that he didn't really want to do the interview. When I asked if he wanted to continue, he told me yes, and during the interview warmed up to answering my questions. He described the challenges that he faced in making both of his wives, who lived in different parts of the larger island, happy. At the end of the interview, I asked him whether there was anything important for me to know that I hadn't asked. He paused for a long minute, thinking deeply. He then said that if a man is going to be polygamous, it is most important to own a car to ensure that he could quickly travel between his wives' residences. This moment of levity made it clear that in the end he was comfortable sharing his experiences.

In both metropolitan France and Mayotte, I had fewer interviews with those living in polygyny (or willing to declare their polygamous families) than other people who worked with these populations. Still, my objective of studying how polygamy is governed meant that my interviews with this latter group were incredibly instructive and provided clear perspective on how these populations are viewed. Many of the themes that came out of my interviews with those living in polygyny were reflected in my interviews with other representatives.

Ultimately, this research required many years of fieldwork and effort to understand the lay of the land and make contacts to fully study the complex dynamics of government regulation. I conducted many hours of fieldwork and archival research to study the social conditions under which laws are implemented and how outlawing polygamy affects different populations. It also required a team of research assistants who were invaluable to conducting literature reviews, transcribing interviews, and coding thousands of pages of data for the project. I adapted questions to the participant's relationship to polygamy and to the laws in each country. All but one interview was audiorecorded, transcribed in English or French, and analyzed together with my field notes using NVivo. A team of five research assistants—four Anglophones and one Francophone—worked together on coding. A research associate managed the coding with me, and together we created a 15-page codebook with detailed descriptions of each code, and we reviewed all coding for consistency.

I have given most of my participants pseudonyms, except in cases where they requested to have their real name used or where they are so well known that trying to protect their identity would be impossible. In the latter case, each participant agreed that I could use their legal name. I have sought to ensure that people living in polygynous communities are not recognizable in this book by slightly changing details when possible; however, as I discussed with them, there is always the possibility that someone in the community could recognize a participant from the stories they tell.

The research itself was sometimes emotionally grueling. My goal was to fully understand each side of the debate—harm as inherent to polygyny or harm caused by its prohibition. On the one hand, for those who had terrible experiences being in a polygynous marriage or being raised in a polygynous family, the only possible solution from their perspective is a total ban that sends a clear signal that polygyny is harmful. These interviews were difficult. I agonized with participants who told stories of abuse, sometimes sexual abuse, and the challenges they faced leaving their community and religion. For those living in outlawed plural families, the threat of prosecution creates fear and encourages people to hide. For them, the only solution is decriminalization. Without polygamy's prohibition, it would be easier to prosecute those who committed crimes, such as underage marriage. I sympathized as they told stories of discrimination and stigma. Clearly, both sides brought forward arguments that held truth, and the problem from a legal perspective is how to best govern these populations, whether it be criminalization, decriminalization, or legalization.

My hope has been that this book, by identifying polygamies that vary within and across race, class, and nation, ultimately sheds light on governmental racial projects that use forbidden intimacies to propel their agendas. One of the most important findings of this research is the need for Western governments to recognize the nefarious consequences of prohibition that make many women and children living in polygyny more vulnerable to abuse and government surveillance. The ways that governments regulate polygamy tend to be tied to racial projects that have little to do with protecting women and children from harm. Thus, recognizing how plural families are structured by labyrinthine love can lead to more justice and better government approaches.

Notes

Introduction

1. Anthropologist Mariam Zeitzen provides the following definition of polygamy and its variants: "Polygamy is the practice whereby a person is married to more than one spouse at the same time, as opposed to monogamy, where a person has only one spouse at a time. In principle, there are three forms of polygamy: polygyny, in which one man is married to several wives; polyandry, where one woman is married to several husbands; and group marriage, in which several husbands are married to several wives, i.e. some combination of polygyny and polyandry" (Zeitzen 2008, 3). Polygamy is often used in exchange with polygyny, and I follow this conflation as used by the participants in this study and the law. *Plural marriage* is a term used by Mormon fundamentalists and others. I use the terms *polygamy, polygyny, plural marriage,* and *plural families* interchangeably to signal that these are families.

2. More broadly, polygamous or nonmonogamous relationships signify interpersonal relationships that involve multiple marital, sexual, and/or romantic partners. Polyamory is the dominant contemporary form of romantic or sexual relationships with multiple partners in which some involve marriage and some do not.

3. For example, Bernstein and Naples 2015; Canaday 2009; Puri 2016; Weeks 2018.

4. For example, Friedman 2005; Harder 2007; Heath 2009, 2012a, 2013; Shah 2011.

5. Eskridge 1999; Mackey 1987.

6. Chauncey 2019; Eskridge 1999.

7. Corriveau 2011.

8. Corriveau 2011, 52.

9. Varrella 2021.

10. Canaday 2009.

11. Puri 2016.

12. Puri 2016. See also Ritchie and Whitlock 2018.

13. Ali 2017; Haritaworn et al. 2008.

14. Mutua 2001, 201.

15. Currier 2010; McKay and Angotti 2016.

16. Denike 2010.

17. Some prominent examples include Graff (2004), Strassberg (1997), and A. Sullivan (1996).

18. Graff 2004, 176.

19. Graff 2004, 176.

20. Puar 2007, 2. See also Duggan 2003.

21. Omi and Winant 2015, 109.

22. Winant 2001, 107.

23. Brekhus 1998; M. McDermott and Samson 2005.

24. Abji et al. 2019.

25. Summarized in J. Bennion and Joffe 2016, 13–14.

26. Korteweg and Yurdakul 2014.

27. Pande 2015.

28. Jamieson 1999.

29. Schippers 2016, 3.

30. Scholars who argue that monogamy has been key to the rise of Western dominance in the world include Buck (2012) and Witte (2015a, 2015b).

31. Strassberg 2016.

32. Barker and Langdridge 2012, 3.

33. Rich 1980, 647.

34. Rich 1980, 648. The concept of a lesbian continuum has produced lively debate among feminists, but it has been helpful in conceptualizing the socially constructed nature of sexuality to consider the relationships among women. Likewise, familial and sexual polygamous relationships are social constructed.

35. Schippers 2016, 6 (emphasis in original).

36. Rubin 1984, 153.

37. Felmlee and Sprecher (2006) point to the debate over whether love is

an emotion. Some argue that love is a cultural construct or a mixture of other emotions, such as joy and anxiety. Others view love as a basic drive, such as hunger, thirst, and sleep. In contrast, some scholars view love as an emotion, pointing to the example of romantic love that is universal across cultures and historical time.

38. Coontz 2006.

39. Coontz 2006; Giddens 1992.

40. Giddens 1992, 61.

41. Deri 2015.

42. Clanton 2006, 411.

43. Clanton 2006, 417.

44. Clanton 2006, 416.

45. Deri 2015, 21.

46. Lee (1977) proposed ideal types of intimate adult affiliation ("love") from fictional and nonfictional literature and created an interview method to enable individuals "in love" to reconstruct their experiences. After coding the responses, he constructed types that were tested and revised, producing a structured typology of styles of loving. The Love Attitudes Scale is based on this typology and is the dominant measure of different styles of love in use today.

47. Schippers 2016, 16.

48. Kramer 2020.

49. Bailey and Kaufman 2010.

50. Dixon-Spear 2009.

51. See Alexandre 2007; Bailey and Kaufman 2010; Bala et al. 2005; J. Bennion and Joffe 2016; Brooks 2009; Calder and Beaman 2014; Calhoun 2005; Chambers 1997; Davis 2010; Dixon-Spear 2009; Duncan 2008; Fry 2010; Gher 2008; Gordon 2002; Hayes 2007; Iversen 1984; Jacobson and Burton 2011; Joffe 2016; Klein 2010; Klesse 2006; Levinson 2005; Mahoney 2008; McGinnis 2012; Myers 2006; Okin 1999; Park 2017; Pinfree 2006; Rower 2004; Rude-Antoine 1991, 1997; Sealing 2001; Sheff 2011; Sigman 2006; Slark 2004; Smearman 2009; Song 2007; Stacey and Meadow 2009; Strassberg 1997, 2003, 2015, 2016; Strauss 2012; Tenney 2002; C. M. Ward 2004.

52. Strassberg 1997.

53. Goldfeder 2017. In addition, political scientist Ron C. Den Otter (2015) has provided an excellent overview of the legal and philosophical arguments for and against legalizing plural marriage. He argues in favor of the constitutional case for polygamy and plural marriage.

54. R. McDermott 2018.

55. R. McDermott 2018, 94.

56. Al-Krenawi 2001, 2010; Al-Krenawi and Graham 2006; Al-Krenawi and Kanat-Maymon 2017; C. Patil and Hadley 2008.

57. In addition to the articles cited in the previous note, see Al-Krenawi (2014), Al-Krenawi et al. (2011), and Slonim-Nevo and Al-Krenawi (2006).

58. Ahinkorah 2021; Owoo et al. 2021.

59. Research on the correlation between polygyny and intimate partner violence includes Abramsky et al. (2011), Jewkes et al. (2002), and Karamagi et al. (2006). For other studies that have found more complexities in this relationship, see Behrman 2019.

60. Behrman 2019.

61. Lawson et al. 2015.

62. Lawson et al. 2015, 13,829.

63. Steady 1987.

64. Gaullier 2008, 2009; Poiret 1995, 1996; Poiret and Guégan 1992, 1–6; Quiminal and Bodin 1993; Sidhoum 1985, 1986.

65. Poiret 1996. See also Quiminal and Bodin (1993) and Sidhoum (1985).

66. Gaullier 2008, 2009.

67. Altman and Ginat 1996.

68. J. Bennion 1998, 2008, 2011.

69. J. Bennion 1998, 6.

70. A. Campbell 2008, 2009, 2010.

71. For example, see Jankowiak and Allen 1995.

72. Dixon-Spear 2009.

73. Majeed 2015.

74. Dinero 2012.

75. Dinero 2012, 507.

76. Charsley and Liversage 2013.

77. Charsley and Liversage 2013, 60.

78. Charsley and Liversage 2013, 69.

79. Desmond 2014, 547.

80. Grewal and Kaplan 1994; C. Kaplan et al. 1999; V. Patil 2013.

81. V. Patil 2013, 847.

82. V. Patil 2018; Puri 2016.

83. Adam 2003; Fetner 2008; Stacey 1996.

84. Kosmin 2007, 8.

85. Kosmin 2007; Scott 2007.

86. Therrien 2004; Zubrzcki 2016.

87. Stahl 2007.

88. Zeitzen 2008.

89. Criminal Code (R.S.C., 1985, c. C-46), https://laws-lois.justice.gc.ca/eng/acts/C-46/section-293.html#docCont.

90. Mohrman 2021.

91. Conseil du statut de la femme 2010.

92. Sargent and Cordell 2003.

93. Zeitzen 2008.

94. See the Appendix on Methodology for more details.

Chapter 1

1. Monéger 2013, 7.

2. *Brown v. Buhman*, Case No. 2:11-cv-0652-CW, 18–20, https://www.stgeorgeutah.com/wp-content/uploads/2013/12/20131213-Memorandum-of-Decision-Brown-v-Buhman-polygamy-statute-Utah-1.pdf (accessed October 21, 2020).

3. *Reference re: Section 293 of the Criminal Code of Canada*, 2011 BCSC 1588, para. 883, https://www.hlaw.ca/wp-content/uploads/2009/01/2011-BCSC-1588-Reference-re-Section-293-of-the-Criminal-Code-of-Canada.pdf. (accessed October 21, 2020).

4. Camiscioli 2009.

5. "Preamble to the 27th of October 1946 Constitution," https://www.equalrightstrust.org/ertdocumentbank/Preamble%201946%20ENG.pdf (accessed August 25, 2020).

6. *Reynolds v. United States*, 98 U.S. 145 (1879). Quoted in Ertman 2010, 293.

7. M. Campbell 2001.

8. Cott 2000.

9. Macaulay 2005, 386.

10. Gruning et al. 2015; Mantu 2015.

11. Jennings 2011, 97.

12. Brubaker 1992; Korteweg and Yurdakul 2014; Laborde 2008; Scott 2007.

13. Scott (2007, 15) explains that "*laïcité*, the French version of 'secularism,' is no less translatable than any other term. It is part of the mythology of the specialness and superiority of French republicanism—the same mythology that paradoxically offers French universalism as different from all others—to insist that *laïcité* can only be used in its original tongue."

14. Bertossi 2012; Laborde 2008; Scott 2007. Scott (2007) translates the concept of *communautarisme* to "communalism," noting that it differs from the American concept of communitarianism, which emphasizes the responsibility of the individual to the community.

15. Zhou (2013, 1333) defines these terms in the following way: "Ethnic en-

claves are urban neighborhoods in which immigrant groups or ethnic minorities are residentially concentrated, while ethnic niches are where particular types of businesses are disproportionately owned and/or staffed by ethnic minorities."

16. Imloul 2009.

17. Robcis (2013) argues that the 1939 Family Code made the family a key vector of social policy.

18. Surkis 2010a.

19. Bowen and Rohe 2014.

20. Bienvenu and Rials 1980. The Conseil d'État is a body of the French national government that acts as both the legal adviser of the executive branch and the supreme court for administrative justice. The *Rivière* decision determined that the reaction to a provision contrary to the public order is not always the same depending on whether or not it took place abroad.

21. See Kawar 2012. The 1978 *GISTI* decision of France's Conseil d'État is seen by immigration scholars and practitioners as an exemplar of immigrant rights jurisprudence. However, the right to lead a normal family life provided only limited rights and was later eclipsed by Article 8 of the European Convention on Human Rights, which guarantees the right of respect for private and family life. See GISTI (2002).

22. Conseil d'Etat, Ass., 8 décembre 1978, GISTI, CFDT et CGT, https://www.conseil-etat.fr/ressources/decisions-contentieuses/les-grandes-decisions-du-conseil-d-etat/conseil-d-etat-8-decembre-1978-g.i.s.t.i.-c.f.d.t.-et-c.g.t (accessed June 9, 2019).

23. "Les conditions d'une vie familiale normale sont celles qui prévalent en France, pays d'accueil, lesquelles excluent la polygamie; que dès lors les restrictions apportées par la loi au regroupement familial des polygames et les sanctions dont celles-ci sont assorties ne sont pas contraires à la Constitution." Conseil constitutionnel, 1993, No. 93–325 DC, "Loi relative à la maîtrise de l'immigration et aux conditions d'entrée, d'accueil et de séjour des étrangers en France, 13 août," para. 76, https://www.conseil-constitutionnel.fr/decision/1993/93325DC.htm (accessed June 10, 2019).

24. "Familles interdites," *Plein Droit* 24 (April–June 1994), https://www.gisti.org/spip.php?article4037.

25. Ministère de l'Intérieur (France), "Circulaire sur le renouvellement des cartes de résident obtenues par des ressortissants étrangers polygames avant l'entrée en vigueur de la loi du 24 août 1993," April 25, 2000, https://www.gisti.org/doc/textes/2000/circulaire-polygames.html.

26. Korteweg and Yurdakul 2014.

27. Bellucci 2017.

28. Ternaux 2012, 23.

29. Before departmentalization, Mayotte was an overseas territory from 1974 to 2003 and was an integral part of the French Republic, though it lacked citizenship rights. Mayotte was the only island in the archipelago of the Comoros Islands that voted in referenda in 1974 and 1976 to retain its link with France and to forgo independence. The Mahorais became French citizens with departmentalization in 2011. The Institut National de la Statistique et des Études Économiques (INSEE) defines overseas departments as "territorial authorities integrated into the French Republic in the same capacity as the departments and regions in Metropolitan France (INSEE, "Overseas Department/DOM," 2016, https://www.insee.fr/en/metadonnees/definition/c2031).

30. Hachimi-Alaoui and Lemercier 2018.

31. Connell and Aldrich 2020.

32. Weber 2016, 382.

33. According to the 2016 Next Mormons Survey, 87% of Mormons are white. There are no demographics on race and ethnicity for fundamentalist Mormons, but the demographics are likely similar to or include a higher number of whites. In terms of race, fundamentalists blend in in states where there is a high percentage of Mormons, such as Utah—91% white (United States Census, 2019, https://www.census.gov/quickfacts/UT). See also Riess 2019.

34. Ertman 2010, 287.

35. The history of fundamentalist Mormonism is provided in Chapter 2.

36. Alba 2005.

37. Ertman 2010, 290.

38. I am indebted to Jyoti Puri for this insight.

39. Thornton 2011.

40. *Brown v. Buhman*, 947 F. Supp. 2d 1170, 1190 (D. Utah 2013).

41. Strassberg 2015.

42. Quoted in Ertman 2010, 356; emphasis in original.

43. Henkel has trademarked this title.

44. Quoted in Strassberg 2015, 1845.

45. For discussion on trafficking and consent, see Chapter 4.

46. See Strassberg 2015.

47. Stacey and Meadow 2009.

48. Haupert et al. 2017.

49. Rault 2019.

50. Heath 2012b.

51. Bramham 2008.

52. The small community of Bountiful was generally tolerated by the surrounding communities in the 1990s and 2000s. Blackmore was a prominent businessman who had nurtured relationships with many people in the surrounding towns (Bramham 2008).

53. Said 1979.

54. For example, Debbie Palmer, after leaving the community in 1988, filed a complaint stating that she was forced to marry a 58-year-old man at age 15 and that her third "spiritual" husband raped her and fondled her daughter, Memory. The husband was convicted on one count of sexual assault and received a five-year suspended sentence and intensive therapy (Bramham 2008). These complaints motivated the Royal Canadian Mounted Police to investigate Dalmon Oler—who married Memory when she was 16—and Winston Blackmore, the bishop of the community. In 1992 the investigation recommended charging the two men with polygamy. However, the crown counsel issued a statement that no charges would be laid after constitutional experts unanimously concluded that the sections of the Criminal Code outlawing polygamy were unconstitutional.

55. Winter 2015.

56. Canadian Multiculturalism Act, R.S.C., 1985, c. 24 (4th Supp.).

57. Bloemraad et al. 2008, 161.

58. Bloemraad et al. 2008, 161.

59. "What Does Polygamy Have to Do With It?" *The Globe and Mail*, January 22, 2005, https://www.theglobeandmail.com/opinion/what-does-polygamy-have-to-do-with-it/article734115/.

60. Status of Women Canada 2005.

61. *Reference re: Section 293 of the Criminal Code of Canada*, 2011 BCSC 1588.

62. The issue of trafficking and consent is discussed in Chapter 4.

63. Quoted in Ashley 2014, 329.

64. *Reference*, at para. 147.

65. *Reference*, at para. 576.

66. See Ahmed 2014; Ashley 2014; J. Bennion and Joffe 2016; Heath 2016; Lenon 2016; Mathen 2012; Sweet 2013.

67. *Reference*, at para. 1041.

68. Frank 2017.

69. *Reference*, at para. 1037.

70. Chagnon 2014.

71. Jones 2012, 348.

72. The lawyer probably meant fundamentalist rather than mainstream Mormons, as the latter do not practice polygyny.

73. J. Bennion and Joffe 2016.

74. Abji et al. 2019.

75. Quoted in Abji et al. 2019, 813.

76. Quoted in Abji et al. 2019, 813.

77. Quoted in Abji et al. 2019, 813.

78. Van Walsum 2008, 21.

79. Nadler 2017, 71. I am indebted to Martha Ertman for this insight.

80. Quoted in Carlisle 2018.

81. Bramham 2018.

82. Bramham 2018.

Chapter 2

1. Swidler 2001, 2.

2. Swidler 2001, 113.

3. Ingraham 2008.

4. For a discussion of the ways that the state shapes marriage policy, see Heath (2012a, 2012b).

5. Terminologies of Indigenous populations differ between Canada and the United States. In both countries Indigenous peoples were called Indians, and it is in this historical sense that I use the term, highlighting the colonial relationship between Indigenous and non-Indigenous populations. In the United States the term *Native American* is in common usage to describe Indigenous peoples. In Canada the term *Aboriginal* or *Indigenous* is generally preferred to *Native*. *First Nation* is a term used to describe Aboriginal peoples of Canada who are ethnically neither Métis nor Inuit.

6. Pearsall 2019.

7. Cott 2000, 26.

8. Carter 2008, 9.

9. See Mathen 2012. The two cases are *R. v. Bone* [1899], 4 Terr. L.R. 173, 3 C.C.C. 329 (S.C.C.); and *R. v. Harris* (1906), 11 C.C.C. 254 (Que. S.C.).

10. Carter 2008. Chapter 2 provides the history of laws against polygamy in the United States.

11. Quoted in Carter 2008, 44.

12. Cott 2000, 10.

13. White and White 2005.

14. Ertman 2010, 307.

15. Ertman 2010, 308. According to Ertman, anti-polygamists did not see a problem when Blacks participated in what they viewed as a barbaric practice, because Blacks were naturally inferior to whites. However, when whites participated in such practices, it fundamentally undermined racial hierarchy and white supremacy.

16. White and White 2005, 167.

17. *Reynolds v. United States*, 98 U.S. 145 (1879). Quoted in Ertman 2010, 293.

18. Gordon 2002; Strassberg 2015.

19. Strassberg 2015, 1845.

20. Hammon and Jankowiak 2011.

21. This is a succinct summary of the rise of Mormon polygyny and fundamentalism. For a more in-depth analysis of its history, see Foster and Watson (2019) and Van Wagoner (1989).

22. Driggs 1990.

23. Foster and Watson 2019.

24. Gospel Tangents Interview 2017.

25. Foster and Watson 2019. The Apostolic United Brethren is also known as the Allred Group.

26. J. Bennion 2012.

27. Foster and Watson (2019) provide a detailed analysis of the differing groups. The members of the Davis County Co-op (also known as the Kingston Family) practice underage marriage as well as intrafamily marriage. Women members wear modern fashion, are often educated, and blend into mainstream society. This group clusters closer to the FLDS (Osmond 2010). In contrast, a more progressive group is The Work of Jesus Christ (also known as Centennial Park), which splintered from the FLDS. These members have become vocal opponents of underage marriage, and the community has a cutting-edge school that readies students for university, supporting education for women and girls. Still, women in this group wear modest clothing (long skirts and long-sleeve shirts) and long, intricate braids. Like the FLDS, they are easily recognized as Mormon fundamentalists. A small group of fundamentalist Mormons affiliated with the FLDS live in Canada. Another group (also about 500) follows Winston Blackmore, who was excommunicated by Warren Jeffs.

28. Eichenberger 2012.

29. *Sola Scriptura* is the Latin phrase for "by scripture alone." Some Christian denominations believe that the Christian scriptures are the sole source of authority for Christian faith.

30. Majeed 2015.

31. Majeed 2015, 26.

32. For example, Jessop 2007.

33. Jackson 1993.

34. For a discussion of homosocial femininity among Mormon fundamentalists, see Heath (2019). See also J. Bennion 1998, 2012; S. C. Bennion 1977; Iturriaga and Saguy 2017; Kilbride 1994.

35. Lee 1977.

36. Stacey 1996.

37. Majeed 2015, 134.

38. In addition to Bantus, Austronesians (or Proto-Malagasy) from Indonesia arrived in the eighth century. In the fifteenth century, Arabs invaded the island, converting its inhabitants to Islam and introducing the Swahili culture.

39. Caminade (2010) provides an important history of the neocolonial context in which Mayotte became independent of the Comoros Islands and how France supported the movement to remain a French territory to maintain its military presence on the island. An independence referendum was held in the Comoros in 1974, and 95% of voters voted in favor of independence. Almost all the no votes were cast in Mayotte, where a majority desired remaining under French control. The French government recognized the independence of the Comoros Islands in 1975 but did not mention Mayotte. Subsequently, a referendum was held in Mayotte in 1976 on remaining part of the Comoros, which was rejected by more than 99% of voters. France later vetoed United Nations Security Council resolutions that would affirm Comorian sovereignty over Mayotte.

40. For example, Blanchy (1990) conducted fieldwork on the Comoros Islands and Mayotte for many years and has stated that one should not attribute to one island what takes place on another. On the island of Ngazidja, the largest island, there is a matrilineal system of filiation. This is not the case in Mayotte, where they instead have matrilocal residence.

41. Blanchy 1990.

42. Blanchy 1990.

43. Blanchy 1990; Lambek 2018. Arranged marriages of young girls were a dominant practice until the late 1970s. Today, Mahoraise women mostly choose who they will marry, and women marry in their 20s, although these choices are limited by the continued admonition against remaining single in Mahorais society.

44. Lambek 2018. In Mahorais society, marriage represents the transformation, expansion, and renewal of individuals and families. According to

anthropologist Michael Lambek, who conducted ethnographic research beginning in 1975 in Mayotte, marriages at that time were arranged, and girls
were often married quite young, much like the account given by Hamina Ibrahima, whose arranged marriage occurred when she was between 12 and 13
years old. Traditionally, marrying girls at a young age ensured that they were
virgins, essential for women's first marriage. Tradition also required men to
marry a virgin at some point in their lives, although they themselves need
not be virgins. This form of marriage required certain rituals. In general, the
groom provided food for a series of feasts for men in the village. In turn, it was
the bride's parents who prepared the food and fed the guests. After the feast,
men danced to recognize the groom's important achievement. According to
anthropologist Sophie Blanchy (1990), the spouse remained passive in this
process. During the week of the festivities, the family served her, and women
danced for her as she waited for her new husband's ceremonial entrance into
her new home. The religious leader who officiated the marriage in her absence
visited her to provide the dowry from the husband's family, which was often
used by her family to pay for the wedding. My interviews reflect the findings
of these scholars concerning the vast changes that have taken place in Mayotte
over the past forty years.

45. Lambek 2018.

46. Marie et al. (2017). The 1991 population census found 13% of the population to be polygynous.

Chapter 3

1. Jankowiak et al. (2005) studied sixty-nine polygynous families, finding
co-wife conflict, especially in the early years of marriage, including verbal and
physical violence. However, most co-wives preferred pragmatic cooperation.
Slonim-Nevo and Al-Krenawi (2006) interviewed ten polygynous families in a
Bedouin Arab town in the south of Israel, finding that five were well functioning and five were poorly functioning. The researchers discovered that polygyny
in all families was painful, particularly for wives, but that some techniques allowed families to function well. My studies provide evidence that some families
function quite well, like that of Mariam, whereas others function poorly and
can lead to co-wife violence and poor outcomes for children.

2. For example, Boccagni 2012; Hewett 2009; Hoang 2016; Hondagneu-
Sotelo and Avila 1997; Liu 2019; Mazzucato and Dito 2018.

3. Bernhard et al. 2009; Boccagni 2012; Dreby 2006; Parreñas 2001, 2005.

4. Dreby 2006; Hondagneu-Sotelo and Avila 1997; Parreñas 2005.

5. Hondagneu-Sotelo 2007; Lan 2006; Stasiulis and Bakan 2005.

6. Carrillo 2017. See also Cantu 2009. Puri (2016) and Canaday (2009) offer important analyses of the sexual state.

7. Clancy-Smith and Gouda 1998; Conklin 1997; Fassin 2011; Surkis 2000.

8. Conklin 1997.

9. Conklin 2011, 174. Conklin explains how this civilizing mission is mastery over nature, including one's own body. The French conception of being civilized meant to be free of tyranny. This idea of freedom justified methods to eliminate barbaric practices.

10. Saada 2011; Surkis 2010b.

11. Surkis 2010b.

12. Schreier 2007; Surkis 2010b.

13. Bowlan 1997, 111.

14. Ruedy 1992.

15. Bowlan 1997.

16. Quoted in Surkis 2010b, 42. Ultimately, polygyny was seen as an insurmountable difference that made it impossible for Muslims to become French citizens.

17. Diouf 1998.

18. Lewis 2007, 2011.

19. Lewis 2007.

20. Ossman and Terrio 2006.

21. Lewis 2011.

22. Raissiguier 2010.

23. Gaullier 2008.

24. Zeitzen 2008. Polygyny is also supported by Islam, and in Zeitzen's research some of the participants originally from Senegal discussed their practice of polygyny in relation to their Muslim faith.

25. Gaullier 2008, 2009. Gaullier cites the following studies in addition to the study by the National Consultative Commission for Human Rights: Christian Poiret and colleagues conducted research in 1992 on the housing of polygamous households in Île-de-France in which he proposed a range of 3,000–15,000 families. Poiret, in a major survey carried out in 1995, also estimated that 8,000 households were concerned by polygamy in France. The 2000 Interministerial Commission for the Housing of Immigrant Populations provided the number of 2,000 households in Île-de-France and about 500 families in the provincial departments (Gaullier 2009, 6). In 2002 the Department of Population and Migration of the Ministry of Social Affairs gave a range of 8,000–15,000 affected

households in 1992–1993, and the Ministry of the Interior's office gave a range of 10,000–20,000 households in 2004 (Gaullier 2009, 6).

26. Commission Nationale Consultative des Droits de l'Homme de l'Assemblée Nationale 2006.

27. Hunter 2018.

28. Hunter 2018, 1.

Chapter 4

1. For a discussion of women's agency in the context of polygamy, see the introduction in Calder and Beaman (2014). Abrams (1995) offers the idea of constrained choice to move beyond liberal ideas of agency.

2. Fuchs 2001.

3. Abu-Lughod 2013.

4. Abu-Lughod 2002.

5. Spivak 1988, quoted in Abu-Lughod 2013, 33.

6. Jones 2012, 107.

7. Abrams 1995; Duggan and Hunter 2006; Ferguson et al. 1984; Heath et al. 2016.

8. According to the Legal Information Institute at Cornell University (2020), the Mann Act became law in June 1910 to "felonize the use of interstate or foreign commerce to transport women for immoral purposes." In fact, the act criminalized "consensual sexual activity and had racist undertones" that held men liable irrespective of whether the woman consented. The language of immoral purpose was amended in 1986, substituting it with "any sexual activity for which any person can be charged with a criminal offense." See https://www.law.cornell.edu/wex/mann_act.

9. Quek 2018. For a general discussion of the problems of conceptualizing trafficking, see Weitzer 2015.

10. Abrams 1995.

11. Quek 2018, 134.

12. Quek 2018, 136.

13. Quek 2018, 145.

14. Canaday 2009; Heath et al. 2016.

15. Heath 2012b.

16. Abrams 1995.

17. Heath et al. 2016.

18. The Women's Legal Education and Action Fund (LEAF) was founded in 1985 to strengthen the substantive equality rights of women and girls, as

guaranteed by the Charter of Rights and Freedoms. See http://www.leaf.ca/about-leaf/faqs/.

19. *Reference re: Section 293 of the Criminal Code of Canada*, 2011 BCSC 1588, West Coast LEAF Opening Statement, para 4.

20. *Reference*, West Coast Leaf Opening Statement, para 30(b).

21. *Reference re: Section 293 of the Criminal Code of Canada*, 2011 BCSC 1588, West Coast LEAF Closing Statement, para 14.

22. *Reference*, West Coast Leaf Closing Statement, para 60.

23. *Reference*, West Coast Leaf Closing Statement, para 51.

24. *Reference*, West Coast Leaf Opening Statement, para. 30.

25. Daphna Rubin, dir., "Polygamy: Life in Bountiful," *Inside*, season 4, episode 3, Hoggard Films for National Geographic Channels.

26. *Reference re: Section 293 of the Criminal Code of Canada*, 2011 BCSC 1588, para. 879.

27. *Reference*, paras. 1196 and 1197.

28. *Reference*, para. 703.

29. *Reference*, para. 706.

30. Zaman and Koski 2020. For an excellent discussion of laws concerning child marriages in North America, see O'Quinn (2021).

31. *Reference*, para. 1357.

32. A. Campbell 2008, 2009.

33. *Reference*, para. 752.

34. *Reference*, para. 757.

35. Heath 2016.

36. Ministère de l'Intérieur (France), "Circulaire sur le renouvellement des cartes de resident obtenues par des ressortissants étrangers polygames avant l'entrée en vigueur de la loi du 24 août 1993," April 25, 2000, https://www.gisti.org/doc/textes/2000/circulaire-polygames.html.

37. *Reference*, para. 564.

38. Kandiyoti 1988, 275.

39. Brasher 1998; Diefendorf 2019; Gallagher 2003, 2004; Griffith 1997; Ingersoll 2003; Kelly 2012; Schreiber 2008; Stacey and Gerard 1990.

40. Avishai 2008; Beaman 2001; Brasher 1998; Chen 2005; Chong 2006; Davidman 1991; Griffith 1997; Heath 2003, 2019; Irby 2014; Leamaster and Einwohner 2018; Prickett 2015.

41. See, for example, Burke 2016; Irby 2014.

42. Burke 2016; Diefendorf 2015.

43. Blackmore 2020.

44. Blackmore 2020, 201.

45. Mahmood 2005.

46. Heath 2019.

47. Hochschild 1983.

48. Burke 2012.

49. Erickson 2005, 338.

Chapter 5

1. Link and Phelan 2001.

2. Hyest et al. 2008, 84.

3. Quoted in Wolfreys 2002.

4. Horvath 2018; Selby 2014.

5. Quoted in Selby 2014, 122.

6. Quoted in Selby 2014, 123.

7. Selby 2014, 123.

8. Currier 2010; McKay and Angotti 2016.

9. Fysh and Wolfreys 2003.

10. Moulères 2010, 15–16.

11. Le Bars 2010. News reports cited different total numbers of children. According to *Le Monde*, in June 2010 Hebbadj had fourteen children with one more on the way.

12. "Many Wives' Tales," *Economist*, May 8, 2010, http://www.economist .com/node/16068972.

13. Ganley 2021.

14. Civil Code, as of July 1, 2013. Translated by David W. Gruning.

15. Lochak 2012, 21.

16. Trouille 2000.

17. Stein 2001.

18. Ertman 2010, 290.

19. Link and Phelan 2001.

20. Ertman 2010, 289.

21. Collins 2004.

22. Misra et al. 2003.

23. Winslow 2019.

24. Blackmore 2020, 130.

25. Bramham 2008, 9.

26. Bramham 2008, 162.

27. Rubin 1984, 153.

28. Porter-Hirsche 2012.

29. Dawson 1998; S. Wright and Palmer 2016.

30. Hannaford 2018.

31. Erin La Rosa, "19 Things You Probably Don't Know About FLDS Polygamists," BuzzFeed, March 6, 2013, https://www.buzzfeed.com/erinlarosa/19-things-you-probably-I-know-about-flds-polygamists.

32. "Ex-FLDS Members Who Broke with Secretive Polygamous Sect Buy Former Compound," Associated Press, February 26, 2021, kutv.com/news/local/ex-flds-members-who-broke-with-secretive-polygamous-sect-buy-former-compound.

Chapter 6

1. I am not including Canada in this chapter because it has a small polygynous population, which makes it difficult to organize against the state. There have been more efforts to protest for and against polygamy. Nancy Mereska led the organization Stop Polygamy in Canada, and several books were written by people who left polygamy, such as Debbie Palmer and Dave Perrin's *Keep Sweet: Children of Polygamy*. A movement for polyamory exists in Canada, the Canadian Polyamory Advocacy Association, which was formed to intervene in the British Columbia reference case in 2010. However, there is no organized movement to protest polygamy's criminalization. Winston Blackmore has allowed journalists to film his community and has given interviews. A recent book calling for decriminalization was written by Winston's daughter, Mary Jayne Blackmore (2020), *Balancing Bountiful: What I Learned About Feminism from My Polygamist Grandmothers*. She describes the efforts women in the community made to educate mainstream Canadians about their lifestyle through a group they called the Bountiful Women's Society. Beyond Borders invited the group to an international conference in 2005 in Winnipeg, because a discussion about Bountiful and polygamy was on the agenda. Blackmore summarized the experience: "The many hours of preparing, organizing, speaking, interviewing, welcoming people into homes, feeding, feeding and feeding, talking and talking, repeating over and over: 'We are here, we are Canadians, we are alive and we are not going away. We choose to be here. This is our family. We love our family and we don't need to be saved: we just deserve to be here.' For all the effort it takes, we feel it mostly falls unheeded. Most media groups cover the summit in similar ways, belittling the value, efforts and innovation of the women to advocate for their families and lifestyle. The headlines and articles that get written over and over take the same spin: 'Under the directive

of the male leadership, the women of Bountiful community speak out'" (Blackmore 2020, 190).

2. See Cantu 2009; Carrillo 2017; Fassin 2014; Frank 2017; Puar 2007; Puri 2016; Richardson 2018; Smith 2020.

3. Hull 2006, 16. See also Harding 2010.

4. Taylor et al. 2009.

5. Massoud and Moore 2020.

6. Abrego 2019.

7. Robcis 2015.

8. Moreau 2013.

9. Moreau 2013.

10. De Boni 2016.

11. Idriss 2016.

12. Moore-Emmett 2004.

13. Moore-Emmett 2004, 61.

14. Decker 2013.

15. See Laschever and Meyer (2021) for an overview. See also Fetner 2008.

16. Laschever and Meyer 2021.

17. Lawrence Wright (2002), in his *New Yorker* article, provides an excellent overview of the controversy over polygamy before the 2002 Olympic Winter Games and the Utah bill that was passed.

18. Perkins 2003.

19. Centennial Park Action Committee: http://www.cpaction.org/CPAC/index.htm.

20. For an analysis of how various groups are using "coming out" to gain personal power, allies, and increased civil rights, see Saguy 2020.

Conclusion

1. *Reference re: Section 293 of the Criminal Code of Canada*, 2011 BCSC 1588, para. 1318, https://www.hlaw.ca/wp-content/uploads/2009/01/2011-BCSC-1588-Reference-re-Section-293-of-the-Criminal-Code-of-Canada.pdf) (accessed October 21, 2020).

2. Burgett 2005, 77. See also Denike 2010; A. Kaplan 1998; Stoler 2001.

3. Burgett 2005, 78. See also Cott 2000; Ertman 2010; McClintock 1995.

4. A. Kaplan 1998, 582.

5. Stoler 2001, 829.

6. Said 1979.

7. Bramham 2008, 11.

8. DelPlato 2002.

9. DelPlato 2002, 20.

10. Conklin 2011; Surkis 2010b.

11. Surkis 2010b.

12. Hamilton et al. 2004.

13. Debra Majeed's (2015) research provides an important lens into the lives of African American Muslims who practice polygyny in the United States.

14. Smearman 2009.

15. For example, Amgott 2015; Faucon 2014; Rogozen 2017; Smearman 2009.

16. Rogozen 2017.

17. Cott 2000, 25.

18. Cott 2000, 73.

19. Ertman 2010, 307.

20. Rogozen 2017.

21. Newport 2020.

22. Hopkins 2017.

23. Carter 2008, 4.

24. Carter 2008, 4.

25. *Reference*, para 152.

26. *Reference*, para 575. See also Lenon 2016.

27. *Reference*, para 561.

28. *Reference*, para 567.

29. Abji and Korteweg 2021.

30. Béchard et al. 2014; Lenon 2016.

31. Berry 2020.

32. Banting and Kymlicka (2010) argue for Canadian exceptionalism, arguing that "Canada's problems are not Europe's problems" (62).

33. Law Commission of Canada 2001. See Cossman and Ryder (2017) for a discussion of this report and its impacts on Canadian society.

34. Grossbard 2013.

35. Bass 2014.

36. Giddens 1992.

37. Aguiar 2018, 5.

38. For analysis of the strange bedfellows that anti-polygamy brings together, see Heath et al. 2016.

39. See Chapter 4.

40. See, for example, M. Sullivan 2004.

41. *Reference*, Closing Submissions, Canadian Polyamory Advocacy Association, para 8.

42. J. Ward 2020, 9.

43. Andrejek et al. 2022.

44. Pollitt et al. 2018; Umberson et al. 2015.

45. For example, Avishai 2008; Beaman 2001; Brasher 1998; Chen 2005; Chong 2006; Davidman 1991; Diefendorf 2019; Gallagher 2003, 2004; Griffith 1997; Heath 2003, 2015, 2019; Irby 2014; Leamaster and Einwohner 2018; Prickett 2015; Schreiber 2008; Stacey and Gerard 1990.

46. Heath 2019.

47. Samantha provided the exposé in personal correspondence on January 16, 2015.

48. Abu-Lughod 2013, 43.

49. Abu-Lughod (2013, 17) describes how the "sad figure of the oppressed Muslim woman" justified the war in Afghanistan in 2001.

50. A. Campbell 2008, 2009.

51. Strassberg 1997, 1501. See also Strassberg 2003, 2015; Witte 2015a, 2015b.

52. Strassberg 2003, 362.

53. Den Otter 2015; Goldfeder 2017.

54. Goldfeder 2017, 126.

APPENDIX

1. Heath 2003, 2015.

2. Heath 2009, 2012a, 2012b, 2013.

3. "Polygamists, Unite!" *Newsweek*, March 19, 2006, https://www.newsweek.com/polygamists-unite-106169.

4. "Polygamists, Unite!"

5. Gross 2007.

6. Gross 2007.

7. Latin 2007.

8. A. Campbell 2008, 2009, 2010.

9. Adams and Jarvis 2006, 1.

10. For a good discussion of how the court sought to protect monogamy by marginalizing qualitative methodologies and privileging quantitative research that purportedly demonstrated widespread social harms associated with the practice of polygyny, see Ashley (2014).

11. Heath et al. 2016.

12. J. Bennion 1998.

13. Desmond 2014.

Bibliography

Abji, Salina, and Anna C. Korteweg. 2021. "'Honour'-Based Violence and the Politics of Culture in Canada: Advancing a Cultural Analysis of Multiscalar Violence." *International Journal of Child, Youth, and Family Studies* 12 (1): 73–92.

Abji, Salina, Anna C. Korteweg, and Lawrence H. Williams. 2019. "Culture Talk and the Politics of the New Right: Navigating Gendered Racism in Attempts to Address Violence Against Women in Immigrant Communities." *Signs: Journal of Women in Culture and Society* 44 (3): 797–822. https://doi .org/10.1086/701161.

Abrams, Kathryn. 1995. "Sex Wars Redux: Agency and Coercion, Feminist Legal Theory." *Columbia Law Review* 95 (2): 304–76.

Abramsky, Tanya, Charlotte H. Watts, Claudia Garcia-Moreno, Karen Devries, Ligia Kiss, Mary Ellsberg, Henrica Afm Jansen, and Lori Heise. 2011. "What Factors Are Associated with Recent Intimate Partner Violence? Findings from the WHO Multi-Country Study on Women's Health and Domestic Violence." *BMC Public Health* 11: art. 109. https://doi.org/10.1186/1471-2458-11-109.

Abrego, Leisy J. 2019. "Relational Legal Consciousness of U.S. Citizenship: Privilege, Responsibility, Guilt, and Love in Latino Mixed-Status Families." *Law and Society Review* 53 (3): 641–70.

Abu-Lughod, Lila. 2002. "Do Muslim Women Really Need Saving? Anthropological Reflections on Cultural Relativism and Its Others." *American Anthropologist* 104 (3): 783–90.

———. 2013. *Do Muslim Women Need Saving?* Cambridge, MA: Harvard University Press.

Adam, Barry D. 2003. "The Defense of Marriage Act and American Exceptionalism: The 'Gay Marriage' Panic in the United States." *Journal of the History of Sexuality* 12 (2): 259–76. https://doi.org/10.1353/sex.2003.0074.

Adams, Susan H., and John P. Jarvis. 2006. "Indicators of Veracity and Deception: An Analysis of Written Statements Made to Police." *Speech, Language, and the Law* 13 (1): 1–22.

Aguiar, Marian. 2018. *Arranging Marriage: Conjugal Agency in the South Asian Diaspora.* Minneapolis: University of Minnesota Press.

Ahinkorah, Bright Opoku. 2021. "Polygyny and Intimate Partner Violence in Sub-Saharan Africa: Evidence from 16 Cross-Sectional Demographic and Health Surveys." *SSM: Population Health* 13. https://doi.org/10.1016/j.ssmph.2021.100729.

Ahmed, Washim. 2014. *Criminalization of Polygamy in Canada: Historical, Legal, and Sociological Analysis.* Osgoode Legal Studies Research Paper no. 78/2014. https://doi.org/10.2139/ssrn.2508804.

Alba, Richard. 2005. "Bright vs. Blurred Boundaries: Second-Generation Assimilation and Exclusion in France, Germany, and the United States." *Ethnic and Racial Studies* 28 (1): 20–49. https://doi.org/10.1080/0141987042000280003.

Alexandre, Michele. 2007. "Big Love: Is Feminist Polygamy an Oxymoron or a True Possibility?" *Hastings Women's Law Journal* 18 (1): 3–30.

Ali, Muna-Udbi A. 2017. "Un-Mapping Gay Imperialism: A Postcolonial Approach to Sexual Orientation-Based Development." *Reconsidering Development* 5 (1). https://pubs.lib.umn.edu/index.php/reconsidering/article/view/907.

Al-Krenawi, Alean. 2001. "Women from Polygamous and Monogamous Marriages in an Out-Patient Psychiatric Clinic." *Transcultural Psychiatry* 38 (2): 187–99.

———. 2010. "A Study of Psychological Symptoms, Family Function, Marital and Life Satisfactions of Polygamous and Monogamous Women: The Palestinian Case." *International Journal of Social Psychiatry* 58 (1): 79–86. https://doi.org/10.1177/0020764010387063.

———. 2014. *Psychosocial Impact of Polygamy in the Middle East.* New York: Springer.

Al-Krenawi, Alean, and John R. Graham. 2006. "A Comparison of Family Functioning, Life and Marital Satisfaction, and Mental Health of Women in Polygamous and Monogamous Marriages." *International Journal of Social Psychiatry* 52 (1): 5–17. https://doi.org/10.1177/0020764006061245.

Al-Krenawi, Alean, John R. Graham, and Fakir Al Gharaibeh. 2011. "A Comparison Study of Psychological, Family Function Marital, and Life Satisfactions of Polygamous and Monogamous Women in Jordan." *Community Mental Health Journal* 47: 594–602.

Al-Krenawi, Alean, and Yaniv Kanat-Maymon. 2017. "Psychological Symptomatology, Self-Esteem, and Life Satisfactions of Women from Polygamous and Monogamous Marriages in Syria." *International Social Work* 60 (1): 196–207. https://doi.org/10.1177/0020872814562478.

Altman, Irwin, and Joseph Ginat. 1996. *Polygamous Families in Contemporary Society*. New York: Cambridge University Press.

Amgott, Jonathan E. 2015. "Post-Windsor Prospects for Morals Legislation: The Case of Polygamous Immigrants." *Stanford Law and Policy Review* 26: 513–53.

Andrejek, Nicole, Tina Fetner, and Melanie Heath. 2022. "Climax as Work: Heteronormativity, Gender Labor, and the Gender Gap in Orgasms." *Gender and Society* 36 (2): 189–213.

Ashley, Sean Matthew. 2014. "Sincere but Naive: Methodological Queries Concerning the British Columbia Polygamy Reference Trial." *Canadian Review of Sociology / Revue Canadienne de Sociologie* 51 (4): 325–42. https://doi.org/10.1111/cars.12050.

Avishai, Orit. 2008. "Doing Religion in a Secular World: Women in Conservative Religions and the Question of Agency." *Gender and Society* 22 (4): 409–33.

Bailey, Martha, and Amy J. Kaufman. 2010. *Polygamy in the Monogamous World: Multicultural Challenges for Western Law and Policy*. Santa Barbara, CA: Praeger.

Bala, Nicolas, Katherine Duvall-Antonacopoulos, Joanne J. Paetsch, and Leslie D. MacRae Krisa. 2005. *Polygamy in Canada: Legal and Social Implications for Women and Children*. Canadian Research Institute for Law and the Family, CanLIIDocs 18. https://canlii.ca/t/285f.

Banting, Keith, and Will Kymlicka. 2010. "Canadian Multiculturalism: Global Anxieties and Local Debates." *British Journal of Canadian Studies* 23 (1): 43–72.

Barker, Meg, and Darren Langdridge, eds. 2012. *Understanding Non-Monogamies*. New York: Routledge.

Bass, Loretta E. 2014. *African Immigrant Families in Another France*. Basingstoke, UK: Palgrave Macmillan.

Beaman, Lori G. 2001. "Molly Mormons, Mormon Feminists, and Moderates: Religious Diversity and the Latter Day Saints Church." *Sociology of Religion* 62 (1): 65–86.

Béchard, Julie, Sandra Elgersma, and Julia Nicol. 2014. *Bill S-7: An Act to Amend the Immigration and Refugee Protection Act, the Civil Marriage Act and the Criminal Code and to Make Consequential Amendments to Other Acts—Legislative Summary*. Ottawa: Library of Parliament. https://lop.parl.ca/staticfiles/PublicWebsite/Home/ResearchPublications/LegislativeSummaries/PDF/41-2/s7-e.pdf.

Behrman, Julia A. 2019. "Polygynous Unions and Intimate Partner Violence in Nigeria: An Examination of the Role of Selection." *Journal of Marriage and Family* 81 (4): 905–19. https://doi.org/10.1111/jomf.12570.

Bellucci, Lucia. 2017. "Shaping Notions of Personal Autonomy in Plural Societies." In *Personal Autonomy in Plural Societies*, ed. Marie-Claire Foblets, Michele Graziadei, and Alison Dundes Renteln, 192–205. London: Routledge.

Bennion, Janet. 1998. *Women of Principle: Female Networking in Contemporary Mormon Polygyny*. New York: Oxford University Press.

———. 2008. *Evaluating the Effects of Polygamy on Women and Children in Four North American Mormon Fundamentalist Groups: An Anthropological Study*. New York: Edwin Mellen Press.

———. 2011. "History, Culture, and Variability of Mormon Schismatic Groups." In *Modern Polygamy in the United States*, ed. Cardell K. Jacobson and Lara Burton, 101–24. New York: Oxford University Press.

———. 2012. *Polygamy in Primetime: Media, Gender, and Politics in Mormon Fundamentalism*. Waltham, MA: Brandeis University Press.

Bennion, Janet, and Lisa Fishbayn Joffe, eds. 2016. *The Polygamy Question*. Logan: Utah State University Press.

Bennion, Sherilyn Cox. 1977. "The New Northwest and Woman's Exponent: Early Voices for Suffrage." *Journalism Quarterly* 54 (2): 286–92.

Bernhard, Judith K., Patricia Landolt, and Luin Goldring. 2009. "Transnationalizing Families: Canadian Immigration Policy and the Spatial Fragmentation of Care-Giving Among Latin American Newcomers." *International Migration* 47 (2): 3–31. https://doi.org/10.1111/j.1468-2435.2008.00479.x.

Bernstein, Mary, and Nancy A. Naples. 2015. "Altared States: Legal Structuring and Relationship Recognition in the United States, Canada, and Australia." *American Sociological Review* 80 (6): 1226–49. https://doi.org/10.1177/000312 2415613414.

Berry, David. 2020. "Canadian Multiculturalism Act." https://www.thecanadianencyclopedia.ca/en/article/canadian-multiculturalism-act.

Bertossi, Christophe. 2012. "French Republicanism and the Problem of Normative Density." *Comparative European Politics* 10 (3): 248–65. https://doi.org/10.1057/cep.2012.6.

Bienvenu, Jean-Jacques, and Stéphane Rials. 1980. "Repertoire Analytique." *La Revue Administrative* 198: 606–9.

Blackmore, Mary Jayne. 2020. *Balancing Bountiful: What I Learned About Feminism from My Polygamist Grandmothers*. Halfmoon Bay, Canada: Caitlin Press.

Blanchy, Sophie. 1990. *La vie quotidienne à Mayotte*. Paris: L'Harmattan.

Bloemraad, Irene, Anna Korteweg, and Gökçe Yurdakul. 2008. "Citizenship and Immigration: Multiculturalism, Assimilation, and Challenges to the Nation-State." *Annual Review of Sociology* 34 (1): 153–79. https://doi.org/10.11 46/annurev.soc.34.040507.134608.

Boccagni, Paolo. 2012. "Practising Motherhood at a Distance: Retention and Loss in Ecuadorian Transnational Families." *Journal of Ethnic and Migration Studies* 38 (2): 261–77. https://doi.org/10.1080/1369183X.2012.646421.

Bowen, John R., and Matias Rohe. 2014. "Juridical Framings of Muslims and Islam in France and Germany." In *European States and Their Muslim Citizens: The Impact of Institutions on Perceptions and Boundaries*, ed. John R. Bowen, Christophe Bertossi, Jan W. Duyvendak, and Mona Lena Krook, 135–63. New York: Cambridge University Press.

Bowlan, Jeanne. 1997. "Polygamists Need Not Apply: Becoming a French Citizen in Colonial Algeria, 1918–1938." *Proceedings of the Western Society for French History* 24: 110–19.

Bramham, Daphne. 2008. *The Secret Lives of Saints: Child Brides and Lost Boys in Canada's Polygamous Mormon Sect*. Toronto: Random House Canada.

———. 2018. "Sentencing Two Polygamists and Child Abusers to House Arrest Is No Punishment at All." *Vancouver Sun*, June 26. https://vancouversun .com/opinion/columnists/daphne-bramham-sentencing-two-polygamists -and-child-abusers-to-house-arrest-is-no-punishment-at-all.

Brasher, Brenda. 1998. *Godly Women: Fundamentalism and Female Power*. New Brunswick, NJ: Rutgers University Press.

Brekhus, Wayne. 1998. "A Sociology of the Unmarked: Redirecting Our Focus." *Sociological Theory* 16 (1): 34–51.

Brooks, Thom. 2009. "The Problem with Polygamy." *Philosophical Topics* 37 (2): 109–22.

Brubaker, W. Rogers. 1992. *Citizenship and Nationhood in France and Germany*. Cambridge, MA: Harvard University Press.

Buck, Thomas, Jr. 2012. "From Big Love to the Big House: Justifying Anti-Polygamy Laws in an Age of Expanding Rights." *Emory International Law Review* 26 (2): 939–96.

Burgett, Bruce. 2005. "On the Mormon Question: Race, Sex, and Polygamy in the 1850s and the 1990s." *American Quarterly* 57 (1): 75–102.

Burke, Kelsy. 2012. "Women's Agency in Gender-Traditional Religions: A Review of Four Approaches." *Sociology Compass* 6 (2): 122–33.

———. 2016. *Christians Under Covers: Evangelicals and Sexual Pleasure on the Internet.* Berkeley: University of California Press.

Calder, Gillian, and Lori G. Beaman, eds. 2014. *Polygamy's Rights and Wrongs: Perspectives on Harm, Family, and Law.* Vancouver: University of British Columbia Press.

Calhoun, Cheshire. 2005. "Who's Afraid of Polygamous Marriage: Lessons for Same-Sex Marriage Advocacy from the History of Polygamy." *San Diego Law Review* 42: 1023–42.

Caminade, Pierre. 2010. *Comores-Mayotte: une histoire néocoloniale.* Marseille: Agone.

Camiscioli, Elisa. 2009. *Reproducing the French Race: Immigration, Intimacy, and Embodiment in the Early Twentieth Century.* Durham, NC: Duke University Press.

Campbell, Angela. 2008. "Wives' Tales: Reflecting on Research in Bountiful." *Canadian Journal of Law and Society* 23 (1/2): 121–42.

———. 2009. "Bountiful Voices." *Osgoode Hall Law Journal* 47 (2): 183–234.

———. 2010. "Bountiful's Plural Marriages." *International Journal of Law in Context* 6 (4): 343–62.

Campbell, Mary. 2001. "Mr. Peay's Horses: The Federal Response to Mormon Polygamy, 1854–1887." *Yale Journal of Law and Feminism* 13 (1): 29–70. https://digitalcommons.law.yale.edu/yjlf/vol13/iss1/3.

Canaday, Margot. 2009. *The Straight State: Sexuality and Citizenship in Twentieth-Century America.* Princeton, NJ: Princeton University Press.

Cantu, Lionel. 2009. *The Sexuality of Migration: Border Crossings and Mexican Immigrant Men.* New York: New York University Press.

Carlisle, Nate. 2018. "'The Cults Won,' Anti-Polygamist Says as Even Some Supporters of Winston Blackmore Mock His Sentence." *Salt Lake Tribune*, June 27. https://www.sltrib.com/news/polygamy/2018/06/27/cults-won-anti/.

Carrillo, Héctor. 2017. *Pathways of Desire: The Sexual Migration of Mexican Gay Men.* Chicago: University of Chicago Press.

Carter, Sarah. 2008. *The Importance of Being Monogamous: Marriage and Nation Building in Western Canada to 1915.* Edmonton: University of Alberta Press.

Chagnon, Rachel. 2014. "Constats sur la difficile intégration d'une analyse intersectionnelle en droit canadien: le traitement de la polygamie dans l'affaire Bountiful." *Nouvelles Pratiques Sociales* 26 (2): 187–99. https://doi-org.libaccess.lib.mcmaster.ca/10.7202/1029270ar.

Chambers, David L. 1997. "Polygamy and Same-Sex Marriage." *Hofstra Law Review* 26 (1): 53–83.

Charsley, Katherine, and Anika Liversage. 2013. "Transforming Polygamy: Migration, Transnationalism, and Multiple Marriages Among Muslim Minorities." *Global Networks* 13 (1): 60–78.

Chauncey, George. 2019. *Gay New York: Gender, Urban Culture, and the Making of the Gay Male World, 1890–1940*. New York: Basic Books.

Chen, Carolyn. 2005. "A Self of One's Own: Taiwanese Immigrant Women and Religious Conversion." *Gender and Society* 19 (3): 336–57.

Chong, Kelly. 2006. "Negotiating Patriarchy: South Korean Evangelical Women and the Politics of Gender." *Gender and Society* 20 (6): 697–724.

Clancy-Smith, Julia Ann, and Frances Gouda. 1998. *Domesticating the Empire: Race, Gender, and Family Life in French and Dutch Colonialism*. Charlottesville: University Press of Virginia.

Clanton, Gordon. 2006. "Jealousy and Envy." In *Handbook of the Sociology of Emotions*, ed. Jan E. Stets and Jonathan H. Turner, 410–42. New York: Springer.

Collins, Patricia Hill. 2004. *Black Sexual Politics: African Americans, Gender, and the New Racism*. New York: Routledge.

Commission Nationale Consultative des Droits de l'Homme de l'Assemblée Nationale. 2006. "Etude et propositions sur la polygamie en France." https://www.cncdh.fr/fr/publications/avis-sur-la-situation-de-la-polygamie-en-france.

Conklin, Alice. 1997. *A Mission to Civilize: The Republican Idea of Empire in France and West Africa, 1895–1930*. Stanford, CA: Stanford University Press.

———. 2011. "The Civilizing Mission." In *The French Republic: History, Values, Dates*, ed. Edward Berenson, Vincent Duclert, and Christophe Prochas, 173–81. Ithaca, NY: Cornell University Press.

Connell, John, and Robert Aldrich. 2020. *The Ends of Empire: The Last Colonies Revisited*. Singapore: Palgrave Macmillan.

Conseil du Statut de la Femme. 2010. *La polygamie au regard du droit des femmes* [Polygamy and the Rights of Women]. Avis: Gouvernement du Quebec. https://www.csf.gouv.qc.ca/wp-content/uploads/avis-la-polygamie-au-regard-du-droit-des-femmes.pdf.

Coontz, Stephanie. 2006. *Marriage, a History: How Love Conquered Marriage*. New York: Penguin.

Corriveau, Patrice. 2011. *Judging Homosexuals: A History of Gay Persecution in Quebec and France*. Vancouver: University of British Columbia Press.

Cossman, Brenda, and Bruce Ryder. 2017. "Beyond Beyond Conjugality." *Canadian Journal of Family Law* 30 (2): 227–63.

Cott, Nancy F. 2000. *Public Vows: A History of Marriage and the Nation.* Cambridge, MA: Harvard University Press.

Currier, Ashley. 2010. "Political Homophobia in Postcolonial Namibia." *Gender and Society* 24 (1): 110–29.

Davidman, Lynn. 1991. *Tradition in a Rootless World: Women Turn to Orthodox Judaism.* Berkeley: University of California Press.

Davis, Adrienne D. 2010. "Regulating Polygamy: Intimacy, Default Rules, and Bargaining for Equality." *Columbia Law Review* 110 (8): 1955–2046.

Dawson, Lorne L. 1998. *Comprehending Cults: The Sociology of New Religious Movements.* Toronto: Oxford University Press.

De Boni, Marc. 2016. "Polygamie et mariage gay: Marine Le Pen désavoue sa niece." *Le Figaro*, March 17. https://www.lefigaro.fr/politique/le-scan/couacs /2016/03/17/25005-20160317ARTFIG00087-polygamie-et-mariage-gay-ma rine-le-pen-desavoue-sa-niece.php.

Decker, Kristyn. 2013. *Fifty Years in Polygamy: Big Secrets and Little White Lies.* St. George, UT: Synergy Books.

DelPlato, Joan. 2002. *Multiple Wives, Multiple Pleasures: Representing the Harem, 1800–1875.* London: Associated University Press.

Denike, Margaret. 2010. "The Racialization of White Man's Polygamy." *Hyptia* 25 (4): 852–74.

Den Otter, Ron C. 2015. *In Defense of Plural Marriage.* New York: Cambridge University Press.

Deri, Jillian. 2015. *Love's Refraction: Jealousy and Compersion in Queer Women's Polyamorous Relationships.* Toronto: University of Toronto Press.

Desmond, Matthew. 2014. "Relational Ethnography." *Theory and Society* 43: 547–79.

Diefendorf, Sarah. 2015. "After the Wedding Night: Sexual Abstinence and Masculinities over the Life Course." *Gender and Society* 29 (5): 647–69.

———. 2019. "Contemporary Evangelical Responses to Feminism and the Imagined Secular." *Signs: Journal of Women in Culture and Society* 44 (4): 1003–26.

Dinero, Steven C. 2012. "Neo-Polygamous Activity Among the Bedouin of the Negev, Israel: Dysfunction, Adaptation—Or Both?" *Journal of Comparative Family Studies* 43 (4): 495–509.

Diouf, Mamadou. 1998. "The French Colonial Policy of Assimilation and the Civility of the Originaires of the Four Communes (Senegal): A Nineteenth Century Globalization Project." *Development and Change* 29: 671–96.

Dixon-Spear, Patricia. 2009. *We Want for Our Sisters What We Want for Ourselves: African American Women Who Practice Polygyny by Consent*, 2nd ed. Decatur, GA: Nuvo Development Inc.

Dreby, Joanna. 2006. "Honor and Virtue: Mexican Parenting in the Transnational Context." *Gender and Society* 20 (1): 32–59. https://doi.org/10.1177/0891243205282660.

Driggs, Ken. 1990. "After the Manifesto: Modern Polygamy and Fundamentalist Mormons." *Journal of Church and State* 32 (2): 367–89.

Duggan, Lisa. 2003. *The Twilight of Equality: Neoliberalism, Cultural Politics, and the Attack on Democracy.* Boston: Beacon Press.

Duggan, Lisa, and Nan D. Hunter. 2006. *Sex Wars: Sexual Dissent and Political Culture.* New York: Routledge.

Duncan, Emily J. 2008. "The Positive Effects of Legalizing Polygamy: Love Is a Many Splendored Thing." *Duke Journal of Gender Law and Policy* 15: 315–37.

Eichenberger, Sarah. 2012. "When for Better Is for Worse: Immigration Law's Gendered Impact on Foreign Polygamous Marriage." *Duke Law Journal* 61 (5): 1067–1110.

Erickson, Rebecca J. 2005. "Why Emotion Work Matters: Sex, Gender, and the Division of Household Labor." *Journal of Marriage and Family* 67 (2): 337–51.

Ertman, Martha M. 2010. "Race Treason: The Untold Story of America's Ban on Polygamy." *Columbia Journal of Gender and Law* 2: 287–366.

Eskridge, William N., Jr. 1999. *Gaylaw: Challenging the Apartheid of the Closet.* Cambridge, MA: Harvard University Press.

Fassin, Eric. 2011. "Order and Disorder in the Family." In *The French Republic: History, Values, Dates,* ed. Edward Berenson, Vincent Duclert, and Christophe Prochas, 308–14. Ithaca, NY: Cornell University Press.

———. 2014. "Same-Sex Marriage, Nation, and Race: French Political Logics and Rhetorics." *Contemporary French Civilization* 39 (3): 281–301.

Faucon, Casey E. 2014. "Marriage Outlaws: Regulating Polygamy in America." *Duke Journal of Gender Law and Policy* 22: 1–54.

Felmlee, Diane H., and Susan Sprecher. 2006. "Love." In *Handbook of the Sociology of Emotions,* ed. Jan E. Stets and Jonathan H. Turner, 389–409. New York: Springer.

Ferguson, Ann, Ilene Philipson, Irene Diamond, Lee Quinby, Carole S. Vance, and Ann Barr Snitow. 1984. "Forum: The Feminist Sexuality Debates." *Signs: Journal of Women in Culture and Society* 10 (1): 106–35.

Fetner, Tina. 2008. *How the Religious Right Shaped Lesbian and Gay Activism.* Minneapolis: University of Minnesota Press.

Foster, Craig L., and Marianne T. Watson. 2019. *American Polygamy: A History of Fundamentalist Mormon Faith.* Charleston, SC: History Press.

Frank, Nathaniel. 2017. *Awakening: How Gays and Lesbians Brought Marriage Equality to America.* Cambridge, MA: Harvard University Press.

Friedman, Sara L. 2005. "The Intimacy of State Power: Marriage, Liberation, and Socialist Subjects in Southeastern China." *American Ethnologist* 32 (2): 312–27. https://doi.org/10.1525/ae.2005.32.2.312.

Fry, Amy. 2010. "Polygamy in America: How the Varying Legal Standards Fail to Protect Mothers and Children from Its Abuses." *Saint Louis University Law Journal* 54 (3): 967–96.

Fuchs, Martin. 2001. "A Religion for Civil Society? Ambedkar's Buddhism, the Dalit Issue, and the Imagination of Emergent Possibilities." In *Charisma and Canon: Essays on the Religious History of the Indian Subcontinent*, ed. Vasudha Dalmia, Angelika Malinar, and Martin Christof, 250–73. New Delhi: Oxford University Press.

Fysh, Peter, and Jim Wolfreys. 2003. *The Politics of Racism in France*. New York: Palgrave Macmillan.

Gallagher, Sally K. 2003. *Evangelical Identity and Gendered Family Life*. New Brunswick, NJ: Rutgers University Press.

———. 2004. "Where Are the Antifeminist Evangelicals? Evangelical Identity, Subcultural Location, and Attitudes Toward Feminism." *Gender and Society* 18 (4): 451–72.

Ganley, Elaine. 2021. "France Passes Anti-Radicalism Bill That Worries Muslims." Associated Press, February 16. https://apnews.com/article/polygamy-radicalism-secularism-elections-france-cbee2c916aa8c35380562277f0025c2b.

Gaullier, Pauline. 2008. "La décohabitation et le relogement des familles polygames: un malaise politique émaillé d'injonctions contradictoires." *Revue des Politiques Sociales et Familiales* 94: 59–69.

———. 2009. *Le relogement des menage polygames: un revelateur des enjeux lies au relogement et a l'intergration en France*. Paris: Fondation Abbé Pierre pour le Logement des Défavorisés. http://www.affil.fr/uploads/4/2/0/7/42072013/synthese_de_letude_pauline_gaullier_(3)_1.pdf.

Gher, Jamie M. 2008. "Polygamy and Same-Sex Marriage: Allies or Adversaries Within the Same-Sex Marriage Movement." *William & Mary Journal of Women and Law* 14: 559–603.

Giddens, Anthony. 1992. *The Transformation of Intimacy: Sexuality, Love, and Eroticism in Modern Societies*. Stanford, CA: Stanford University Press.

GISTI. 2002. "Pas de vie familiale sans droit au travail." *Plein Droit* 53–54. https://www.gisti.org/doc/plein-droit/53-54/j2.html (accessed June 9, 2019).

Goldfeder, Mark. 2017. *Legalizing Plural Marriage: The Next Frontier in Family Law*. Waltham, MA: Brandeis University Press.

Gordon, Sarah Barringer. 2002. *The Mormon Question: Polygamy and Constitutional Conflict in Nineteenth-Century America*. Chapel Hill: University of North Carolina Press.

Gospel Tangents Interview. 2017. *Anne Wilde: Expert on Modern Day Polygamy*, ed. Rick Bennett. Independently published.

Graff, E. J. 2004. *What Is Marriage for? The Strange Social History of Our Most Intimate Institution*. Boston: Beacon Press.

Grewal, Inderpal, and Caren Kaplan. 1994. *Scattered Hegemonies: Post-Modernity and Transnational Feminist Practices*. Minneapolis: University of Minnesota Press.

Griffith, R. Marie. 1997. *God's Daughters: Evangelical Women and the Power of Submission*. Berkeley: University of California Press.

Gross, Terry. 2007. "Mark Olsen and Will Scheffer, Feeling the 'Big Love.'" *Fresh Air*, August 1. https://freshairarchive.org/segments/mark-olsen-and -will-scheffer-feeling-big-love.

Grossbard, Shoshana. 2013. "Polygamy Is Bad for Women." *New York Times*, December 17. https://www.nytimes.com/roomfordebate/2013/12/17/should -plural-marriage-be-legal/polygamy-is-bad-for-women.

Gruning, David W., Alain A. Levasseur, Paul M. Hebert, John R. Trahan, and Estelle Roy. 2015. *Traduction du Code civil français en anglais: version bilingue*. https://halshs.archives-ouvertes.fr/halshs-01385107/document.

Hachimi-Alaoui, Myriam, and Elise Lemercier. 2018. "Que faire des cadis de la république? enquête sur la reconfiguration de l'institution cadiale à Mayotte." *Ethnologie Française* 48 (1): 37–46.

Hamilton, Kimberly, Patrick Simon, and Clara Veniard. 2004. "The Challenge of French Diversity." Migration Policy Institute, November 1. https://www .migrationpolicy.org/article/challenge-french-diversity.

Hammon, Heber B., and William Jankowiak. 2011. "One Vision: The Making, Unmaking, and Remaking of a Fundamentalist Polygamous Community." In *Modern Polygamy in the United States: Historical, Cultural, and Legal Issues*, ed. Cardell Jacobson and Lara Burton, 41–75. New York: Oxford University Press.

Hannaford, Alex. 2018. "The Woman Who Escaped a Polygamist Cult—and Turned Its HQ into a Refuge." *The Guardian*, October 13. https://www.the guardian.com/world/2018/oct/13/woman-escaped-cult-hq-flds-refuge.

Harder, Lois. 2007. "Rights of Love: The State and Intimate Relationships in Canada and the United States." *Social Politics: International Studies in Gender, State, and Society* 14 (2): 155–81. https://doi.org/10.1093/sp/jxm009.

Harding, Rose. 2010. *Regulating Sexuality: Legal Consciousness in Lesbian and Gay Lives*. New York: Routledge.

Haritaworn, Jin, Tamsila Tauqir, and Esra Erdem. 2008. "Gay Imperialism: Gender and Sexuality Discourse in the 'War on Terror.'" In *Out of Place: Interrogating Silences in Queerness/Raciality*, ed. Adi Kuntsman and Esperanza Miyake, 71–95. New York: Raw Nerve Books.

Haupert, M. L., Amanda N. Gesselman, Amy C. Moors, Helen E. Fisher, and Justin R. Garcia. 2017. "Prevalence of Experiences with Consensual Non-monogamous Relationships: Findings from Two National Samples of Single Americans." *Journal of Sex and Marital Therapy* 43 (5): 424–40. https://doi.org/10.1080/0092623X.2016.1178675.

Hayes, Jeffrey Michael. 2007. "Polygamy Comes Out of the Closet: The New Strategy of Polygamy Activists." *Stanford Journal of Civil Rights and Civil Liberties* 3: 99–129.

Heath, Melanie. 2003. "Soft-Boiled Masculinity: Renegotiating Gender and Racial Ideologies in the Promise Keepers Movement." *Gender and Society* 17 (3): 423–44.

———. 2009. "State of Our Unions: Marriage Promotion and the Contested Power of Heterosexuality." *Gender and Society* 23 (1): 27–48. https://doi.org/10.1177/0891243208326807.

———. 2012a. "Making Marriage Promotion into Public Policy: The Epistemic Culture of a Statewide Initiative." *Qualitative Sociology* 35 (4): 385–406.

———. 2012b. *One Marriage Under God: The Campaign to Promote Marriage in America*. New York: New York University Press.

———. 2013. "Sexual Misgivings: Producing Un/Marked Knowledge in Neoliberal Marriage Promotion Policies." *Sociological Quarterly* 54 (4): 561–83. https://doi.org/10.1111/tsq.12042.

———. 2015. "Manhood Over Easy: Reflections on Hegemonic, Soft-Boiled, and Multiple Masculinities." In *Exploring Masculinities: Identity, Inequality, Continuity, and Change*, ed. C. J. Pascoe and Tristan Bridges, 155–65. Oxford, UK: Oxford University Press.

———. 2016. "Testing the Limits of Religious Freedom: The Case of Polygamy's Criminalization in Canada." In *The Polygamy Question*, ed. Janet Bennion and Lisa Fishbayn Joffe, 157–79. Logan: Utah State University Press.

———. 2019. "Espousing Patriarchy: Conciliatory Masculinity and Homosocial Femininity in Religiously Conservative Families." *Gender and Society* 33 (6): 888–910.

Heath, Melanie, Jessica Braimoh, and Julie Gouweloos. 2016. "Judging Women's Sexual Agency: Contemporary Sex Wars in the Legal Terrain of Prostitution and Polygamy." *Signs: Journal of Women in Culture and Society* 42 (1): 199–225.

Hewett, Heather. 2009. "Mothering Across Borders: Narratives of Immigrant Mothers in the United States." *Women's Studies Quarterly* 37 (3/4): 121–39.

Hoang, Lan Anh. 2016. "Moral Dilemmas of Transnational Migration: Vietnamese Women in Taiwan." *Gender and Society* 30 (6): 890–911. https://doi .org/10.1177/0891243216670602.

Hochschild, Arlie. 1983. *The Managed Heart: Commercialization of Human Feeling.* Berkeley: University of California Press.

Hondagneu-Sotelo, Pierrette. 2007. *Domestica: Immigrant Workers Cleaning and Caring in the Shadows of Affluence.* Berkeley: University of California Press.

Hondagneu-Sotelo, Pierrette, and Ernestine Avila. 1997. " 'I'm Here, but I'm There': The Meanings of Latina Transnational Motherhood." *Gender and Society* 11 (5): 548–71.

Hopkins, Anna. 2017. " 'I Love All My Moms': Hundreds of Polygamists and Their Families Led by the 'Sister Wives' Descend on the Steps of Utah Capitol to Demand the Legal Right to Plural Marriage." *DailyMail*, February 10. https://www.dailymail.co.uk/news/article-4213990/Polygamous-families -protest-bigamy-law-Utah-Capitol.html.

Horvath, Christina. 2018. "Riots or Revolts? The Legacy of the 2005 Uprising in French Banlieue Narratives." *Modern and Contemporary France* 26 (2): 193–206.

Hull, Kathleen E. 2006. *Same-Sex Marriage: The Cultural Politics of Love and Law.* Cambridge, UK: Cambridge University Press.

Hunter, Alistair. 2018. *Retirement Home? Aging Migrant Workers in France and the Question of Return.* Dordrecht, The Netherlands: Springer.

Hyest, M. Jean-Jacques, Michèle André, Christian Cointat, and Yves Détraigne. 2008. *Départementalisation de Mayotte: sortir de l'ambiguïté, faire face aux responsabilités.* Les rapports du Sénat no. 115. Paris: Sénat. https://www .senat.fr/notice-rapport/2008/r08-115-notice.html.

Idriss, Mamaye. 2016. "Le mouvement des chatouilleuses: genre et violence dans l'action politique à Mayotte (1966–1976)." *Le Mouvement Social* 255 (2): 57–70.

Imloul, Sonia. 2009. *La polygamie en France: une fatalité?* Paris: Institut Montaigne. www.institutmontaigne.org.

Ingersoll, Julie. 2003. *Evangelical Christian Women: War Stories in the Gender Battles.* New York: New York University Press.

Ingraham, Chrys. 2008. *White Weddings: Romancing Heterosexuality in Popular Culture*, 2nd ed. New York: Routledge.

Irby, Courtney Ann. 2014. "Moving Beyond Agency: A Review of Gender and Intimate Relationships in Conservative Religions." *Sociology Compass* 8 (11): 1269–80.

Iturriaga, Nicole, and Abigail C. Saguy. 2017. "'I Would Never Want to Be an Only Wife': The Role of Discursive Networks and Post-Feminist Discourse in Reframing Polygamy." *Social Problems* 64 (3): 333–50.

Iversen, Joan. 1984. "Feminist Implications of Mormon Polygyny." *Feminist Studies* 10 (3): 505–22.

Jackson, Stevi. 1993. "Even Sociologists Fall in Love: An Exploration in the Sociology of Emotions." *Sociology* 27 (2): 201–20. https://doi.org/10.1177/0038038593027002002.

Jacobson, Cardell K., and Lara Burton, eds. 2011. *Modern Polygamy in the United States: Historical, Cultural, and Legal Issues*. Oxford, UK: Oxford University Press.

Jamieson, Lynn. 1999. "Intimacy Transformed? A Critical Look at the 'Pure Relationship.'" *Sociology* 33 (3): 477–94.

Jankowiak, William, and Emilie Allen. 1995. "The Balance of Duty and Desire in a Mormon Polygamous Community." In *Romantic Passion: The Universal Emotion?* ed. William Jankowiak, 277–96. New York: Columbia University Press.

Jankowiak, William, Monika Sudakov, and Benjamin C. Wilreker. 2005. "Co-Wife Conflict and Co-Operation." *Ethnology* 44 (1): 81–98. https://doi.org/10.2307/3773961.

Jennings, Jeremy. 2011. "Liberty." In *The French Republic: History, Values, Debates*, ed. Edward Berenson, Vincent Duclert, and Christophe Prochasson, 95–102. Ithaca, NY: Cornell University Press.

Jessop, Carolyn. 2007. *Escape: A Memoir*. New York: Broadway Books.

Jewkes, Rachel, Jonathan Levin, and Loveday Penn-Kekana. 2002. "Risk Factors for Domestic Violence: Findings from a South African Cross-Sectional Study." *Social Science and Medicine* 55 (9): 1603–17. https://doi.org/10.1016/S0277-9536(01)00294-5.

Joffe, Lisa Fishbayn. 2016. "What's the Harm in Polygamy? Multicultural Toleration and Women's Experience of Plural Marriage." *Journal of Law and Religion* 31 (3): 336–53.

Jones, Craig E. 2012. *A Cruel Arithmetic: Inside the Case Against Polygamy*. Toronto: Irwin Law.

Kandiyoti, Deniz. 1988. "Bargaining with Patriarchy." *Gender and Society* 2 (3): 274–90.

Kaplan, Amy. 1998. "Manifest Domesticity." *American Literature* 70 (3): 581–606.

Kaplan, Caren, Norma Alarcón, and Minoo Moallem, eds. 1999. *Between Woman and Nation: Nationalisms, Transnational Feminisms, and the State.* Durham, NC: Duke University Press.

Karamagi, Charles A. S., James K. Tumwine, Thorkild Tylleskar, and Kristian Heggenhougen. 2006. "Intimate Partner Violence Against Women in Eastern Uganda: Implications for HIV Prevention." *BMC Public Health* 6 (1). https://doi.org/10.1186/1471-2458-6-284.

Kawar, Leila. 2012. "Juridical Framings of Immigrants in the United States and France: Courts, Social Movements, and Symbolic Politics." *International Migration Review* 46 (2): 414–55. https://doi.org/10.1111/j.1747-7379.2012 .00892.x.

Kelly, Kimberly. 2012. "In the Name of the Mother: Renegotiating Conservative Women's Authority in the Crisis Pregnancy Center Movement." *Signs: Journal of Women in Culture and Society* 38 (1): 203–30.

Kilbride, Philip L. 1994. *Plural Marriage for Our Times: A Reinvented Option?* Westport, CT: Bergin & Garvey.

Klein, Diane J. 2010. "Plural Marriage and Community Property Law." *Golden Gate University Law Review* 41 (1): 33–87.

Klesse, Christian. 2006. "Polyamory and Its 'Others': Contesting the Terms of Non-Monogamy." *Sexualities* 9 (5): 565–83.

Korteweg, Anna C., and Gökçe Yurdakul. 2014. *The Headscarf Debates: Conflicts of National Belonging.* Stanford, CA: Stanford University Press.

Kosmin, Barry A. 2007. "Introduction: Contemporary Secularity and Secularism." In *Secularism and Secularity: Contemporary International Perspectives*, ed. Barry A. Kosmin and Ariela Keysar, 1–13. Hartford, CT: Institute for the Study of Secularism in Society and Culture.

Kramer, Stephanie. 2020. "Polygamy Is Rare Around the World and Mostly Confined to a Few Regions." Pew Research Center, September 7. https:// www.pewresearch.org/fact-tank/2020/12/07/polygamy-is-rare-around-the -world-and-mostly-confined-to-a-few-regions/.

Laborde, Cécile. 2008. *Critical Republicanism: The Hijab Controversy and Political Philosophy.* Oxford, UK: Oxford University Press.

Lambek, Michael. 2018. *Island in the Stream: An Ethnographic History of Mayotte.* Toronto: University of Toronto Press.

Lan, Pei-Chia. 2006. *Global Cinderellas: Migrant Domestics and Newly Rich Employers in Taiwan.* Durham, NC: Duke University Press.

Laschever, Eulalie, and David S. Meyer. 2021. "Growth and Decline of Opposing Movements: Gun Control and Gun Rights, 1945–2015." *Mobilization* 26 (1): 1–20.

Latin, Don. 2007. "Gay Monogamous Couple Are Brains Behind Polygamy Show." *SFGate,* June 10. https://www.sfgate.com/entertainment/article/Gay -monogamous-couple-are-brains-behind-polygamy-2573064.php.

Law Commission of Canada. 2001. *Beyond Conjugality: Recognizing and Supporting Close Adult Relationships.* Ottawa: Public Works and Government Services Canada.

Lawson, David W., Susan James, Esther Ngadaya, Bernard Ngowi, Sayoki G. M. Mfinanga, and Monique Borgerhoff Mulder. 2015. "No Evidence That Polygynous Marriage Is a Harmful Cultural Practice in Northern Tanzania." *Proceedings of the National Academy of Sciences of the United States of America* 112 (45): 13,827–832.

Leamaster, Reid J., and Rachel L. Einwohner. 2018. " 'I'm Not Your Stereotypical Mormon Girl': Mormon Women's Gendered Resistance." *Review of Religious Research* 60 (2): 161–81.

Le Bars, Stéphanie. 2010. "Les vies multiples de Liès Hebbadj." *Le Monde*, June 9. https://www.lemonde.fr/societe/article/2010/06/08/les-vies-multiples-de -lies-hebbadj_1369440_3224.html.

Lee, John Alan. 1977. "A Typology of Styles of Loving." *Personality and Social Psychology Bulletin* 3 (2): 173–82. https://doi.org/10.1177/014616727700300204.

Lenon, Suzanne. 2016. "Intervening in the Context of White Settler Colonialism: West Coast LEAF, Gender Equality, and the Polygamy Reference." *Onati Socio-Legal Series* 6 (6): 1324–47.

Levinson, Sanford. 2005. "Thinking About Polygamy." *San Diego Law Review* 42: 1049–58.

Lewis, Mary Dewhurst. 2007. *The Boundaries of the Republic: Migrant Rights and the Limits of Universalism in France, 1918–1940.* Stanford, CA: Stanford University Press.

———. 2011. "Immigration." In *The French Republic: History, Values, Debates*, ed. Edward Berenson, Vincent Duclert, and Christophe Prochas, 232–41. Ithaca, NY: Cornell University Press.

Link, Bruce G., and Jo C. Phelan. 2001. "Conceptualizing Stigma." *Annual Review of Sociology* 27: 363–85.

Liu, Xiangyan. 2019. "Narratives of Mothers in Diaspora: Motherhood Reconstruction in Chinese Transnational Families." *Women's Studies International Forum* 73: 16–23. https://doi.org/10.1016/j.wsif.2019.01.007.

Lochak, Danièle. 2012. "L'image de l'étranger au prisme des lois sur l'immigration." *Ecarts d'Identité* 120: 19–23.

Macaulay, Stewart. 2005. "The New Versus the Old Legal Realism: Things Ain't the Way They Used to Be." *Wisconsin Law Review* 2: 365–404.

Mackey, Thomas C. 1987. *Red Lights Out: A Legal History of Prostitution, Disorderly Houses, and Vice Districts, 1870–1917.* New York: Garland.

Mahmood, Saba. 2005. *Politics of Piety: The Islamic Revival and the Feminist Subject.* Princeton, NJ: Princeton University Press.

Mahoney, Jon. 2008. "Liberalism and the Polygamy Question." *Social Philosophy Today* 23: 161–74.

Majeed, Debra. 2015. *Polygyny: What It Means When African American Muslim Women Share Their Husbands.* Gainesville: University of Florida Press.

Mantu, Sandra. 2015. *Contingent Citizenship: The Law and Practice of Citizenship Deprivation in International, European, and National Perspectives.* Leiden: Brill Nijhoff.

Marie, Claude-Valentin, Didier Breton, Maude Crouzet, Édouard Febre, and Sébastien Merceron. 2017. *Migrations, natalité et solidarités familiales: la société de Mayotte en pleine mutation.* INSEE Analyses Mayotte, no. 12. Paris: Institut National de la Statistique et des Études Économiques.

Massoud, Mark Fathi, and Kathleen M. Moore. 2020. "Shari'a Consciousness: Law and Lived Religion Among California Muslims." *Law and Social Inquiry* 45 (3): 787–817.

Mathen, Carissima. 2012. "Reflecting Culture: Polygamy and the Charter." *Supreme Court Law Review: Osgoode's Annual Constitutional Cases Conference* 57 (1): 357–74.

Mazzucato, Valentina, and Bilisuma B. Dito. 2018. "Transnational Families: Cross-Country Comparative Perspectives." *Population, Space, and Place* 24 (7): 1–7. https://doi.org/10.1002/psp.2165.

McClintock, Anne. 1995. *Imperial Leather: Race, Gender, and Sexuality in the Colonial Contest.* New York: Routledge.

McDermott, Monica, and Frank L. Samson. 2005. "White Racial and Ethnic Identity in the United States." *Annual Review of Sociology* 31: 245–61.

McDermott, Rose. 2018. *The Evils of Polygyny: Evidence of Its Harm to Women, Men, and Society.* Ithaca, NY: Cornell University Press.

McGinnis, Katilin R. 2012. "Sister Wives: A New Beginning for United States

Polygamist Families on the Eve of Polygamy Prosecution." *Jeffrey S. Moorad Sports Law Journal* 19 (1): 249–80.

McKay, Tara, and Nicole Angotti. 2016. "Ready Rhetorics: Political Homophobia and Activist Discourses in Malawi, Nigeria, and Uganda." *Qualitative Sociology* 39: 397–420.

Misra, Joya, Stephanie Moller, and Marina Karides. 2003. "Envisioning Dependency: Changing Media Depictions of Welfare in the 20th Century." *Social Problems* 50 (4): 482–504.

Mohrman, K. 2021. "'Same-Sex Marriage?! What Next, Polygamy?': Mormonism in U.S. Political Culture." *Mormon Studies Review* 8: 57–67.

Monéger, Françoise. 2013. "Le conseil constitutionnel et l'état des personnes." *Les Nouveaux Cahiers du Conseil Constitutionnel* 39 (2): 51–61.

Moore-Emmett, Andrea. 2004. *God's Brothel*. San Francisco: Pince-Nez Press.

Moreau, Manuel. 2013. "Mariage gay et polygamie: à Mayotte, le débat est rouvert." *Causeur,* May 16. https://www.causeur.fr/mariage-gay-polygamie -mayotte-22535.

Moulères, Sandrine. 2010. *Les boucs émissaires de la république*. Paris: Michalon.

Mutua, Makau. 2001. "Savages, Victims, and Saviors: The Metaphor of Human Rights." *Harvard International Law Journal* 42 (1): 201–45.

Myers, Michael G. 2006. "Polygamist Eye for the Monogamist Guy: Homosexual Sodomy . . . Gay Marriage . . . Is Polygamy Next?" *Houston Law Review* 42: 1451–86.

Nadler, Janice. 2017. "Expressive Law, Social Norms, and Social Groups." *Law and Social Inquiry* 42 (1): 60–75.

Newport, Frank. 2020. "Understanding the Increase in Moral Acceptability of Polygamy." *Gallup: Polling Matters, June 26.* https://news.gallup.com/opin ion/polling-matters/313112/understanding-increase-moral-acceptability -polygamy.aspx.

Okin, Susan Moller. 1999. *Is Multiculturalism Bad for Women?* Princeton, NJ: Princeton University Press.

Omi, Michael, and Howard Winant. 2015. *Racial Formation in the United States*, 3rd ed. New York: Routledge.

O'Quinn, Jamie. 2021. "Mapping the Literature on Child Marriage: A Critical Engagement." *Sociology Compass* 15 (11): e12935. https://doi.org/10.1111/soc4 .12935.

Osmond, Amy Kathlyn. 2010. "Organizational Identification: A Case Study of the Davis County Cooperative Society, the Latter Day Church of Christ, or Kingston Order." PhD diss., University of Utah. https://collections.lib.utah .edu/details?id=192296.

Ossman, Susan, and Susan Terrio. 2006. "The French Riots: Questioning Spaces of Surveillance and Sovereignty." *International Migration* 44 (2): 5–21.

Owoo, Nkechi S., Victor Agadjanian, and Chitalu M. Chama-Chiliba. 2021. "Revisiting the Polygyny and Intimate Partner Violence Connection: The Role of Religion and Wife's Rank in Nigeria." *Journal of Marriage and Family* 83 (5): 1310–31.

Palmer, Debbie, and Dave Perrin. 2004. *Keep Sweet: Children of Polygamy*. Lister, Canada: Dave's Press.

Pande, Raksha. 2015. "'I Arranged My Own Marriage': Arranged Marriages and Post-Colonial Feminism." *Gender, Place, and Culture* 22 (2): 172–87. https://doi.org/10.1080/0966369X.2013.855630.

Park, Shelley M. 2017. "Polyamory Is to Polygamy as Queer Is to Barbaric?" *Radical Philosophy Review* 20 (1): 1–32.

Parreñas, Rhacel Salazar. 2001. "Mothering from a Distance: Emotions, Gender, and Intergenerational Relations in Filipino Transnational Families." *Feminist Studies* 27 (2): 361–90. https://doi.org/10.2307/3178765.

———. 2005. "Long Distance Intimacy: Class, Gender, and Intergenerational Relations Between Mothers and Children in Filipino Transnational Families." *Global Networks* 5 (4): 317–36. https://doi.org/10.1111/j.1471-0374.2005.00122.x.

Patil, Crystal, and Craig Hadley. 2008. "Symptoms of Anxiety and Depression and Mother's Marital Status: An Exploratory Analysis of Polygyny and Psychosocial Stress." *American Journal of Human Biology* 20 (4): 475–77. https://doi.org/10.1002/ajhb.20736.

Patil, Vrushali. 2013. "From Patriarchy to Intersectionality: A Transnational Feminist Assessment of How Far We've Really Come." *Signs: Journal of Women in Culture and Society* 38 (4): 847–67.

———. 2018. "The Heterosexual Matrix as Imperial Effect." *Sociological Theory* 36 (1): 1–26. https://doi.org/10.1177/0735275118759382.

Pearsall, Sarah M. S. 2019. *Polygamy: An Early American History*. New Haven, CT: Yale University Press.

Perkins, Nancy. 2003. "Polygamy Summit No Peak: St. George Meeting Leaves Bad Taste in Many Mouths." *Deseret News*, September 1. https://www.deseret.com/2003/9/2/19745671/polygamy-summit-no-peak.

Pinfree, Gregory C. 2006. "Rhetorical Holy War: Polygamy, Homosexuality, and the Paradox of Community and Autonomy." *Journal of Gender, Social Policy, and the Law* 14: 314–83.

Poiret, Christian. 1995. "L'immigration familiale d'Afrique noire en région Ile-de-France: famille et habitat au coeur des mutations." *Migrations Etudes* 57: 1–8.

———. 1996. *Familles Africaines en France*. Paris: L'Harmattan.

Poiret, Christian, and Christiane Guégan. 1992. *L'habitat des familles polyga-mes en région Ile-de-France*. Paris: Vivre la Ville.

Pollitt, Amanda M., Brandon A. Robinson, and Debra Umberson. 2018. "Gender Conformity, Perceptions of Shared Power, and Marital Quality in Same- and Different-Sex Marriages." *Gender and Society* 32: 109–31.

Porter-Hirsche, Janis L. 2012. "Seditious Spirits Within Bountiful: Challenges to the Divine Authority Claimed by the Fundamentalist Church of Jesus Christ of Latter Day Saints." Victoria: Royal Roads University.

Prickett, Pamela J. 2015. "Negotiating Gendered Religious Space: The Particu-larities of Patriarchy in an African American Mosque." *Gender and Society* 29 (1): 51–72.

Puar, Jasbir K. 2007. *Terrorist Assemblages: Homonationalism in Queer Times*. Durham, NC: Duke University Press.

Puri, Jyoti. 2016. *Sexual States: Governance and the Struggle over the Antisod-omy Law in India*. Durham, NC: Duke University Press.

Quek, Kaye. 2018. *Marriage Trafficking: Women in Forced Wedlock*. New York: Routledge.

Quiminal, Catherine, and Claudette Bodin. 1993. *Mode de constitution des ménages polygames et vécu de la polygamie en France*. https://francearchives .fr/fr/facomponent/b604dcfdeeeocb00949050b350245307ef54d4ae.

Raissiguier, Catherine. 2010. *Reinventing the Republic: Gender, Migration, and Citizenship in France*. Stanford, CA: Stanford University Press.

Rault, Wilfried. 2019. "20 Years of France's Civil Union, the PACS (Pacte Civil de Solidarity): An Increasingly Popular Option." INED, October. https:// www.ined.fr/en/everything_about_population/demographic-facts-sheets/ focus-on/20-years-pacs-considerable-expansion/.

Rich, Adrienne. 1980. "Compulsory Heterosexuality and Lesbian Existence." *Signs: Journal of Women in Culture and Society* 5 (4): 631–60. https://doi.org /10.1086/493756.

Richardson, Diane. 2018. "Sexuality and Citizenship." *Sexualities* 21 (8): 1256–60.

Riess, Jana. 2019. "'Stranger Things' Sees Mormons as 'Super-Religious White People.'" Religion News Service, July 8. https://religionnews.com/2019/07/ 08/stranger-things-sees-mormons-as-super-religious-white-people/.

Ritchie, Andrea J., and Kay Whitlock. 2018. "Criminalization and Legaliza-tion." In *The Routledge History of Queer America*, ed. Don Romesburg, 300–314. New York: Routledge.

Robcis, Camille. 2013. *The Law of Kinship: Anthropology, Psychoanalysis, and the Family in France*. Ithaca, NY: Cornell University Press.

———. 2015. "Catholics, the 'Theory of Gender,' and the Turn to the Human in France: A New Dreyfus Affair?" *Journal of Modern History* 87: 892–923.

Rogozen, Sarah. 2017. "Prioritizing Diversity and Autonomy in the Polygamy Legalization Debate." *UCLA Women's Law Journal* 24: 107–49.

Rower, Alyssa. 2004. "The Legality of Polygamy: Using the Due Process Clause of the Fourteenth Amendment." *Family Law Quarterly* 38 (3): 711–31.

Rubin, Gayle. 1984. "Thinking Sex: Notes for a Radical Theory of the Politics of Sexuality." In *Pleasure and Danger: Exploring Female Sexuality*, ed. Carole S. Vance. Boston: Routledge & Kegan Paul.

Rude-Antoine, Edwige. 1991. "Muslim Maghrebian Marriage in France: A Problem for Legal Pluralism." *International Journal of Law, Policy, and the Family* 5 (2): 93–103.

———. 1997. "Validity and Reception of Polygamy by the French Judicial Order: A Theoretical and Controversial Question." *Journal des Anthropologues* 71: 39–56.

Ruedy, John. 1992. *Modern Algeria: The Origins and Development of a Nation*. Bloomington: Indiana University Press.

Saada, Emmanuelle. 2011. "The Republic and the Indigènes." In *The French Republic: History, Values, Dates*, ed. Edward Berenson, Vincent Duclert, and Christophe Prochas; trans. Renée Champion and Edward Berenson, 223–31. Ithaca, NY: Cornell University Press.

Saguy, Abigail C. 2020. *Come Out, Come Out, Whoever You Are*. New York: Oxford University Press.

Said, Edward. 1979. *Orientalism*. New York: Vintage Books.

Sargent, Carolyn, and Dennis Cordell. 2003. "Polygamy, Disrupted Reproduction, and the State: Malian Migrants in Paris, France." *Social Science and Medicine* 56: 1961–72.

Schippers, Mimi. 2016. *Beyond Monogamy: Polyamory and the Future of Polyqueer Sexualities*. New York: New York University Press.

Schreiber, Ronnee. 2008. *Righting Feminism: Conservative Women and American Politics*. New York: Oxford University Press.

Schreier, Joshua. 2007. "Napoléon's Long Shadow: Morality, Civilization, and Jews in France and Algeria, 1808–1870." *French Historical Studies* 30 (1): 77–103.

Scott, Joan Wallach. 2007. *The Politics of the Veil*. Princeton, NJ: Princeton University Press.

Sealing, Keith E. 2001. "Polygamists Out of the Closet: Statutory and State Constitutional Prohibitions Against Polygamy Are Unconstitutional Under the Free Exercise Clause." *Georgia State University Law Review* 17 (3): 692–758.

Selby, Jennifer A. 2014. "Polygamy in the Parisian Banlieues: Debate and Discourse on the 2005 French Suburban Riots." In *Polygamy's Rights and Wrongs: Perspectives on Harm, Family, and Law*, ed. Gillian Calder and Lori G. Beaman, 120–41. Vancouver: University of British Columbia Press.

Shah, Nayan. 2011. *Stranger Intimacy: Contesting Race, Sexuality, and the Law in the North American West*. Berkeley: University of California Press.

Sheff, Elisabeth. 2011. "Polyamorous Families, Same-Sex Marriage, and the Slippery Slope." *Journal of Contemporary Ethnography* 40 (5): 487–520.

Sidhoum, Rahal S. M. 1985. *Les ménages polygames résident en France*. Paris: Anthropologie Comparative des Sociètes Musulmanes.

———. 1986. *Les aspects socio-juridiques de la polygamie au sein de l'immigration en France*. Paris: Anthropologie Comparative des Sociètes Musulmanes.

Sigman, Shayna M. 2006. "Everything Lawyers Know About Polygamy Is Wrong." *Cornell Journal of Law and Public Policy* 16 (1): 102–85.

Slark, Samantha. 2004. "Are Anti-Polygamy Laws an Unconstitutional Infringement on the Liberty Interests of Consenting Adults?" *Journal of Law and Family Studies* 6 (2): 451–60.

Slonim-Nevo, Vered, and Alean Al-Krenawi. 2006. "Success and Failure Among Polygamous Families: The Experience of Wives, Husbands, and Children." *Family Process* 45 (3): 311–30.

Smearman, Claire A. 2009. "Second Wives' Club: Mapping the Impact of Polygamy in U.S. Immigration Law." *Berkeley Journal of International Law* 27 (2): 382–447.

Smith, Mariam. 2020. "Homophobia and Homonationalism: LGBTQ Law Reform in Canada." *Social and Legal Studies* 29 (1): 65–84.

Song, Sarah. 2007. *Justice, Gender, and the Politics of Multiculturalism*. Cambridge, UK: Cambridge University Press.

Spivak, Gayatri Chakravorty. 1988. "Can the Subaltern Speak?" In *Marxism and the Interpretation of Culture*, ed. Cary Nelson and Lawrence Grossberg, 21–78. Urbana: University of Illinois Press.

Stacey, Judith. 1996. *In the Name of the Family: Rethinking Family Values in the Postmodern Age*. Boston: Beacon Press.

Stacey, Judith, and Susan Elizabeth Gerard. 1990. "We Are Not Doormats: The Influence of Feminism on Contemporary Evangelicalism in the United States." In *Uncertain Terms: Negotiating Gender in American Culture*, ed. Faye Ginsburg and Anna Lowenhaupt Ting. Boston: Beacon Press.

Stacey, Judith, and Tey Meadow. 2009. "New Slants on the Slippery Slope: The Politics of Polygamy and Gay Family Rights in South Africa and the United States." *Politics and Society* 37 (2): 167–202.

Stahl, William. 2007. "Is Anyone in Canada Secular?" In *Secularism and Secularity: Contemporary International Perspectives*, ed. Barry A. Kosmin and Ariela Keysar, 59–72. Hartford, CT: Institute for the Study of Secularism in Society and Culture.

Stasiulis, Daiva K., and Abigail B. Bakan. 2005. *Negotiating Citizenship: Migrant Women in Canada and the Global System*. Toronto: University of Toronto Press.

Status of Women Canada. 2005. *Polygamy in Canada: Legal and Social Implications for Women and Children—A Collection of Policy Research Reports*. Ottawa: Status of Women Canada. http://www.crilf.ca/Documents/Polygamy%20in%20Canada%20-%20Nov%202005.pdf.

Steady, Filmina Chioma. 1987. "Polygamy and the Household Economy in a Fishing Village in Sierra Leone." In *Transformations of African Marriage*, ed. David Parkin and David Nyamwaya, 211–32. Manchester, UK: Manchester University Press.

Stein, Arlene. 2001. *The Stranger Next Door: The Story of a Small Community's Battle over Sex, Faith, and Civil Rights*. Boston: Beacon Press.

Stoler, Ann Laura. 2001. "Tense and Tender Ties: The Politics of Comparison in North American History and (Post) Colonial Studies." *Journal of American History* 88 (3): 829–65.

Strassberg, Maura I. 1997. "Distinctions of Form or Substance: Monogamy, Polygamy, and Same-Sex Marriage." *North Carolina Law Review* 75: 1501–1624.

———. 2003. "The Crime of Polygamy." *Temple Political and Civil Rights Law Review* 12 (2): 353–431.

———. 2015. "Scrutinizing Polygamy: Utah's *Brown v. Buhman* and British Columbia's Reference Re: Section 293." *Emory Law Journal* 64 (6): 1815–76.

———. 2016. "Distinguishing Polygyny and Polyfidelity Under the Criminal Law." In *The Polygamy Question*, ed. Janet Bennion and Lisa Fishbayn Joffe, 180–98. Logan: Utah State University Press.

Strauss, Gregg. 2012. "Is Polygamy Inherently Unequal?" *Ethics* 122 (3): 516–44.

Sullivan, Andrew. 1996. *Virtually Normal*. New York: Vintage Books.

Sullivan, Maureen. 2004. *The Family of Woman: Lesbian Mothers, Their Children, and the Undoing of Gender*. Berkeley: University of California Press.

Surkis, Judith. 2000. *Sexing the Citizen: Morality and Masculinity in France, 1870–1920*. Ithaca, NY: Cornell University Press.

———. 2010a. "Hymenal Politics: Marriage, Secularism, and French Sovereignty." *Public Culture* 22 (3): 531–56.

———. 2010b. "Propriété, polygamie et statut personnel en Algérie coloniale, 1830–1873." *Revue d'Histoire du XIXe Siècle* 41 (2): 27–48.

Sweet, Joanna. 2013. "Equality, Democracy, Monogamy: Discourses of Canadian Nation Building in the 2010–2011 British Columbia Polygamy Reference." *Canadian Journal of Law and Society / La Revue Canadienne Droit et Société* 28 (1): 1–19. https://doi.org/10.1017/cls.2012.7.

Swidler, Ann. 2001. *Talk of Love: How Culture Matters*. Chicago: University of Chicago Press.

Taylor, Verta, Katrina Kimport, Nella Van Dyke, and Ellen Ann Andersen. 2009. "Culture and Mobilization: Tactical Repertoires, Same-Sex Weddings, and the Impact on Gay Activism." *American Sociological Review* 74 (6): 865–90.

Tenney, Ryan D. 2002. "Tom Green, Common-Law Marriage, and the Illegality of Putative Polygamy." *BYU Journal of Public Law* 17 (1): 141–62.

Ternaux, Catherine. 2012. *La polygamie, pourquoi pas?* Paris: Grasset & Fasquelle.

Therrien, Sophie. 2004. *Laïcité et diversité religieuse: l'approche québécoise*. Montreal: Conseil des Relations Interculturelles. https://numerique.banq.qc.ca/patrimoine/details/52327/46792?docref=_h5bsA_P3TOrb0G2kg9USw.

Thornton, Arland. 2011. "The International Fight Against Barbarism: Historical and Comparative Perspectives on Marriage Timing, Consent, and Polygamy." In *Modern Polygamy in the United States: Historical, Cultural, and Legal Issues*, ed. Cardell Jacobson and Lara Burton, 259–79. Oxford, UK: Oxford University Press.

Trouille, Helen. 2000. "Private Life and Public Image: Privacy Legislation in France." *International and Comparative Law Quarterly* 49 (1): 199–208.

Umberson, Debra, Mieke Beth Thomeer, and Amy C. Lodge. 2015. "Intimacy and Emotion Work in Lesbian, Gay, and Heterosexual Relationships." *Journal of Marriage and Family* 77: 542–56.

Van Wagoner, Richard S. 1989. *Mormon Polygamy: A History*, 2nd ed. Salt Lake City: Signature Books.

Van Walsum, Sarah. 2008. *The Family and the Nation: Dutch Family Migration in the Context of Changing Family Norms*. Newcastle, UK: Cambridge Scholars.

Varrella, Simona. 2021. "Number of Countries That Permit Same-Sex Marriage, 2021, by Continent." https://www.statista.com/statistics/1229293/number-of-countries-that-permit-same-sex-marriage-by-continent/.

Ward, Cassiah M. 2004. "I Now Pronounce You Husband and Wives: *Lawrence v. Texas* and the Practice of Polygamy in Modern America." *William & Mary Journal of Women and the Law* 11 (1): 131–52.

Ward, Jane. 2020. *The Tragedy of Heterosexuality*. New York: New York University Press.

Weber, Brenda R. 2016. "The Epistemology of the (Televised, Polygamous) Closet: Progressive Polygamy, Spiritual Neoliberalism, and the Will to Visibility." *Television and New Media* 17 (5): 375–91.

Weeks, Jeffrey. 2018. *Sex, Politics, and Society: The Regulation of Sexuality Since 1800*, 4th ed. New York: Routledge.

Weitzer, Ronald. 2015. "Researching Prostitution and Sex Trafficking Comparatively." *Sexuality Research and Social Policy* 12: 81–91.

White, O. Kendall, and Daryl White. 2005. "Polygamy and Mormon Identity." *Journal of American Culture* 28 (2): 165–77. https://doi.org/10.1111/j.1542-734X.2005.00161.x.

Winant, Howard. 2001. "White Racial Projects." In *The Making and Unmaking of Whiteness*, ed. Birgit Brander Rasmussen, Eric Klineberg, Irene J. Nexica, and Matt Wray, 97–112. Durham, NC: Duke University Press.

Winslow, Ben. 2019. "Utah Drops Its Investigation into FLDS Food Stamp Fraud." *Fox News*, April 24. https://www.fox13now.com/2019/04/24/utah-drops-its-investigation-into-flds-food-stamp-fraud/amp/?__twitter_impression=true.

Winter, Elke. 2015. "Rethinking Multiculturalism After Its 'Retreat': Lessons from Canada." *American Behavioral Scientist* 59 (6): 637–57.

Witte, John, Jr. 2015a. *The Western Case for Monogamy over Polygamy*. New York: Cambridge University Press.

———. 2015b. "Why Two in One Flesh: The Western Case for Monogamy over Polygamy." *Emory Law Journal* 64 (6): 1675–1746.

Wolfreys, Jim. 2002. "The Centre Cannot Hold: Fascism, the Left, and the Crisis of French Politics." *International Socialism* 95. https://www.marxists.org/history/etol/newspape/isj2/2002/isj2-095/wolfreys.htm.

Wright, Lawrence. 2002. "Lives of the Saints." *The New Yorker*, January 22. https://www.newyorker.com/magazine/2002/01/21/lives-of-the-saints.

Wright, Stuart A., and Susan J. Palmer. 2016. *Storming Zion: Government Raids on Religious Communities*. Oxford, UK: Oxford University Press.

Zaman, Michele, and Alissa Koski. 2020. "Child Marriage in Canada: A Systematic Review." *PLoS ONE* 15 (3): e0229676.

Zeitzen, Miriam Koktvedgaard. 2008. *Polygamy: A Cross-Cultural Analysis*. London: Bloomsbury.

Zhou, Min. 2013. "Ethnic Enclaves and Niches." In *The Encyclopedia of Global Human Migration*, ed. Immanuel Ness, 3: 1333–37. Oxford: Wiley Blackwell.

Zubrzcki, Geneviève. 2016. *Beheading the Saint: Nationalism, Religion, and Secularism in Quebec*. Chicago: University of Chicago Press.

Index

GLOBALIZATION
IN EVERYDAY LIFE

As global forces undeniably continue to change the politics and economies of the world, we need a more nuanced understanding of what these changes mean in our daily lives. Significant theories and studies have broadened and deepened our knowledge on globalization, yet we need to think about how these macro processes manifest on the ground and how they are maintained through daily actions.

Globalization in Everyday Life foregrounds ethnographic examination of daily life to address issues that will bring tangibility to previously abstract assertions about the global order. Moving beyond mere illustrations of global trends, books in this series underscore mutually constitutive processes of the local and global by finding unique and informative ways to bridge macro- and microanalyses. This series is a high-profile outlet for books that offer accessible readership, innovative approaches, instructive models, and analytic insights to our understanding of globalization.

CPSIA information can be obtained
at www.ICGtesting.com
Printed in the USA
JSHW060216271222
35298JS00001B/1